Hugh Culve
the Tampa Ba

Hugh Culverhouse and the Tampa Bay Buccaneers

*How a Skinflint Genius with a
Losing Team Made the Modern NFL*

DENIS M. CRAWFORD

Foreword by Hugh F. Culverhouse, Jr.

McFarland & Company, Inc., Publishers
Jefferson, North Carolina, and London

LIBRARY OF CONGRESS CATALOGUING-IN-PUBLICATION DATA

Crawford, Denis M.
    Hugh Culverhouse and the Tampa Bay Buccaneers : how a
skinflint genius with a losing team made the modern NFL / Denis
M. Crawford ; foreword by Hugh F. Culverhouse, Jr.
        p.   cm.
    Includes bibliographical references and index.

    ISBN 978-0-7864-6516-3
    softcover : 50# alkaline paper ∞

    1. Culverhouse, Hugh, 1919–1994.   2. Football team owners—
United States—Biography.   3. Tampa Bay Buccaneers (Football
team)—History.   I. Title.
GV939.C74C74 2011
796.332092—dc23   2011030553
[B]

BRITISH LIBRARY CATALOGUING DATA ARE AVAILABLE

On the cover: (inset) Hugh Culverhouse; (bottom) A Tampa Bay
player during the "Snow Bowl" game on December 1, 1985, against
Green Bay at Lambeau Field (*Tampa Tribune*)

Manufactured in the United States of America

McFarland & Company, Inc., Publishers
  Box 611, Jefferson, North Carolina 28640
    www.mcfarlandpub.com

Table of Contents

Foreword
Hugh F. Culverhouse, Jr.

BACK IN THE GREAT DEPRESSION, when my dad was a student at the University of Alabama, his roommate was an odd fellow that other guys picked on. One night, his roommate showed up bruised and bloody; two guys from another fraternity had beaten him up, just for sport. In a fury, my dad went straight to their fraternity house and, standing on the front lawn, called out for them by name. A crowd poured out to watch the violence that was about to unfold.

Cockily, and to the cheers of his fraternity brothers, the first assailant stepped forward, and he and my dad began to circle. Minutes later, my dad stood over the guy's prone body; he had knocked him unconscious. The crowd, which moments earlier had been taunting and cheering, grew eerily quiet.

The next assailant, now pale with fear, stepped into the circle. My dad cursed him foully, then proceeded to methodically pummel him until that man fell to the ground too, bloody and unconscious. Having avenged his roommate, my dad calmly walked home, washed the blood from his raw knuckles, and took care of his injured friend.

That story says a lot about my dad. He was at once loyal and merciless, brave and crude, hated and loved, disciplined and impulsive, generous and feared—all of which depended on the moment, the situation and his mood. When he died on August 25, 1994—a public figure of no small controversy— I struggled to reconcile those contradictions.

I had seen such contradictions for a long time. For example, my mother would always try to get my dad to control his weight by cooking very healthy

1

meals. He would compliment her on the poached eggs on dry toast and then, on leaving the house, immediately stop at the Village Inn on Dale Mabry Highway in Tampa to order pancakes, sausage and fried eggs. But his appetite for a second breakfast was the least of it. For decades he kept a mistress— then the wife of a national broadcaster—and even took her on an African safari. Just before leaving on the safari, though, he asked the parents of his other girlfriend—who was nearly 50 years younger—for permission to marry.

As a businessman, my father was both prescient and successful—and wildly impulsive. Often, as soon as he made a profit from one endeavor, he would rush to borrow multiples of that profit and invest in oil wells with a 100-to-1 shot of production, orange groves he had no experience running, or crazy real estate ventures.

Yet, when it came to the National Football League—my dad's abiding passion—he was totally disciplined. To view my dad only through the prism of the Buccaneers' won–loss record would be unfair. While a bad team, his Buccaneers introduced Tampa Bay to big-time professional sports, and he fought hard to keep the team in the city. While some people may still harbor bitter feelings from those days, he had a big impact on the entire community and many individual lives—a story well told in this honest, engaging book.

My dad ran the Buccaneers on the cheap. Splitting the national television revenue gave him a financial base to operate from, enabling him to cover business losses and pay interest to the banks. Of course, he could only do this if he kept the Buccaneers payroll low. That meant not winning. Each victory increased the salaries and performance bonuses.

The 1979 season was the closest Dad came to winning it all in the National Football League. Ironically, he was the head trustee of the team that beat us. Sometimes I wondered which team he really wanted to win.

My father rose through the power structure of the NFL guided by his knowledge of law and his abilities to both divide and build consensus. His main opponent in the beginning was the famed lawyer Edward Bennett Williams, who once owned the Washington Redskins. In short order, my father's financial acumen outshined Williams's oratorical skills, and he found himself head of the Finance Committee and NFL Management Council. The NFL needed fiscal discipline, and my dad imposed it. He imposed a borrowing cap on each team and orchestrated the methods for breaking the National Football League Players Association (NFLPA) in two strikes.

His mannerisms were a lot like those of Nikita Khrushchev. His scowls were famous. He cursed more crudely than a drunken sailor and yet—when it came to the business of football—he was never out of control. The boxer in him watched and waited for his adversary to flinch, and usually the other guy did, whether it was the NFLPA, the United States Football League (USFL) or other NFL owners.

During the USFL's lawsuit against the NFL, some NFL owners wanted to settle. One morning, my dad and I were in an elevator with them at the federal courthouse. Crowded into that little box, the tension rose as a number of owners pressed their case with my dad. At the mention of the word settlement, he exploded. "Over your dead bodies!" he shouted. By the time the elevator door opened, the discussion was over.

To my dad, preparing for trial meant you went to trial. Just as in the fight at the frat house back in his college days, you didn't show up on the lawn to shout. You finished what you came to do, and you won. My father was adamantly opposed to allowing teams from the USFL to enter the NFL, let alone pay them several hundred million to do so. And he didn't care about the opinions of the other owners. The USFL won $1 (trebled to $3 under federal anti-trust laws) and my father was vindicated.

To the fans of Tampa Bay, however, my father's ownership of the team was a disaster. Truthfully, it was. Dad's fatal flaw was that he was cheap. Whether paying players or his lawyers, he scrimped. Players resented it, and lawyers in his firm did as well. People in his real estate firm actually defrauded him to make up for what they perceived as deficient pay. Even I left his law firm because I felt my pay was too low for the cases I brought in. We didn't speak for 18 months after that, but his respect for me grew.

My dad wasn't only cheap on payroll. In many ways, he was cheap with himself, perhaps a product of having grown up poor, on a dirt road. He owned a private jet and yet often flew coach, using frequent flyer miles. Often, he would bring only one suit, shirt and tie on a business trip, rather than buy more clothing. One time he and I met in Boston to represent a sports announcer who had a criminal tax problem. Before the initial meeting, he called me to his hotel room and said, "I can't go to the meeting." I asked why and he showed me his pants. The seam had unraveled on the inside from his crotch right down to the knee.

"Just wear another suit," I said.

"This is all I have," he answered.

Luckily, my mother had taught me how to sew and the hotel had a small sewing kit. After my tailoring, his pants were serviceable. Away we went and, in an excellent result, our client and the IRS settled.

Even towards the end of his life, my father continued to exercise his strong will in major NFL decisions. As you will read in this book, he sent me as an emissary of mayhem to derail the candidacy of Jim Finks to succeed Pete Rozelle as commissioner. As a former SEC attorney, assistant U.S. attorney and experienced trial attorney, I read the rules carefully, and originated a strategy based on securities take-over litigation to defeat Finks. Combined with my dad's nuanced understanding of NFL politics, the strategy worked. It took many months of meetings, but ultimately we got Paul Tagliabue appointed.

Ironically, if my dad hadn't died when he did, the appointment of Tagliabue could have had dire consequences for him. Paul Tagliabue was very smart, and he moved the league far along the curve in advancing revenue. At the same time, Tagliabue saw the merit in a salary cap and salary floor. Cancer never comes at a good time, but in my father's case, cancer saved him from confronting the salary floor. The $12 million floor was higher than the Bucs' annual net profit of $11 million. That would have led my father to default on his debts and lose his empire. Cancer also saved him from witnessing the loss of his power in the league he loved.

For all his flaws, my dad—a World War II veteran—believed deeply in public service, and was very generous and charitable. He and my mother helped send dozens of people to college, and gave millions to the University of Alabama and the University of Florida. The University of Alabama's School of Business and Commerce is named after him.

But through the very end, my dad remained an enigma. He was warm and harsh, simple and brilliant, selfish and generous, trusting and doubtful, faithful and disloyal. How does one resolve those contradictions in a single person, let alone in someone you love? Every August 25, the anniversary of his death, I send flowers or visit his grave. I am able to cry. I have no resentment. I have warm thoughts for a flawed man. He taught me, and he guided me, and for that I am eternally grateful.

The book you are about to read is a candid account of his impact on the NFL. I hope that, in reading it, people will come to more fully understand my dad's complexity, the evolution of the league, and the enduring impact he made on the sport, the business and the community he loved. He was a unique man and left a mark that few will ever equal.

---

*Hugh F. Culverhouse, Jr., is the owner of Palmer Ranch Holdings and Culverhouse Limited Partnership. A securities litigator, he has worked for the Department of Justice and the Securities and Exchange Commission and partnered at the law firm Culverhouse, Botts & Culverhouse. He was a key member of the NFL Finance Committee from 1989 to 1994.

Preface

TAMPA BAY IS A SPORTING COMMUNITY. With its tropical climate, it affords its citizens the luxury of year-round outdoor activity. Football, baseball, soccer, golf, tennis, track and field and auto racing are just some of the daily sporting activities available to the citizens of Tampa Bay. At the top of this sporting pyramid sits the Tampa Bay Buccaneers.

A Tampa Bay institution since 1976, the Buccaneers are the primary professional sporting choice for local fans. A Super Bowl championship in 2002 only cemented an almost monogamous relationship between team and town. Despite the Tampa Bay Lightning winning a Stanley Cup in 2004 and the Tampa Bay Rays clinching an American League pennant in 2008, the Buccaneers remain number one in the hearts and minds of Tampa Bay fans.

For proof, just tune into one of Tampa Bay's all sports radio stations on a random March, April or May afternoon and chances are a major topic of conversation competing for air time with the Rays' season opener or the Lightning's playoff push will be the state of the Buccaneers heading into mini-camps.

This passionate relationship would not exist without the efforts of team owner Hugh F. Culverhouse, Sr. This fact will come as a bit of a shock to a fan base which for years has been disposed towards viewing Culverhouse's tenure as a mostly dark era. The fans remember the Dickensian thriftiness, the contentious contract negotiations, labor strife and loss after loss. While these memories are valid they have warped over time to the point of carica-ture.

This caricature of Culverhouse is fair to a point but suffers for the same reason all caricatures suffer. Caricatures are easy to draw but lack the details found in a full portrait. A full portrait requires time and effort. The status of Hugh Culverhouse and his Tampa Bay Buccaneers increases significantly when a little more care is taken in reviewing his time at the head of the franchise.

It is my hope this book represents such care and effort. Hugh Culverhouse was a much more complex and influential figure than he has been heretofore given credit. Likewise, Culverhouse's Buccaneer teams were a much more significant franchise than is widely accepted. For the first time, a fair review of the Culverhouse era is offered.

A book such as this is the product of many sets of hands, eyes and hearts. While only one name appears on the cover, it would be folly to assume only one man or woman could create something like this alone. This book is my pride and joy, but it is the accomplishment of many.

First off, I would like to thank Hugh F. Culverhouse, Jr., for his willingness to answer numerous questions about his father. His openness did more than just provide intimate details; it gave me credibility with so many of the other former executives who later agreed to speak with me. Likewise, former Buccaneers linebacker Richard "Batman" Wood's openness and agreement to be a reference provided me the needed cachet to speak with other former Buccaneers players. The wonderful array of photographs in this book would not have been possible without the courteous help of Ron Kolwak of the *Tampa Tribune*. Steven Johnston, Lauren Hartmann and Christy Schnell of the Buccaneers were also invaluable in bringing these photographs to print.

This book is also a family affair. My wife, Amy, in addition to the duties of putting up with my obsession with this franchise, took on the extra jobs of copy editor and sounding board. My nephew William was an able research assistant and my parents, Jim and Louisa, continue to provide encouragement. Close friend Paul Stewart of Bucs UK provided numerous research ideas and was an excellent partner in brainstorming, and Alex Kubli offered much appreciated editing notes.

In short, the team behind this book has much in common with Hugh Culverhouse and the Tampa Bay Buccaneers. They're necessary.

Introduction

THE DEFINING MOMENT of the Hugh Culverhouse era occurred shortly before noon on Sunday, December 29, 1991.

The only owner the Tampa Bay Buccaneers had ever known scheduled a press conference at One Buccaneer Place to announce the biggest news in franchise history: two-time Super Bowl winner Bill Parcells had accepted the job as head coach of the Tampa Bay Buccaneers. The long-time Giants coach had retired following the end of the 1990 season. Ironically, Parcells' last game was played at Tampa Stadium, the home of the Buccaneers. The Giants' 20–19 victory over the Buffalo Bills in Super Bowl XXV was viewed as Parcells' crowning achievement. The Super Bowl victory had allowed him to leave on top. But after spending a year as an analyst for NBC Sports, Parcells had expressed an interest in returning to the sideline, and it appeared that Culverhouse was taking him up on it.

The hiring of one of the best coaches in the game was a coup for Culverhouse, but it was also the worst-kept secret in football. On the day after the Buccaneers defeated the Indianapolis Colts in the season finale, CBS reported Culverhouse and Parcells had been meeting to work out the details of an agreement. The next day, local newspapers reported that Culverhouse had flown to New Jersey to continue discussions with Parcells about money and the level of control the coach would have over the organization.

Christmas Day brought more reports: Culverhouse was going to fire head coach Richard Williamson and re-assign general manager Phil Krueger to make room for Parcells. The next day those reports proved accurate as Richard Williamson was terminated following a 19-game tenure in which he amassed a 4–15 record. The day after Williamson was fired, Krueger resigned his position with the team. Meeting with reporters to discuss his decision to leave the Buccaneers, Krueger let it be known that a deal with Bill Parcells was signed. Krueger wished the new man in charge luck.

"I think hiring Parcells is a positive move," Krueger said to the press. "The fans want a marquee guy, and I hope fans respond to Parcells. I hope the fans respond because Culverhouse has gone all out to get a marquee guy."[1]

On the morning of December 29, details of the contract became known, and it validated the comments made by Krueger in his farewell address. Culverhouse had not only gone all out financially to win Parcells; he had practically signed the deed to One Buccaneer Place over to the former Giants coach. Parcells was coming to Tampa Bay in exchange for $7 million over five years. The contract would make Parcells one of the richest coaches in NFL history. Not only would Parcells become the head coach, but Culverhouse had also granted him absolute authority over all aspects of the Buccaneers' front office. It was reported that Parcells had 38 stipulations he wanted Culverhouse to meet before he would agree to the job. Culverhouse agreed to all 38.

The ceding of total decision-making control to Parcells—everything from player personnel to filters for the coffee makers at One Buccaneer Place—was unheard of at the time in Tampa Bay. Hugh Culverhouse long had final say on the Buccaneer operation, for good and bad. Whatever qualms Culverhouse may have had over turning his franchise over to Parcells were easily outweighed by the positive reaction the team was receiving. For the first time in almost a decade, the Buccaneers were relevant again in the professional football conversation.

Sunday, December 29, was a big weekend for the National Football League. It was Wild Card Weekend, the opening round of the playoffs. The New York Jets and Houston Oilers were preparing to meet in the AFC game while the Dallas Cowboys and Chicago Bears got ready for the NFC battle. At 12 o'clock, ESPN, NBC and CBS would begin their ritualistic pre-game shows, but shortly after the start of the programs the focus would move from Soldier Field and the Astrodome to the big news announced earlier at One Buccaneer Place.

Of the three network pre-game shows, NBC's *NFL Live* would be mustsee. Parcells had spent the season as a studio analyst alongside Bob Costas. On the day that he would be announced as head coach, Parcells would be in the studio fulfilling his obligation to NBC. It was reported that after being named coach, Parcells would fly to Tampa on Tuesday to formally accept the position.

It would be great theater for NBC. Their star analyst, one of the most respected football coaches in the NFL, would be announced as the new head coach of the Tampa Bay Buccaneers and answer questions live on their pre-game show. While ESPN and CBS would also cover the press conference, NBC would have the main man on their staff and in studio.

NBC wasn't the only party that would benefit from great theater. Hugh Culverhouse and his Tampa Bay Buccaneer franchise would receive national exposure during the playoffs, which they had not participated in for almost a decade, and ink Bill Parcells in the process.

As the events unfolded, great theater was produced for NBC, Parcells and Culverhouse. Unfortunately for Hugh Culverhouse and fans of the Tampa Bay Buccaneers, the owner played the part of jester.

As Culverhouse walked to the podium something didn't seem right. The owner of the Tampa Bay Buccaneers did not have the look of a man that just landed the biggest fish in the pond. Instead, Culverhouse's facial expression and posture were similar to that of a convict walking the last mile. Culverhouse stood behind the lectern, looked out at the assembled members of the press and into the cameras that were transmitting his image from coast to coast. He then uttered the three words that would come to be his NFL epitaph.

"I've been jilted," Culverhouse stammered out. For what seemed like ages, the owner of the Tampa Bay Buccaneers just stood there as cameras flashed and video recorders whirred.[2]

Reporter questions quickly broke the silence. How did this happen? Didn't Culverhouse and Parcells have an agreement? Wasn't Parcells scheduled to arrive in Tampa on Tuesday? Didn't Culverhouse meet every single one of the coach's demands?

"I thought we had a deal," Culverhouse answered in a tone that was a combination of anger and humiliation. "Now I feel as though we've been jilted at the altar. I regret it not for only the team but the fans, for this community. I'm still here at the altar. For what it's worth, there is no honeymoon."[3]

Culverhouse went on to affirm that he and Parcells had agreed on the amount of control the coach would have and the compensation he would receive. Culverhouse had expected to announce Parcells as coach on this Sunday and introduce him at a press conference on Tuesday. "I was to hear from him Saturday afternoon to determine if we would do it Tuesday or announce it sooner," Culverhouse said. "I called him at 10 P.M. Saturday night at home. He said he had a change of heart and was not coming to Tampa Bay, although he had received a fabulous offer. It was a five-year guarantee for $6.5 million. He would be director of football operations with complete control."[4]

Culverhouse stated that not only had the agreement been to bring Parcells on board, but to hire Jerry Vainisi as Parcell's hand-picked general manager. "We agreed last Monday night, person to person somewhere in New York or New Jersey, I forget where. Then he wrote down the points we agreed on and put it in a letter, which I received Thursday. We talked and went over it point by point. Then he brought up Jerry Vainisi's name, and I said he would be welcome as general manager.[5]

"He said we were all set; we will execute the contract," Culverhouse continued. "It was executed by Tampa Bay. We now feel we have been jilted at the altar. I regret it for the team's sake and the fans and the community because I thought we had reached a milestone."[6]

Shortly after the press conference ended Parcells gave his side of the story more than a thousand miles away from Tampa. Parcells contradicted Culverhouse by stating that they had never reached an agreement. "We had not agreed," Parcells said. "I agreed to consider the job on the basis of a number of things that we enumerated in writing. I never said I would take the job."[7]

During his time on NBC's *NFL Live* program Parcells explained his reasoning for not taking the job. "In the end I thought it may be too big a job, too many hats to wear in this modern time in professional football, and I just didn't feel right about the job at that time and that's why I didn't take it."[8]

Parcells continued, "Hey, we've all been in job negotiations, we've all been in contract negotiations. All of us have and there was just something about it. In the end, I didn't feel right."[9]

Parcells' reasoning left some members of the Tampa Bay media contingent baffled. Didn't Parcells demand total control of football operations as one of his more than three dozen demands? Wasn't that one of the reasons he had resigned from the Giants in the first place following their victory in Super Bowl XXV? New York papers had been filled with reports of a long-running battle of wills between Parcells and Giants general manager George Young. Young held final say on player personnel, and Parcells wanted that authority for himself. In Tampa Bay, Parcells would have had that wish fulfilled, so why did he say no?

Hubert Mizell, a columnist for the *St. Petersburg Times*, did a little more digging in the weeks that followed and surmised that it wasn't the job that worried Parcells, it was Hugh Culverhouse.

"Parcells is noted for his homework," wrote Mizell. "In assessing the Bucs, he not only got scouting reports of players, but contacted former Tampa Bay coach Ray Perkins, Atlanta Falcons GM Ken Herock, Los Angles Raiders owner Al Davis and (Green Bay) GM Ron Wolf. All but Davis have worked for Culverhouse.[10]

"My guess is Parcells heard four predominantly negative reviews."[11]

Almost 20 years later, Ray Perkins, Ken Herock, and Ron Wolf deny they advised Parcells to spurn Culverhouse, statements that are backed by the former head coach himself. "That didn't make any difference," Parcells said of the stories circulating about Culverhouse's reputation.[12]

The reason Parcells turned down the Buccaneers was not a sense of unease at working for Hugh Culverhouse, far from it. Parcells explained that he desired the opportunity to turn around the Buccaneers franchise but was worried that he physically couldn't handle the job at that time in his life.

"I really wanted to work for the Bucs. I really did," Parcells said in a 2009 interview for this book. "Mr. Culverhouse and I had a meeting. I was interested in returning to the NFL as a coach. Unfortunately, simultaneously with that interest, I was having some physical problems. I didn't know to what extent my problems were at the time. I just knew there was something a little wrong. But I didn't want to pass up the opportunity to go back to the NFL.[13]

"We (Mr. Culverhouse and I) had a conversation and we started talking about things," Parcells continued. "We got down the road pretty well with the contract to the point where we were going to do this. And I told him I felt like I was going to do it, just give me a day or two and we can get this resolved."[14]

"I think he relied on that; I know he did," Parcells said. "In that other day, I had another doctor's deal and there was some additional information that came to light where what I had with my heart was a little more serious than we first thought. I was passing these stress tests only because I had been used to exercising. Compared to my age group I was efficient, but in actuality I was having problems."[15]

When asked if negotiating salary or being granted total control of the franchise led him to question the stability of the franchise, Parcells said it did not.

"The contract discussions were not a problem," Parcells explained. "The only reason why I didn't go to the Tampa Bay Bucs was my physical problem. That is not an excuse. That is just what happened. After that, I started to have some serious second thoughts about being able to do it."[16]

Unfortunately, while Parcells was meeting with his doctors, Hugh Culverhouse was preparing to announce to the NFL that the Tampa Bay Buccaneers were turning a whole new corner. A combination of Parcells' concern over his health, his doctor's not being able to pinpoint the cause and Culverhouse's planning for the restructuring of his football operations led to miscommunication and, ultimately, the owner's embarrassment on national television.

Parcells felt bad about the predicament Culverhouse was placed in, but he had tried his best to explain his situation. Many years later, however, he admits that he didn't help by not being able to offer specifics.

"I tried to explain it [the decision to walk away] to him," Parcells said.

"I said, 'I'm just not able to do it at this time.' I wasn't able to give him a good enough reason.[17]

"I really couldn't prove to him at the time what was wrong," Parcells continued. "I knew something was wrong, but we weren't able to pinpoint it. It was a little bit vague. It was my intention to coach the Bucs. As the time got near I said, 'You know, I just don't think I can do it.' So I called him and told him I don't think I can do it. That is when he said publicly that he felt he was jilted at the altar."[18]

It is important for Parcells that people understand the truth of what happened during the final week of 1991. Bill Parcells did not rebuke Hugh Culverhouse, although it appeared that way at the time, especially to Hugh Culverhouse. Like many events in history, Parcells' negotiations with Mr. Culverhouse became a thing of legend in Tampa Bay and when the legend becomes the story, the legend is printed.

The Bill Parcells soap opera was the last great public example of the intriguing dichotomy that marked Culverhouse's years as owner of the Tampa Bay Buccaneers. The impetuosity, passion, fervor and painstaking attention to the bottom line shown in the Parcells affair were strong traits in Culverhouse. These traits had led him to become one of the wealthiest men in America and arguably the most influential owner in the NFL.

Unfortunately, the same traits that made Culverhouse such an imposing figure were often negated by an obstinate nature. Tight-fisted with his money and stubborn in his refusal to acquiesce to the wisdom of football-men, Culverhouse almost single-handedly crafted one of the most financially successful NFL franchises in the history of the sport but did so at the expense of victory. That myopia would lead to an often inaccurate view of the man's legacy as owner.

Culverhouse would spend almost two decades at the helm of the Buccaneers ship. During that time he would rise to a level of power that would rival that of NFL commissioner Pete Rozelle. In fact, some in the NFL would refer to Culverhouse as vice-commissioner.[19] The late 1970s and the decade of the 1980s proved to be a turbulent time for the NFL. Franchise upheaval, contentious work stoppages and the emergence of a rival professional football league were three significant issues the NFL had to contend with in a relatively short period of time.

In each one of those instances, the NFL turned to Hugh Culverhouse. Tenacious in his work for the league office, Culverhouse pulled the NFL into the modern business era, amassing admirers and enemies along the way. To his fellow owners, Culverhouse was more than just a member of the club, he was necessary.

Culverhouse's status in the NFL was so vaunted, it is hard to fathom that he oversaw the least successful franchise of the 1970s and 1980s. A string of personnel blunders marked the Buccaneers during this era. Several All-Pros, Super Bowl MVPs and even a Hall of Famer called Tampa Bay home briefly before being dealt away for little or nothing in return. Those deals hamstrung the Bucs and shifted the balance of power in the NFL. When other teams needed young talent, they often found a willing trading partner in Hugh Culverhouse. To the personnel departments of the NFL, Hugh Culverhouse was necessary.

Those players that stayed behind played to the best of their abilities but were often overmatched on the football field. As unwilling accomplices to the franchise's inability to retain talent, these players were victimized by losses of historic proportions. To a victory-starved opponent, the Tampa Bay Buccaneers were necessary.

This is the story of Hugh Culverhouse's time as the boss of the Tampa Bay Buccaneers. During his reign, Culverhouse and the Buccaneers would become the National Football League's necessary team. It is a story that all started with the death of one of the pioneering owners of the National Football League.

CHAPTER ONE

"You Just Bought a Lawsuit!"

FIVE YEARS BEFORE THE Buccaneers first took to the field, the man that would become their owner placed himself at the center of the greatest ownership controversy in the history of professional sports. Hugh Culverhouse's involvement in the sale of the Los Angeles Rams in 1972 acted as the catalyst for the only franchise swap in NFL history. Without his bid for the Rams, the Los Angeles franchise may have been sold with little to no notice other than the agate type of the sports transaction page. However, the fight Culverhouse showed reverberated through the NFL for years and ultimately landed him in Tampa Bay. The circuitous route Culverhouse took to ownership was indicative of his ability, and the later ability of his team, to be involved in the defining moments of the modern NFL.

In April of 1971, the National Football League was saddened by the death of Los Angeles Rams majority owner Dan Reeves. Reeves had been the NFL's most prominent pioneer and master showman. Reeves's decision to transplant the Rams from Cleveland to Los Angeles in 1946 was heralded by many as the first move towards establishing professional football as a national sport.[1] For years the NFL had confined itself to the Northeast and industrial Midwest until Reeves moved the Rams.

The move by Reeves was daring. As the only team on the West Coast, the Rams were forced to supplement the travel expenses of their visiting opponents.[2] The cost and hassle of the first couple of years in California paid off handsomely for Reeves as he cultivated a championship contender that grew and thrived in the shadows of Hollywood. From 1946 to 1971, the Rams boasted a high-powered offense and competed for a championship in several seasons. While they claimed only one title during the Reeves era, the Rams were arguably the greatest marketing success in the NFL. The team attracted astonishing crowds to the mammoth Los Angeles Memorial Coliseum. When Reeves passed away, the Rams were a crown jewel of the National Football League.

The passion that Reeves had for the Rams was not shared by his family. Shortly after Reeves passed away, the Rams were put up for sale by the executors of his estate. While the Reeves family may have had no interest in the Los Angeles Rams, suitors from across the country lined up for the chance to spend upwards of $15 to $19 million for the ownership stake. After almost a year of listening to offers, it appeared the general manager of the Rams, Bill Barnes, had agreed to sell the franchise to a Jacksonville, Florida, tax attorney named Hugh F. Culverhouse for an astonishing $17 million.[3]

At the time of the deal, Culverhouse was an unknown quantity. Within just a matter of weeks everybody in the National Football League would know his name.

Born and raised in Alabama during the Great Depression, Hugh Culverhouse was a fighter, literally and figuratively. Culverhouse boxed at the collegiate level at the University of Alabama alongside future governor George Wallace. Shortly after graduating, Culverhouse enlisted in the Army Air Corps during World War II. Commissioned as an officer, Culverhouse served two years in India. Upon returning to civilian life, Culverhouse re-enrolled at Alabama and earned a law degree. The newly minted lawyer quickly moved into the corridors of power, taking a job as Alabama's assistant attorney general. After a couple of years in Montgomery, Culverhouse once again was called to military duty, this time during the Korean War.

Upon completing his military service, Culverhouse felt the time had come to shift the focus of his career. Following the advice of a family friend, Culverhouse decided to leave criminal law and focus on tax law. He explained his reasoning in a 1976 interview.

"A friend of my father's told me back in the 30's that this was going to be a tax-oriented society," Culverhouse said. "I decided I wanted to be a good tax lawyer. I wanted to be better than anyone in the field. But I always went on the assumption that people were smarter than me. So I had to outwork them. I had to be better prepared than they were."[4]

In the early 1950s, Culverhouse took a job with the Internal Revenue Service. Possessing a law degree, experience in state politics and fresh off of military service, he attacked the U.S. Tax Code with the same pugnacious style that had served him well in the boxing ring. In a 1984 interview, he viewed his time with the IRS as one of acquiring the skills and education that would make him a formidable businessman.

"I could take on cases involving things I knew nothing about," Culverhouse said. "I would have to learn everything I could about a business, how it worked, how all its parts interacted. It was wonderful fun."[5]

During his time with the IRS, Culverhouse built up an array of financial and legal skills and an impressive client list. As one of the investigators during the Kefauver hearings on organized crime in the 1950s, he interacted with the movers and shakers of both national business and politics.

"I handled a lot of the tax investigations of organized-crime figures," Culverhouse said. "That was what I liked about the IRS. The magnitude of the cases was far bigger than anything you would see in private practice."[6]

Culverhouse parlayed those contacts into a lucrative private practice when he set out on his own in 1956. Experienced in tax law, politics, corporate policy and even organized crime, he became an exceptionally well-rounded businessman in the 1950s. That variety of expertise made him one of the nation's wealthiest men. Within 20 years Culverhouse had grown from an IRS agent making $20,000 a year to a nationally renowned tax attorney worth an estimated $30 million to $40 million. With an understanding of the tax code that was unparalleled, his services were in demand by a veritable who's who of the nation's elite. The Jacksonville-based law firm that Culverhouse ran boasted clients that ranged from Fortune 500 CEOs to President Richard Nixon. The United States Supreme Court even cited his cases.[7]

Culverhouse's wealth was not just the result of invoicing his celebrity clients. He parlayed his contacts with politicians and businessmen into lucrative land deals and business investments. By the time he had entered his mid-fifties, he was a partner at the preeminent tax law firm Culverhouse, Botts, Mills and Cone and owner of condominiums and undeveloped land throughout Florida. Included in Culverhouse's real estate holdings was a vast majority of the land in Sarasota County, home of some of the most pristine beaches on the Gulf of Mexico at that time. The possession of these land holdings would increase his wealth tenfold in the decades to come. In addition to his law firm and real estate holdings, Culverhouse occupied his time with directorships of Barnett Bank, the Miami Merchandise Mart and Port Everglades Steel Corp.[8]

At an age when many men of his station would have been seeking to spend the rest of their days playing golf or boating, Hugh Culverhouse had decided to go into the business of professional football. In June of 1972, he met with Bill Barnes in Los Angeles and asked how much money it would cost to purchase the Rams. He was told $20 million, an answer that he scoffed at. After some haggling, Culverhouse offered Barnes $17 million and the deal was agreed to verbally. The two men set a meeting in New York City for June 6 to sign the paperwork.[9] After his meeting with Barnes, Culverhouse placed a phone call to his son, a conversation the younger Culverhouse would remember clearly decades later.

Hugh Culverhouse, Jr., was a master's student at New York University in the summer of 1972. More concerned with his coursework than anything else, he was completely unprepared for the bombshell his father dropped on him. While he was used to his father making impetuous purchases, he couldn't understand why his father would be attracted by a football team.

"My dad heard while he was in Los Angeles that the Reeves family estate is going to sell the Rams," Hugh Jr. recalled. "And being Dad, he rushed over and met with them and hammered out a deal to buy the Rams.[10]

"My dad would do stuff like that all the time," he said. "If somebody had the Eiffel Tower for sale, he'd go try to buy it."[11]

What made this impulse buy unusual to Hugh Jr. was that he had never known his father to care for any sport besides boxing.

"I sure as shit didn't think my dad was going to be a football team owner," the son said. "To be honest I never saw him watch a game on TV. I never saw him too much care for it. If he ever went to a game, it was with a client."[12]

But Culverhouse Sr.'s relationship with professional football was about to change dramatically as was his son's.

"I got a phone call in 1972 and my dad said, 'Rent out the 21 [the famous New York restaurant].' I said, 'Are you fucking nuts? What do you mean rent out the 21? Why?'[13]

"My dad said, 'I just bought the Los Angeles Rams; we're going to hold a press conference at 21 and have the room packed.'[14]

"And then I said, 'Are you smoking dope? Are you crazy?' and he said, 'Hugh, just do what I said,' and he hung up, so I went down to 21 and picked out a menu."[15]

As Hugh Jr. picked out a menu at one of the most expensive restaurants in the nation and his father prepared legal documents while heading to New York City, Carroll Rosenbloom was busy hatching an audacious plan.

Carroll Rosenbloom was a restless and charismatic man. Owner of the Baltimore Colts since 1953, Rosenbloom was weary of the mid–Atlantic and desperately wanted to own the Los Angeles Rams and enjoy the southern California lifestyle that went along with that prize. Carroll's son, Steve Rosenbloom, claimed his father had been talking to Dan Reeves for years about acquiring the Rams, a deal that Reeves himself hoped for.

"I remember before a game [against Los Angeles], we were out on the field and Danny Reeves came over and the three of us sat on the bench," Rosenbloom recalled. "Danny knew he was sick and he said, 'Carroll, if something happens to me it would be a wonderful thing if you could get the Rams because nobody in my family is really interested in it, and I don't know what will happen.'"[16]

While Reeves may have wanted the elder Rosenbloom to take over the Rams, there were the small matters of league rules and income tax law which precluded a simple purchase. The NFL prohibited one family from owning multiple franchises, so a plan for Carroll to buy the Rams for himself and leave Steve in charge of the Colts was off the table. A second option, selling the Colts and then buying the Rams was not a financially sound plan. If Rosenbloom sold the Colts, a good deal of the proceeds would be subject to income tax. The money that would go to the IRS would eat away so much of Rosenbloom's liquid assets he would find it impossible to surpass Culverhouse's bid of $17 million. The Reeves estate, sympathetic to Rosenbloom and knowing the late owner's wishes, could not accept a lower offer because they had a fiduciary responsibility to accept the highest bid, which at the moment was Culverhouse's.

Realizing that Culverhouse was heading to a meeting with the Reeves estate, Rosenbloom pulled off an audacious blitz from the blind side that caught Culverhouse off guard and planted the Colts owner in charge of the Los Angeles market he so coveted. Rosenbloom realized there was no league rule against one franchise owner trading the rights for his NFL team to the owner of another NFL team for the rights of that franchise. What Rosenbloom needed was a willing partner, a man that would be willing to buy the Rams and then trade the entire franchise to Rosenbloom in exchange for the Colts and some cash to make the deal worthwhile. With time ticking down, Rosenbloom found a willing partner in Chicago air conditioning magnate Robert Irsay.

David Harris' book *The League* documents how Rosenbloom and Irsay presented a bid to the lawyers representing the Reeves estate while Hugh Culverhouse sat in the lobby, oblivious to the history-making machinations occurring on the other side of the door.

Irsay put up $19 million, a full $2 million more than Culverhouse's offer, to buy the Rams from the Reeves estate. Irsay could afford to do this knowing that he was only on the hook for $15 million. When the Reeves estate accepted the bid, jettisoning Culverhouse, Irsay immediately traded the Rams to Carroll Rosenbloom for the Colts and $4 million. Hugh Jr. explained the benefit to Rosenbloom of such a transaction.[17]

"Carroll Rosenbloom did not have to pay taxes on what would have been a very hefty sale under IRS Code 1031—a tax-free exchange," he said.[18]

With whiplash speed and the approval of the National Football League's 26 owners, Robert Irsay owned the Colts, Carroll Rosenbloom owned the Rams and Hugh Culverhouse was left holding worthless legal documents for a deal that was no more. When he was notified by the Rams that his offer to purchase the franchise was no longer being considered, Culverhouse shot back, "You've just bought yourself a lawsuit!"[19]

When he called his son later that day, Culverhouse was as hot as the Manhattan asphalt in summer.

"My dad went ballistic," Hugh Jr. said. "The next day I get another phone call from Dad. He said, 'Carroll fucked me.' I said, 'Dad, what woman is *Carol*?' He said, 'No! Carroll Rosenbloom, the owner of the Colts, came in and pulled a fast one and now he's buying the Rams.'"[20]

"My dad said, 'Whatever you do, cancel the reservations at 21,' and he hung up. Fortunately, I was able to cancel, and they didn't charge me. I'm a kid in my early 20s in grad school in New York with only a couple of pair of blue jeans to my name!"[21]

While Carroll Rosenbloom and Robert Irsay took possession of their new franchises, an angry Hugh Culverhouse made plans. The NFL may not have intentionally set out to start a fight with Culverhouse, but that is exactly what happened. Culverhouse saw to it that the NFL would be in for a long and painful experience and they would underestimate him at their own peril.

Shortly after returning home, an incensed Culverhouse filed a lawsuit and named Rosenbloom, Irsay, the Reeves estate, and the National Football League as co-conspirators under the Sherman Antitrust Act.

"Rosenbloom and the NFL have acted to further monopolize the monopoly power acquired by them in the business of professional football," Culverhouse complained.[22]

If few people knew who Hugh Culverhouse was, they were about to find out.

The lawsuit was filed in California because Culverhouse stated he had reached a verbal agreement with the Reeves estate in Los Angeles. The tax attorney was adamant that his offer of $17 million had been accepted in Los Angeles only to be told days later that, "The Los Angeles Rams Football Company was best kept within the family."[23] Culverhouse had no doubt that statement meant the Rams and the NFL would bend over backward to violate his deal to satisfy an owner of their choosing, even if it meant taking part in an unorthodox business deal. To Culverhouse, this was a conspiracy, and he refused to take it lying down. Culverhouse's son explained the gist of his father's suit.

"My dad claimed tortious interference with a contract took place in California," Hugh Jr. said. "Rosenbloom, the NFL, all of them under Dad's theory tortiously interfered with his contract [to purchase the Rams]."[24]

Hugh Culverhouse and the Reeves estate had no written documentation of their deal; it was strictly a verbal understanding arranging a contract signing. However, as Culverhouse's son explained, in tort law even though the elder Culverhouse had nothing in writing, he could charge Rosenbloom with being a tortfeasor, a party that prevents the two agreeing parties from formalizing a deal through interference. Rosenbloom's last second introduction of Irsay and quick purchase of the Rams was an act that interfered with Culverhouse's agreement. Under tort law, Culverhouse had the right to sue Rosenbloom, the NFL, and all the other parties for damages.

"The NFL said, 'You didn't have a written contract,' but that doesn't matter if you go under the theory of torts," said Hugh Jr.[25]

Just as Hugh Jr. is able to succinctly sum up the legal argument of his father, Carroll Rosenbloom's son Steve is just as able to explain the thought process of his father before and after the Rams purchase.

"He [Culverhouse] thought he had the rights to buy the Rams, and that may have been through some negotiations with the Reeves family," Steve Rosenbloom said.[26]

"Culverhouse thought that he had purchased the Rams at the time we were in Baltimore. Joe Thomas brought us Bob Irsay and the deal was Irsay would buy the Rams and then we would swap franchises, which is exactly what happened. It turned out to be a fine deal and a good one actually for everybody.[27]

"Culverhouse was of course upset, but this was a foregone conclusion," Steve Rosenbloom said.[28]

Bill Barnes, lead negotiator for the Reeves estate, seemed to back up Rosenbloom's claim when he admitted negotiations for the Colts owner to purchase the Rams had been going on for a year. One of the reasons it had taken so long according to Barnes was because a swap in franchises was an unprecedented and confusing move. "It's all very complicated," Barnes told reporters. "There are so many angles ... depreciation and recapture of depreciation. All kinds of things have to be worked out."[29]

When Culverhouse filed a lawsuit, the elder Rosenbloom wasn't too concerned, said his son.

"There might have been a threat of legal action from Culverhouse," Steven Rosenbloom recalled. "But I don't think it reached the point where something might happen."[30]

One of the reasons the case did not go to court was that the elder Rosenbloom realized that even if Hugh Culverhouse couldn't win the case, he could do a lot of damage to the Rams and the NFL in a court of law. The NFL had been fighting charges of monopolization for decades. The NFL had been granted anti-trust exemptions from Congress in some instances, such as when the AFL-NFL merger took place, but it did not enjoy the unfettered exemption enjoyed by Major League Baseball.[31] The NFL needed to walk a fine line to get exemptions, and a lawsuit claiming that the sale of a franchise was fixed could attract a suspicious congressional eye.

There was also the inconvenient matter that Reeves, Rosenbloom and Rozelle all had a connection. Dan Reeves had hired Rozelle in the 1950s to be his public relations director. In 1960, Reeves was the man who championed Rozelle's nomination to be commissioner. While his tenure with the Rams and friendship with Dan Reeves would have no legal bearing on the case, in the minds of a jury it could appear that Rozelle had given his OK to the franchise swap just to placate the wishes of the man who helped him become commissioner. Explaining the relationship would make for uncomfortable testimony if a trial was to come.

Commissioner Pete Rozelle, right, announces Tampa Bay as the recipient of the NFL's 27th franchise. The NFL awarded the franchise to Tom McCloskey, who would turn the franchise back over to the league after encountering financial difficulties. Jacksonville tax attorney Hugh Culverhouse, thwarted in his attempts to purchase the Los Angeles Rams, was happy to take over the reins. To the left is Tampa delegate Leonard Levy (*Tampa Tribune*).

Carroll Rosenbloom also didn't believe being called to testify was in his or the NFL's best interests for the simple fact that it would cost a lot of time and money.

"In 1972 my father said one thing he needed to do was go talk to Culverhouse and try to smooth things over," Steve Rosenbloom said of his father's actions to facilitate an out of court settlement. "My father was a problem-solver and not a problem-maker. The NFL would not want a lawsuit. Carroll Rosenbloom would not want a lawsuit if it could be resolved.[32]

"So he went down to see Culverhouse and apparently they had a nice meeting and it was resolved eventually by my father promising, and he had Pete Rozelle go along with it, that Hugh Culverhouse would get a crack at the next expansion team."[33]

While many accounts support the fact that Culverhouse was promised an expansion team in exchange for dropping the lawsuit, there is conjecture about whether he was promised an expansion franchise or a *specific* expansion franchise. Steve Rosenbloom contends that the promise was simply for an expansion franchise with no regard to geographic market.

"The bottom line out of all of this, maybe Hugh wasn't completely happy but it was resolved to the point where he would get an NFL team, and it would be an expansion team," the younger Rosenbloom said.[34]

Hugh Jr. claims the NFL promised to award his father a franchise in Florida.

"Dad filed a lawsuit, suing the NFL, suing Rosenbloom and as they proceeded to litigation they struck a settlement that to Dad sounded reasonable," he said. "The settlement was we will grant within the next two years two new franchises. One will be in Tampa, and we will give you the first franchise granted.[35]

"Two years later, Dad's licking his chops about Tampa. He even bought a condo there."[36]

In April of 1974, the NFL announced the first of the two expansion franchises. And just as had been promised, the first to be awarded was Tampa Bay. The 27th NFL franchise was located a mere five-hour car drive away from Jacksonville. The NFL made good on the first half of the deal, but then the roof caved in on Culverhouse. Shockingly, when the NFL announced the ownership group for the Tampa Bay franchise in October of 1974, they ignored Culverhouse and instead chose Tom McCloskey, a Philadelphia real estate millionaire. Less than two months later, the NFL awarded the 28th franchise to Seattle, *a six- to seven-hour flight* from Jacksonville, and offered it to Culverhouse. Culverhouse balked at the offer, explaining that his family was opposed to relocating across the country.[37] Reluctantly, Culverhouse turned down the Seattle franchise.

Whether the decision to locate Culverhouse in Seattle was punishment for having threatened to drag Rosenbloom and the NFL into court depends on which side of the story you believe.

Steve Rosenbloom said Culverhouse being granted the Seattle franchise was simply the NFL keeping up its end of the out of court settlement.

"They [the NFL] were going to award Seattle to Culverhouse," Rosenbloom said. "I was in the league office at the time, and I know that he could have taken the Seattle Seahawks, but he turned it down because it was too far away."[38]

Steve Rosenbloom said that it made no sense for Culverhouse to turn down Seattle after being so adamant about fighting for the Rams.

"I never put together the fact, 'Okay, I'm going to buy the Rams and I live in Florida, but Seattle is too far,'" Rosenbloom said.[39]

While the younger Rosenbloom feels the NFL acted in good faith, Hugh Jr. has no doubt that the NFL was punishing his father.

"The NFL is absolutely crafty," he claims. "They never forget anybody who sues them, and they always bear a grudge. They held a big affair and awarded two teams. If you look at a map of the United States, you couldn't have picked a location further away. They laughed like hell."[40]

After agreeing to give up his pursuit of the Rams, Culverhouse was stunned to be overlooked when the Tampa franchise was awarded. According to his son, Culverhouse did attempt to sell his family on the idea of Seattle, but ultimately had to concede defeat.

"My dad talked to my mom, and my mom said, 'If you go, I stay,'" Hugh Jr. recalled. "My father told the NFL, 'Nice job. You totally fucked me. You win.'"[41]

With the NFL not planning to expand again for the foreseeable future, it seemed that Culverhouse was locked out of professional football. Over the next few days however, an economic calamity that evaporated a great deal of the nation's capital turned out to be the best thing to happen to his impulse to buy into the NFL.

Just days after saying no to the Seattle franchise, Culverhouse received an unexpected phone call from the National Football League asking if he would be interested in owning the Tampa Bay Buccaneers. The events that led up to that telephone call couldn't have been timed more perfectly if Culverhouse himself had been in charge.

Tom McCloskey had been named owner of the Tampa football franchise in October. McCloskey was the owner of McCloskey and Co., a national builder and real estate developer with offices across the country, including one in Tampa. McCloskey's company had been responsible for such projects as RFK Stadium, the home of the Washington Redskins, and the Sam Rayburn Office Building, home of the U.S. Senate's office space. McCloskey was best known as the owner of the Philadelphia Atoms of the North American Soccer League and his failed attempt to purchase the Philadelphia Eagles in 1968. Despite the appearance that McCloskey was a denizen of the City of Brotherly Love, Rozelle and the other owners of the NFL went out of their way to express that McCloskey was a Floridian at heart.

"His company, McCloskey and Co., has its southern headquarters in the First Financial Tower in Tampa," Rozelle told reporters. "Tom's sister went to the University of Tampa. He has a residence and is a registered voter there.[42]

While his Florida ties were tenuous at best, McCloskey had won over the other owners of the NFL, winning in a vote over Fort Lauderdale businessman Harry Mangurian.

"We feel he'll be a great owner," said Pittsburgh Steelers president Dan Rooney. "He is the man we recommended to the full executive committee."[43]

Interestingly, Hugh Culverhouse was barely mentioned as a candidate in the press following McCloskey's announcement.

At first, it appeared that McCloskey was on his way to living up to everyone's expectations. By late November he had established the team's offices in Tampa's First Financial Tower. McCloskey had also named a vice president, started to accept applications for employment, ruminated on the type of head coach he wanted, and began researching possible team nicknames. He told Tom McEwen, sports editor of the *Tampa Tribune*, that his plan was to build the franchise with great deliberation.

"We will move slowly," McCloskey said. "We want to do things right. We know how much work was done by so many people to win this franchise. We know great things like this don't just happen."[44]

While McCloskey appeared busy, there was one thing that wasn't being accomplished. McCloskey was not making the initial payment on the $16 million he owed the National Football League in expansion fees. As the days turned into weeks, many in the Tampa Bay community and NFL headquarters realized something was horribly wrong with the choice to head Tampa Bay's franchise. Hints had been popping up, including a statement McCloskey had made in early November.

"We are taking things carefully," he had said again. "We are just beginning to sit down and work on outlines. *Remember, we haven't signed the papers yet.*"[45]

Shortly after that statement, disturbing rumors began to abound. McCloskey wasn't really worth $100 million, his pending divorce was taking away half of his assets,[46] the NFL was demanding full payment of the $16 million instead of installments. Many of these rumors proved to be unfounded, but the fact was that McCloskey had not paid a dime to the NFL when December rolled around. Finally, on December 5, 1974, the truth came out: Because the nation's deteriorating economy was hitting McCloskey's development business particularly hard, he no longer felt comfortable putting up the capital required to get the Tampa Bay franchise off the ground.

"Since our proposal some six weeks ago to purchase the Tampa franchise in the National Football League, we have made more detailed investigations into all aspects of the project," McCloskey announced in a written statement. "We have decided that it is in our best interests, from a sound business decision, to withdraw application for the franchise."[47]

In an almost inconceivable turn of events, the man who the National Football League had picked over Culverhouse could no longer make the financial commitment necessary to start an NFL franchise. While it seemed astounding that a man of McCloskey's background would have been caught off guard by the expense associated with an NFL franchise, the league also looked incompetent. Exactly what kind of due diligence had the NFL run on McCloskey? How could the NFL have chosen a man whose fortune was made in an industry that was crumbling during the economic downturn? As Hugh Jr. succinctly put it in 2009, "The economy fucked the NFL."[48]

With their primary choice for the Tampa Bay franchise done in, the NFL had little choice but to turn to the man they had spurned not once, but twice.

Three days before Tom McCloskey's announcement to back out of the NFL, Culverhouse Sr. received a telephone call at his Jacksonville home from Pete Rozelle. Hugh Jr. stated the commissioner, on behalf of the league's 26 owners, contacted the elder Culverhouse and asked him to bail out the Tampa Bay franchise.

"Sheepishly they [the NFL] came back to Hugh Culverhouse, and they said, 'Would you take it [Tampa Bay]?'" Hugh Jr. said. "And he said, 'Yes, on my terms.'"[49]

The expansion fee for both Tampa Bay and Seattle was $16 million, but Culverhouse negotiated favorable terms that allowed him to buy the team with minimal impact on his cash flow.

"It was $16 million stretched out over seven years," Hugh Jr. said. "Two years before, he had bought 12,500 acres of land in Sarasota, The Palmer Ranch, and frankly he couldn't have afforded it [the franchise]. He said, 'Take it or leave it.'"[50]

The NFL, faced with the embarrassing possibility of having to delay or even possibly pull the franchise, agreed to Culverhouse's terms. The next morning Culverhouse flew to New York and signed the paperwork. The tax attorney then returned to Jacksonville to wire his deposit for the team and then flew to Puerto Rico to work on a real estate deal. As McCloskey was making his desire to walk away known, Hugh Culverhouse was in a tropical island paradise inking deals and celebrating his entrée to the National Football League.

The announcement that Culverhouse had taken control of the franchise was met with little excitement in Tampa Bay. Following the uncertainty of McCloskey's short tenure as owner, many in the region were worried that the Jacksonville-based Culverhouse would request that the franchise be transferred to Jacksonville, which had also been hoping for an expansion team. Culverhouse quickly allayed those fears, signing a 30-year lease for the team to play its home games at Tampa Stadium.

"I'm totally committed and in for the duration," he told the press. "I'm extremely elated and will become a working member of the community. I've promised the NFL that I will not be a passive owner. I already have the okay from my law firm to cut down on work elsewhere and put my heart and soul into Tampa's pro football team."[51]

Culverhouse backed up his words with actions as he went to great effort to relocate his business concerns and home from Jacksonville to Tampa Bay.

"That's why he bought a condo and opened a law firm on Westshore Boulevard in Tampa," his son explained. "He wanted to have a presence. Three years later they sold their home in Jacksonville."[52]

Just a little over two years removed from being on the short end of Carroll Rosenbloom's shrewd franchise swap, Hugh Culverhouse found himself on top of the world. Not only was he the owner of a National Football League franchise, he led a franchise in his home state. After being treated as a pawn by the NFL, he had placed the league into check when they needed to be bailed out following the embarrassing McCloskey affair. With the expansion fee negotiated down to a little over $2 million a year, Culverhouse didn't need a large group of investors to make the payments. Cincinnati financier Marvin Warner paid $9.6 million for 48 percent of the franchise.[53] With the NFL television contract paying teams $2 million a year, Culverhouse was already seeing a profit before the team even took the field. Within two years, the NFL television contract increased each team's share to $5 million a year. With returns like that, Culverhouse didn't need a partner for long and eventually bought out Warner.

In an interview early in the Bucs' inaugural 1976 season, Culverhouse had said when asked if the investment in the franchise paid off, "People ask me if it's a business or a hobby. I tell them that if it didn't make good business sense, I wouldn't have invested in it. But I also wouldn't do it solely as a business investment."[54]

While the answer was enigmatic, there was no doubt that Culverhouse's purchase of the Tampa Bay Buccaneers was paying off handsomely for him. The effort and fight had been worth it. He had taken on the NFL and won.

With the Tampa Bay franchise securely his, Culverhouse set out to build a winning football team. With fewer than two years until opening day in 1976, he needed to chart the organizational structure of his football team which was christened the Tampa Bay Buccaneers in a popular "Name the Team" contest. Administrators needed to be hired, a coaching staff assembled and players brought onboard.

As the clock ticked down to the opener, One Buccaneer Place became the center of activity for a franchise destined to become the NFL's necessary team.

Chapter Two

"We're Here for One Reason Only!"

THE TAMPA BAY BUCCANEERS were a distinct team before they came close to the field. In early 1975 the team chose as their official colors Florida Orange, Red and White. While the Bucs were not the only team to employ orange—the Denver Broncos and Cleveland Browns also sported the color—their particular shade was quite eye-catching and an instant source of debate. Many Floridians appreciated the nod to the color of citrus and sunshine, but almost as many viewed the orange jerseys as hideous, caricaturing the tops as "creamsicle orange" or "pumpkin orange." Topping off the look was a helmet decal featuring an Errol Flynn–type swashbuckler with a dagger clenched in his teeth and wearing a plumed hat atop his head.

The designer of the logo, Lamar Sparkman, explained the genesis behind the symbol in an early Buccaneers yearbook.

"I approached it [the logo] with the idea that he must be a cavalier, not a hairy-legged slob," said Sparkman. "The plumed feather adds class, I think. I put the dagger in his mouth to add aggression and then had him wink. It's a half wink and a half sneer."[1]

The logo that came to be known as Bucco Bruce was a second sartorial lightning rod. Like the color scheme, the logo appeared to be a love it or hate it creation. For every fan that shared Sparkman's romantic view of a dashing pirate straight out of 1930s Hollywood, another viewed the winking, plumed figure as a bit effeminate.

Wherever one landed on the Bucco Bruce spectrum one thing was certain: the Buccaneers uniform was an attention grabber. Culverhouse had approved a bold fashion choice. He made an even bolder move when he hired the head football coach.

Hugh Culverhouse had made a fortune by being a quick study of how businesses worked. While he made a name for himself as a tax lawyer, Culverhouse freely admitted that the bulk of his millions came from real estate, an industry that he learned over the course of decades.

"I didn't make most of my money from practicing law. It came from real estate ventures more than anything," he announced after being introduced as owner.[2]

Culverhouse was candid about viewing the Buccaneers equally as status symbol and financial investment. A notorious early riser, he described himself as someone incapable of relaxing and commented that he would treat the franchise no differently than any other business opportunity.

"I guess I could sit back and look fat and happy," Culverhouse said. "But I wouldn't know how. What I've done in everything in which I've invested is to try and learn the business."[3]

To that end, he hired one of the NFL's brightest young minds to run the operation, a man who would one day craft a Hall of Fame-worthy career in personnel.

Ron Wolf had been the chief lieutenant to Al Davis for the highly successful Oakland Raiders franchise. As the Raiders director of player personnel for over a decade, Wolf played a key role in acquiring the players that made Oakland a perennial Super Bowl contender. Culverhouse was able to convince Wolf to move to an expansion franchise from one of the NFL's elite clubs by making the 36-year-old the youngest vice president of football operations in the league.

Shortly after being hired, Wolf brought on board another executive well regarded by the NFL. Tom Bass had been involved with the personnel department in Cincinnati when the Bengals were founded in 1968. A veteran of the expansion system, Bass was brought on board to help the Buccaneers stock their roster with the two methods of player acquisition the NFL presented: the annual collegiate draft and a special veteran allocation draft.

The NFL had decreed that the Buccaneers and Seahawks would participate in the annual collegiate draft in the spring of 1976. In addition to the collegiate draft, the NFL would host an allocation draft in which the other 26 teams would identify expendable players that could be hired by Tampa Bay and Seattle. The players available to Tampa Bay and Seattle would most likely be veterans on the downside of their careers and inexperienced players that were perceived to have not lived up to their potential.

Tom Bass recounted that he and Ron Wolf were convinced that it would be in the best interest of the Buccaneers to target young players at the expense of veterans.

"We were trying to get younger players and players we thought could develop into a player that could have more than a one-year career," Bass said. "We weren't really interested in older players. I had been through this in Cincinnati. I had a feeling for the type of player that would be available.[4]

"We knew we weren't going to get any top-of-the-line players," Bass said. "We had to build through the draft and the waiver wire, so we focused a great deal of our attention on the college draft and we tried to get players we could develop through the expansion draft."[5]

With a focus on young and inexperienced players, the Buccaneers would need a coach with a great deal of patience and a reputation for teaching. Culverhouse focused on collegiate head coaches and was reported to have entertained thoughts of former Notre Dame head coach Ara Parseghian. Former Florida State head coach Bill Peterson was also interested in the job, but there was really only one man Hugh Culverhouse was fixated on: Southern Cal coach John McKay.

Shockingly, he got his man without having to work very hard.

Time has dimmed the memory of just what an imposing figure John McKay cut in college football and just what a coup Culverhouse made in talking McKay into taking an NFL job. As head coach of the USC Trojans, McKay won four national championships, coached two Heisman Trophy winners (Mike Garrett and O.J. Simpson), and was regarded as a revolutionary thinker both on the field and off. McKay's variation of the I-formation, having the tailback stand rather than line up in a three-point stance so he could read the defense, created a prolific running game and earned USC the nickname "Tailback U." In addition to his on-field innovations, McKay also garnered headlines for his progressive stance on race. Southern Cal became one of the first teams to be led by an African American quarterback, Jimmy Jones, from 1969 to 1971.

Some of the biggest names in college football history fell before McKay's USC Trojan juggernaut. Among the who's who of college coaching legends McKay bested were Bob Devaney of Nebraska, Woody Hayes of Ohio State, Bobby Dodd of Georgia Tech and Paul "Bear" Bryant of Alabama.

Along the way, McKay also became as well known for his quips and one-liners. Popular with the Los Angeles press, McKay's quotes were repeated around the nation. One of his most famous quotes came following a 51–0 loss to Notre Dame in 1966. McKay reportedly told his players in the locker room, "OK, those of you that need showers take them."[6]

It was this combination of success, innovation, and charisma that attracted Culverhouse to McKay. But on the surface it appeared ludicrous that a man with the world at his feet would want to take over an undermanned expansion franchise clear across the continent. In 1974 McKay won his fourth national championship with an 18–17 victory over Ohio State in the Rose Bowl. With USC's 1975 season already underway McKay appeared content to spend the rest of his career adding to the Trojans' already burgeoning trophy case.

The NFL had tried with little success to pry coaches with the stature of John McKay away from their universities. Joe Paterno of Penn State refused an offer to coach the Pittsburgh Steelers in 1969 (the Steelers' back-up plan was an unknown assistant named Chuck Noll). In the late 1960s, Paul "Bear" Bryant had turned down the opportunity to coach the Miami Dolphins (they hired Don Shula). John McKay had also been approached on multiple occasions by his hometown Los Angeles Rams and once by the New England Patriots, the latter offering an astounding 10-year contract to be head coach and general manager.[7] Each time McKay had said thanks, but no thanks. For all intents and purposes, McKay would stay a college coach.

It seemed a fool's errand for Culverhouse to contemplate making a run at John McKay. But on Halloween 1975, Culverhouse once again shook the sporting world to its foundations by announcing that John McKay, the most dominant college coach of the past decade and a half, was coming to Tampa Bay.

The deal that landed John McKay was an amazingly lucrative offer for the time. Culverhouse had wanted to make a splash, and the money he paid to do so was almost as big a story as McKay's leaving USC. McKay was signed to a five-year contract worth $750,000, life insurance policies worth an additional $750,000, staked McKay to a $250,000 land investment with guarantees against depreciation, a $10,000 expense account and, just for good measure, three automobiles.[8] The $150,000 annual salary almost tripled the $52,000 McKay made at USC.

The contract was the talk of the NFL, but to say that McKay left USC purely for financial gain would be grossly unfair and inaccurate. Culverhouse first offered the deal to McKay in August at the annual College All-Star game, and McKay had refused to accept. But as the 1975 season got underway, McKay began to consider just what a job in the NFL would mean.

McKay was growing frustrated as the athletic director at USC. In addition to running the football team, McKay also was an administrator responsible for the daily operations of all athletic programs at the university. In his early 50s, McKay was no longer as enthusiastic about the AD position. He quipped to a reporter shortly after being named the Buccaneers coach, "I got tired of going to conference meetings and listening to endless conversations about whether we're going to have the hammer throw in our conference track meet."[9]

The Buccaneers job meant McKay could focus on one thing and one thing only: football. That appealed to McKay almost as much as not having to cope with numerous boosters and alumni groups who over the years had begun to expect so much from McKay that he was beginning to find coaching less joyful.

In Tampa Bay McKay would have to answer to just one man: Culverhouse. That suited the Bucs head coach just fine.

"I have been more impressed by Hugh Culverhouse and his plans than I have with any pro group that approached me," McKay told reporters.[10] The two men would become great friends, a relationship that would last for more than 20 years.

Ironically, the only other time McKay had seriously considered leaving USC was in the early 1970s when Dan Reeves was still owner of the Rams. In an interesting quote, McKay admitted that the only reason he didn't take the job was because he was unsure about the Rams ownership situation, something Culverhouse was all too familiar with.

"Of course there was a time when I might have seriously considered a Rams offer, if Dan Reeves hadn't been sick." McKay said. "I liked Danny a lot, but I knew he wasn't going to be around. I wasn't going to accept, not knowing who might get Rams ownership. They might dislike me and I'd be in a mess and out of a job."[11]

Had circumstances been slightly different three years earlier, Culverhouse could have purchased a team with John McKay already installed as coach. As it was, the Tampa Bay owner was only too happy to have McKay as the head coach of the Buccaneers.

"Coach McKay was the first name mentioned when we began discussing coaches and he was the only man I made a firm offer to," the Tampa Bay owner told the media. "His selection is consistent with what I announced last year, when I was awarded the franchise, that I would go after the best talent possible."[12]

In less than a year of ownership Culverhouse had loaded his front office with some of the best minds and names in football, culminating a three year span of participating in momentous off-field NFL incidents. Within four years the team would blaze a similar trail, rewarding the owner with the quickest path to post-season victory in NFL history, but only after suffering through a record-setting streak of futility.

The Buccaneers were almost late to their debut. Immediately following pre-game warm-ups, Coach John McKay led his team off the field at the Astrodome for a return to the locker room. Unfortunately for the Bucs, the team made a wrong turn and ended up lost in a myriad of tunnels and dead ends in the massive domed structure. Eventually McKay and his team made it to their locker room, and the first game in franchise history went off on time. In hindsight, the team may have been better off staying under the stands. The Bucs' 20–0 loss to the Houston Oilers on September 12, 1976, was the first of an astounding 26 consecutive losses for Tampa Bay, an NFL record.

The first few losses during the inaugural season were viewed as the necessary growing pains of an expansion team. However, as the losses continued to mount, including an exceptionally sloppy 13–10 defeat to fellow expansion brother Seattle at Tampa Stadium, patience with the Buccaneers began to evaporate, especially for head coach John McKay.

John McKay came into the NFL with great fanfare, but he also came in a marked man. While he had been a dominant coach in college, many of his fellow coaches were taken aback at the size of his contract, which was higher than that of some well-established head men. In addition to his income, McKay was also viewed unfavorably by his peers for not buying into the mystique of the National Football League. Shortly after being hired, McKay had pointed out that despite opinions to the contrary, winning at the professional level was quite simple.

"What does it take to win in the pros?" McKay asked rhetorically in a *Sports Illustrated* profile in 1976. "The same thing it takes to win in the colleges, the high schools and the Pop Warner leagues. Good players."[13]

In addition to his total lack of awe, McKay also brought his USC style of offense and defense with him to the NFL, bucking the tradition of the pro game. At Southern Cal, McKay used a version of the I-formation in which the tailback and fullback were interchangeable as lead rushers. Additionally, the backs were required to stand upright rather than lining up in a three-point stance. McKay wanted his backs to read the defense and flow to the line looking for the best route as opposed to the standard run to daylight method popularized by Vince Lombardi's Green Bay sweep. This style of running gave opposing defenses fits because, as Ara Parseghian of Notre Dame once said, "You can never tell where that tailback is coming from, and by the time you figure it out, he's gone." The drawback was that offensive linemen needed to be more athletic and sustain their blocks longer while the back read his keys.

On defense, the 3–4 alignment focused on linebackers, a radical departure from the NFL's prominent 4–3 formation. The 4–3 defense was centered on a strong defensive front four for putting pressure on the opposing quarterback and stuffing running lanes. The most romantic names in the NFL of the 1970s were The Purple People Eaters of Minnesota, The Doomsday Defense of Dallas, The Fearsome Foursome of Los Angles and The Steel Curtain Defense of Pittsburgh, each moniker bestowed on a defensive unit that possessed a dominating quartet of defensive linemen. In a 3–4, the front line, containing three down linemen instead of four, was more concerned with occupying as many blockers as they could to allow linebackers to make the majority of tackles. With speedy linebackers flying around the field, turnovers could be created in droves. In college, the USC defense routinely possessed athletes of such speed and athleticism that the Trojans linebackers were as big a threat to score as their offensive teammates. The downside to this alignment was that a smaller defense could wear down if required to be on the field for an extended period of time.

Critics abounded during his first few years as a pro coach as NFL coaches and beat writers argued that McKay wasn't going to be able to make his system work in the pros. Jim Murray of the *Los Angeles Times* made the case the I-formation was doomed to fail at the NFL level in a 1977 column.

"You cannot start back five yards on a pro line," Murray wrote. "They're quicker than you are, and besides they don't have to wait for the ball."[14]

The criticism of the press was one thing. McKay also had a legion of NFL coaches who despised him for his contract and less than reverential quotes about professional football. During a series of interviews following his hiring, McKay shared the feeling of mutual indifference between himself and other coaches.

"I've coached in four College All-Star games and I've never been amazed by the pro coaches," McKay said. "They've never been amazed by me either."[15]

During that first season, some coaches took particular glee in attempting to put McKay in his place and show his style of football was not up to NFL standards. A notorious example was a 48–13 loss to the Denver Broncos at Mile High Stadium in November. McKay felt that the Broncos were running up the score during the fourth quarter at the command of head coach John Ralston, the former Stanford coach who McKay had beaten regularly at USC.

"He's a prick," McKay said of Ralston. "He always was a prick."[16]

"I think they just want to show me I'm a college coach—a losing college coach," an embittered McKay said after the game.[17]

As the season wore on, injuries decimated the Buccaneers. Tampa Bay ended the season with more players on injured reserve (17) than touchdowns scored (15).[18] These injuries combined with the lack of playing experience possessed by the young Bucs led to disheartening final scores of 42–0, 49–16, 34–0 and 31–14. The Buccaneers finished the season 0–14, the first team to lose every single game in the modern NFL era. Things got so bad that Buccaneers highlights, such as they were, became a staple of Johnny Carson's *Tonight Show*. Every week Carson would show clips of Buccaneers losses, incorporated Buccaneers jokes into his opening monologue, and tossed in references to the struggling franchise during his interviews of celebrities. An example of the type of shots Carson would take was personified in a 1977 bit as his psychic alter-ego, Carnac the Magnificent.[19] "What two disasters were accompanied by band music?" asked Carnac-Carson holding a sealed envelope to his turbaned head. "The *Titanic* and the Buccaneers," was the reply to an accompanying belly laugh from his sidekick Ed McMahon.

In Tampa Bay, however, McKay wasn't laughing.

The 1977 season opened with Tampa Bay losing an additional 12 consecutive games. As the most visible member of the Tampa Bay Buccaneers, McKay became a lightning rod for criticism from fans and media alike. Everything about McKay was dissected and vilified, from his chosen sideline attire of golf hat and sunglasses to his dogged determination to prove his version of the I-formation and 3–4 defense could work in the National Football League.

Bumper stickers started to appear in the Tampa Bay area with "Throw McKay in the Bay" printed on them. Shortly thereafter, a t-shirt with a sinking pirate ship emblazoned on it held the caption "Go for 0." Letters to the editor were full of angry comments from fans such as one who commented that he had a picture of John McKay in his office: "I stick pins in his picture every day." Another particularly creative fan wrote, "They should transfer the franchise to Chattahoochee [site of the Florida State Mental Hospital] and trade McKay for one of the inmates, they couldn't do any worse." A headline in a local paper asked the question many in the NFL were asking, "Is Tampa Bay Really Worst Team, or is it McKay's Incapable Coaching?"[20]

All of the attacks from the media, fans, fellow coaches and Johnny Carson himself boiled over when McKay angrily referred to the media as "idiots" at a press conference following a 10–0 loss to the Washington Redskins. Redskins defensive lineman Bill Brundige had piled on with the rest of McKay's critics after the game stating, "Sooner or later McKay has got to learn that his old Southern California offense won't work in this league. He's not playing Stanford now. Running from that I-formation on 3rd and 10 makes no sense."[21]

When informed of this, McKay finally snapped. "What the hell does Bill Brundige know about football? A dumb-ass tackle down on all fours probably doesn't know the offensive set and probably doesn't care."[22] Turning his attention to the gathered media, an angry McKay continued, "I'm going to tell you people something and I want you to listen to me: None of you knows anything about football.[23]

"Anybody in his right mind who says the I-formation won't work is an idiot," McKay snapped. "What formation was Washington in out there when they scored their first touchdown? This time last year some idiot said the 3–4 wouldn't work."[24]

While McKay would eventually reach a truce with the beat writers, there would be an arm's-length relationship between the head coach and the media for the rest of his tenure in Tampa Bay.

As the fans, media, and assorted critics were occupied with assailing McKay, they were missing out on an amazing metamorphosis. The Buccaneers were assembling a young, talented team that would become a legitimate title contender faster than any franchise in professional football history.

From the very beginning, the Buccaneers established a culture of focusing on youth over experience. Ron Wolf, then a relatively unknown personnel man, spent the years 1976 and 1977 offering glimpses of the shrewd front-office guru he would become in crafting Super Bowl champions. The very first collegian Wolf chose left the young personnel man with one hell of a standard to live up to.

With the first choice in the 1976 draft the Buccaneers selected University of Oklahoma defensive lineman Lee Roy Selmon. A winner of both the Outland Trophy as the most outstanding collegiate interior lineman and the Lombardi Award for most outstanding lineman or linebacker, Selmon embarked on a career that made him arguably the greatest Buccaneer of all time. Selmon would be voted to six Pro Bowls, named to five All-Pro teams and win NFL Defensive Player of the Year in 1979 during his decade-long career. Not too many teams can claim to have started their franchise by drafting a future Hall of Fame defensive end, but the Buccaneers were only too happy to claim the achievement and spent countless hours scouring the nation for players to line up next to Selmon.

Not intimidated by the prospects of building an expansion team from scratch, Wolf, along with Tom Bass, Ken Herock and John McKay, funneled over 140 players through One Buccaneer Place during the early days of the franchise. Unlike many expansion teams, the Bucs were able to find a number of high quality players. In addition to Lee Roy Selmon, the inaugural Buccaneers collegiate draft brought to Tampa Bay players such as Dewey Selmon (Lee Roy's brother), Steve Wilson and Curtis Jordan. The Bucs also traded draft choices for young veterans, such as Richard Wood and Mike Washington. Each one of these men would be long time starters for the franchise.

The veteran allocation draft offered slim pickings to Wolf and the front office, but the Bucs' brain trust made the most of it. Mark Cotney, Dave Reavis and Dave Pear quickly became key contributors and team leaders. Free agents Cedric Brown, Isaac Hagins, Morris Owens and Danny Reece also became integral parts of the team.

In 1977 the Buccaneers once again made shrewd use of the draft, bringing on board future starters Ricky Bell, David Lewis, Charley Hannah and Larry Mucker. Free agents Cecil Johnson, Bill Kollar and Dana Nafziger rounded out the callow newcomers. All they needed now was the time to gain experience and develop the skills necessary to make John McKay's offensive and defensive system work in the pros as well as it did at USC.

Ron Wolf and the rest of the Buccaneers front office were certain the franchise would have little on-field success in the first year or two, but none of them could have imagined a 26-game losing streak and status as a national laughingstock.

"When you lose 26 games in a row that is going to check your hold card a little," Tom Bass said looking back many years later.[25]

While the players did hear some grumbling and grief from fans, they were relatively protected from severe scrutiny by their head coach. From the moment McKay came to town, he had made himself a target, and many of the men that worked for him feel the head coach should receive a lot of credit for being a human shield.

"It took a coach the stature of John McKay to be able to hold the team together," Tom Bass said. "I had experienced the same thing in Cincinnati where we had better initial success. Coach [Paul] Brown was there, but no one was going to criticize him because of what he had done in the past. Coach McKay gave the team time to develop and that is what it takes."[26]

While he was combative at times with critics, McKay was patient with his players. The players knew what their head coach was going through and appreciated his efforts.

"He took pressure off the team," said Lee Roy Selmon. "He did a fabulous job of building our team and taking a lot of the pressure off of winning and losing. He did not make that the focal point that was determining week to week where we were as a ball club. His focus as he shared it with us was that he was looking for this team to improve from week to week. His evaluation of us as a team was, 'Did we perform better this week than last week?' When he positioned it that way even though we were losing games we were still encouraged to try and get a little bit better. That philosophy and psychology reduced our disappointment."[27]

The Tampa Bay defense finished in the top half of the NFL in 1977, despite being hampered by the supposedly inferior 3–4 defense. The play of the defense kept Tampa Bay in many games, and by the end of the year McKay's plan began to come together. In December, Tampa Bay won their final two games of the season over New Orleans and St. Louis to finish 2–12 and for the first time a feeling of optimism was evident.

In 1978 the defense continued to improve, finishing in the top five against the pass, and 7th in total team defense. The offense continued to mature and the Buccaneers grabbed everyone's attention when they completed the first half of the season 4–4, including a victory on the road against perennial NFC Central Division champion Minnesota. Another unfortunate spate of injuries decimated the roster, and Tampa Bay finished 5–11, but the Buccaneers had proven themselves legitimate. The next season the Bucs provided the NFL with the biggest surprise since the New York Jets upset the Baltimore Colts in Super Bowl III.

In 1979 the Buccaneers raced out to a 5–0 start on the way to a 10–6 final mark and the NFC Central Division championship. Over the course of the season the young players that McKay had trained in his system rewarded the coach by proving that his philosophy could work at the NFL level. The Buccaneers' 3–4 defensive alignment, anchored by NFL Defensive Player of the Year Lee Roy Selmon, led the league in every defensive category, ranking as the number one unit ahead of the more famous (and traditionally 4–3) defenses in Pittsburgh, Dallas and Minnesota.

Tailback Ricky Bell, running out of the previously maligned I-formation, gained more than 1,200 yards rushing behind a young and athletic offensive line that sustained their blocks longer than most had believed possible at the NFL level. A signature play of the season, a 61-yard touchdown run against the Bears at Soldier Field by tailback Jerry Eckwood, saw offensive lineman Steve Wilson and Greg Roberts throw blocks at the line of scrimmage, disengage, and then sprint down the sideline step-for-step with Eckwood all the way to the end zone on the lookout for any Bears defender with the misfortune of getting in the way.

In the days after the Buccaneers clinched the division title in the season finale against the Kansas City Chiefs, a jubilant McKay let it be known that the first three years hadn't been easy, but it was more than worth it to see the joy in the celebratory locker room.

"I've never felt such elation as I did after the win over Kansas City that gave us the division championship," McKay said. "The elation wasn't for me but for the players, especially the players like the Selmon brothers and Richard Wood and the rest who had been here since the first year. No players have ever had to suffer through what they did."[28]

Despite the division championship, some detractors did try to take some of the luster off of McKay's accomplishment by pointing out that the Buccaneers played one of the least impressive schedules in the NFL. To top it off, when post-season awards were announced McKay suffered the indignity of finishing fourth in Coach of the Year balloting.

When asked why he believed he had been snubbed so publicly, McKay answered that it was just contempt over the fact he had come into the NFL and proved a college coach could succeed in the pros.

"I think I take the biggest bum rap in the country," McKay said. "I can't get a positive image because I didn't play in the NFL. Screw 'em."[29]

McKay and the Buccaneers removed any doubt over the efficacy of their system in the opening round of the playoffs. Tampa Bay dominated the Philadelphia Eagles in the 1979 NFC Divisional Round. The 24–17 final score doesn't indicate how uncompetitive the game had been. The Buccaneers raced out to a 17–0 lead behind Ricky Bell's then playoff record 38 carries for 142 yards and two touchdowns. Nobody mentioned in the days after the game that Bell ran the majority of those 38 times from the I-formation.

While the Buccaneers fell short of the Super Bowl, losing to the Rams in the NFC Championship Game, they had provided the NFL with the story of the year. In doing so they vindicated their head coach and became a point of demarcation in the modern history of the NFL.

The meteoric two-year rise from 0–26 to post-season victors had repercussions far beyond just Tampa Bay. The Bucs' success was necessary to change the thoughts of NFL observers and officials alike.

Many teams began to implement variations of McKay's I-formation and the 3–4 defense became more prevalent. In fact the Pittsburgh Steelers, possessors of the famous Steel Curtain Defense, converted from the 4–3 to the 3–4 in the early 1980s.

McKay's success in transitioning from the college ranks to the pros blazed a trail for other big-name college coaches to follow with varying degrees of success. Former Oklahoma legend Bud Wilkinson bombed in his attempt to lead the St. Louis Cardinals, but Jimmy Johnson and Barry Switzer led the Dallas Cowboys to Super Bowl championships. Steve Spurrier's offensive plans went awry with the Washington Redskins, but Bobby Ross went from national championship-winning coach at Georgia Tech to Super Bowl coach at San Diego. It wasn't always pretty, but John McKay's simultaneous suffering of expansion growing pains and disdain for college coaches made it much easier for the men that followed. The men that failed were viewed as failing because they didn't get the job done, not because they were college coaches.

On a cultural level, the worst to first metamorphosis of the Buccaneers became a national catchphrase. The title of the NFL Films 1979 team highlight film became the signature for any team that moved from the bottom of the standings to the top in a short time span.

The 1979 NFC Central Division championship was also the first major accomplishment in the well-regarded front office career of Ron Wolf. The division title is as much a credit to Ron Wolf as to John McKay. The quick rise was accomplished by a group of special players assembled by the up-and-coming personnel man. Unfortunately, Ron Wolf wasn't around for the championship season, having been fired following the 1977 campaign. While McKay was able to provide cover for the players to grow, his shield didn't cover a young executive that was also growing in the role. After a two-year record of 2–26, Wolf was let go by Hugh Culverhouse.

In the NFL Films documentary *The Birth of the Bucs*, Wolf said in a self-deprecating manner that he had "bombed" in his job with Tampa Bay.[30] However, Wolf's tenure proved necessary to the Buccaneers as almost every defensive starter on the 1979 roster was acquired by the Bucs' former personnel executive. If anything, the NFC Central Division championship proved Wolf had the skills necessary to build winning franchises, and during a Hall of Fame caliber career, Wolf proved it.

Wolf would bounce back from his dismissal in Tampa Bay. Wolf moved back to the Oakland Raiders organization and crafted a roster that would win Super Bowls XV and XVIII. Wolf then moved on to Green Bay and became the Packers general manager, where he pulled off a coup in trading for little known Atlanta Falcon back-up quarterback Brett Favre. Favre and the rest of Wolf's roster would go on to win Super Bowl XXXI. Not bad for a man that "bombed" in Tampa Bay.

Culverhouse may have felt the need to "do something" in letting Wolf go. In hindsight, keeping Wolf in the front office may have led the Buccaneers to years of title-contention, but no one could have known that in 1977. However, Culverhouse deserves credit for giving McKay time to implement his system and allow the young players to mature.

At the end of the 1978 season, Culverhouse granted an impromptu state of the Buccaneers interview with columnists Hubert Mizell of the *St. Petersburg Times* and Tom McEwen of the *Tampa Tribune*. With a three-year record of 7–37, McKay was an easy target of hostility among fans and media and Culverhouse could have easily shown him the door. Instead, he went in exactly the opposite direction and practically guaranteed his coach a job for life.

"I think we have the perfect head coach in John McKay," Culverhouse said. "He has the highest degree of character. I have more respect and admiration for him today than when I hired him. There will always be a place in our organization for John McKay."[31]

In 1979 McKay rewarded Culverhouse's faith in him with a championship, but that victory on the field paled in comparison to the winning streak Culverhouse was enjoying at NFL headquarters. By the time the Bucs claimed their first post-season victory, Culverhouse was already one of the most powerful men in professional football, providing a very necessary skill. In an amazing coincidence that very skill would lead the owner of the Buccaneers into operating Tampa Bay's opponent in the NFC Championship Game.

CHAPTER THREE

Walking Conflict of Interest

THE NFL THAT HUGH CULVERHOUSE joined in 1974 was a business entity in transition. For almost 40 years after its inception in a Canton, Ohio, auto dealership in 1920, the National Football League had been a shoestring operation. In the years from 1920 to 1940, the number of teams in the league fluctuated from a high of 22 to a low of 10 leading up to World War II. Quipped early NFL commissioner Joe Carr, "No owner has made money from pro football, but a lot have gone broke thinking they could."[1]

The vast majority of franchises were small-scale family operations. The patriarchs of these families were often gamblers and sportsmen. The Bidwill family, owners of the Chicago Cardinals were owners of race tracks and made a fortune in pari-mutuel wagering. The Mara family, owner of the New York Giants, flagship of the early NFL, was headed by Tim Mara, a bookmaker at Saratoga. Pittsburgh Steelers owner Art Rooney had famously purchased the football team with his winnings from horse racing.[2]

The finances of the league were rudimentary. In the days before television, the primary source of income for a professional football team was the gate receipts. The more games a team could play, the greater the amount of gate receipts. For this reason teams scheduled as many games as possible, sometimes two and three a week to lay claim to multiple paydays. George Halas' Chicago Bears squad played an amazing 19 games in just 67 days over late 1925 and early 1926 to take advantage of the popularity of rookie sensation Harold "Red" Grange. Radio broadcasts of games were common, but very little money went into the owners' pockets. Even with stars like Grange, the NFL was far behind baseball and college football in popularity so there wasn't a great deal of demand for the broadcasts.

Broadcast demand changed rapidly as television supplanted radio as the electronic medium of choice. Owners of professional football teams were hesitant at first to embrace the latest broadcast innovation because they made the majority of their money through gate receipts. In 1950 the Los Angeles Rams became the first team to have all its games broadcast over television, both home and away. At the end of the season the Rams learned that broadcasting their home games led to a decline in attendance.[3] This realization led the Rams to broadcast only away games from that point on. The Rams' strategy was mirrored by other franchises as well and became league policy when Commissioner Bert Bell mandated that teams could not sell broadcast rights for home games.[4]

This arm's length approach to television showed the relative lack of sophistication on the part of the owners. As small business leaders, the men that operated the NFL's franchises viewed their investments as a community service. Steve Rosenbloom remembers that the majority of his father Carroll Rosenbloom's contemporaries were involved in football for reasons of pride and ego, not for dollars and cents.

"The owners in those days [the 1950s] were considered civic minded citizens that were willing to support the team for the community with very little likelihood of making anything," Steve Rosenbloom said.[5]

The younger Rosenbloom recalled that his father was even good-naturedly mocked by members of the Baltimore business community when he decided to use some of the proceeds from the family garment business to purchase the Colts in 1953.

"When my father was introduced at a banquet, the local radio announcer said, 'This is Carroll Rosenbloom, and he is the new owner of the Colts,'" the younger Rosenbloom said. "'He is lucky he is in the shirt business, because he is likely to lose his shirt on this deal.' These teams weren't making any money. The players weren't making any money."[6]

But Carroll Rosenbloom was a different breed from the owners of the NFL at the time. He viewed the Colts as a business investment and wanted to generate as much revenue as possible, like he had done in the shirt business. As the 1950s came to a close, Rosenbloom and a few like-minded owners had a chance to change the way the NFL did business when Commissioner Bert Bell died suddenly in 1959. Behind Rosenbloom's campaigning, little-known Los Angeles Rams publicity director Pete Rozelle was named commissioner.

The way the NFL did business was about to rapidly change.

Almost from the day he took office, Pete Rozelle tapped into streams of revenue that had long been dormant. One of his first accomplishments was to get the owners to embrace the concept of revenue sharing. With each team guaranteed an even split of the money generated by the NFL product,

Rozelle argued, competitive balance would be maintained. With each team on equal financial footing, the imbalance that had permeated the professional ranks would ameliorate creating multiple late-season championship races that would keeps fans coming through the turnstiles.

With each team willing to share profits, Rozelle turned his attention on Washington, D.C., and lobbied Congress to allow an exemption to the Sherman Anti-Trust Act so that the NFL could negotiate a league-wide television contract with the three major networks. After much cajoling, Rozelle got his way and in 1962 CBS paid the NFL $4.65 million for the rights to televise the 1962 and 1963 season, guaranteeing each franchise $330,000 a year before selling even one ticket.[7]

Rozelle had only just begun. Shortly after inking the deal with CBS, Rozelle oversaw the creation of NFL Properties, the merchandising arm of the league. NFL Properties distributed the rights to create souvenirs, clothing, and miscellaneous merchandise with NFL logos. At about the same time, Ed Sabol's Blair Motion Pictures was brought in-house and re-christened NFL Films. Sabol and his associates recorded NFL game action on film, edited highlight reels out of the millions of shots they recorded and sold the films to an eager public that relished the slow-motion replays set to orchestral music and John Facenda's classic "Voice of God" narration. By the end of the 1960s, NFL Properties and NFL Films were bringing in millions of dollars to the NFL offices to be doled out evenly among each owner.[8]

A mid-decade merger with the American Football League brought about the multi-million dollar Super Bowl spectacle that helped generate television contracts with all three networks that brought each franchise multi-million dollar earnings each year. Coupled with gate receipts, NFL Properties proceeds, and NFL Films proceeds, the money from the television contracts should have had each owner floating on a river of money. Instead most owners were still in debt beyond imagination. The reason for this was simple—a majority of the owners weren't sophisticated businessmen; they were sportsmen with money. In the mad ascent from the periphery of sporting America to multi-million dollar conglomerate, the National Football League was being led by a group of men ill-equipped to handle the amount of money pouring into their coffers. Fortunately, Hugh Culverhouse had an idea of how to structure the league's finances. This necessary skill would lead him to become the most powerful man in football for the next decade.

Pete Rozelle was a visionary, but he was not a businessman in the classic sense. While he realized the impact the untapped potential of television and merchandising would have on the National Football League, Rozelle was at heart a PR guy. He was also an employee who reported to each of the NFL's owners. When money started to flow into the league, few of the owners charged with running the league had the acumen or experience necessary to handle the good fortune.

For example, Art Modell, owner of the Cleveland Browns, was a high-ranking owner and a member of the prestigious television committee. However, upon further inspection, Modell's finances were built on a foundation of sand. An advertising executive, Modell purchased the Browns in 1961 for $4.1 million with mostly borrowed money.

"I gave him [Rozelle] my financial statement—which was a load of shit," Modell admitted in Michael MacCambridge's book *America's Game*.[9]

Modell's situation was similar to those of many other owners, remembered Culverhouse's son, Hugh Jr.

"Most of your owners were financially unsophisticated," Hugh Jr. recalled. "You got to understand that the league was started by gamblers. There is this façade that these guys are from high society, and no more bullshit could be found. It is a collection of gamblers and rejects."[10]

Carroll Rosenbloom realized that Culverhouse was different and encouraged Rozelle to utilize the newcomer in the league's inner circle. Shortly after the Buccaneers began play, Culverhouse was named to the Finance Committee, one of the NFL's more important governing bodies.

Carroll Rosenbloom's son, Steve, explained his father's thinking in championing Culverhouse.

"The league never managed its people well and Rozelle wasn't a business type guy," Steve Rosenbloom said. "He was a PR guy when he came into the league. My father was a businessman, and I know that more than once he talked to Rozelle about doing business in a different way. My father paid attention to the strengths and weaknesses of the different owners. It was kind of obvious with Culverhouse's background that he be on that committee.[11]

"The league is a small group, and I think Culverhouse was the only one at that time that had that background so he would be a perfect guy on the Finance Committee," Steve Rosenbloom continued. "It made perfect sense, and it was common sense. He championed Hugh because he thought Hugh would have some value."[12]

Wasting precious little time, the Tampa Bay owner proved just how valuable a skill set he possessed. Culverhouse went to work immediately, spending an amazing amount of his time pouring over the financial books of all 28 franchises and the league itself. He visited all the owners, consulted with the commissioner and formed an opinion on the financial future of professional football. These studies led Culverhouse to the conclusion that not only did the NFL need to change the way it did business as a whole, but the vast majority of owners needed to change the way they did business individually or a great deal of money was going to go to waste.

One of the first ways he saved the owners money was by taking them on as clients of his tax practice. This allowed him access to their financial statements, interviews with anyone associated with a team's finances and intimate conversations with his fellow owners. In addition, Culverhouse encouraged other owners to use computerized record keeping and was an integral force behind the software some teams used to track their finances.[13] These moves gave him cachet in league circles, bringing him a generous fee income as well.

Having seen the books of his fellow owners, Culverhouse was concerned about the amount of debt his fellow owners had secured with their franchises. The decade of the 1970s was not an economically friendly environment. Interest rates were high, inflation rampant and, while the NFL was a profitable concern, the owners' ancillary business interests were hurt. To make up for their losses in the corporate world, owners would borrow prodigious sums using their NFL holdings as collateral. In the early 1970s the Sullivan family had re-purchased the New England Patriots in a hostile stockholder confrontation with a series of loans from multiple banks.[14] Art Modell of the Cleveland Browns borrowed millions during the 1970s to fund a series of business ventures in Northeast Ohio, including taking control of the operations of Cleveland Stadium.[15] By securitizing multi-million dollar real estate and business loans with an NFL franchise, the owners opened the league to the risk of banks foreclosing on teams whose owners couldn't make good on their debt service. That would be a public relations nightmare and throw the entire NFL into chaos. To thwart this, Culverhouse used his growing influence on Rozelle and the owners to place a limit on the amount of debt a team could carry.

"He instituted the limitation on debt per team," Hugh Jr. said. "Everybody was furious, but he forced through that you can put no more debt against a team than $35 million. They never wanted a football team to be overleveraged."[16]

With a limit on the amount of money an owner could borrow against a team, Culverhouse had shored up the weakness caused by the owners' profligate borrowing and spending during an economic downturn.

The next step in the plan was to initiate a reserve fund for handling future contractual debts. Each team deposited a percentage of their deferred contract payments into the pool to help offset any liquidity issues that could arise. In his spare time, Culverhouse also helped to broker the sales of the San Francisco 49ers and Denver Broncos.[17]

Culverhouse had used all of his legal, financial and political skills to modernize the way the National Football League handled its money. In doing so, he became arguably the most necessary figure in the NFL. Some owners went so far as to refer to Culverhouse as vice commissioner.[18] However, he didn't achieve these milestones without alienating some of his fellow owners and earning a reputation as a man that was capable of doing great things for the league, as long as he got his cut.

The death of a legendary owner in 1979 would further prove Culverhouse had an innate ability to be at the center of the biggest NFL stories of the 1970s and 1980s. It would also provide a startling glimpse at how the NFL gave the Buccaneers owner a tremendous amount of leeway in circumventing NFL rules in order for him to get the job done as he saw fit. These jobs would richly reward Culverhouse off the field but did precious little to help his team on it.

On April 2, 1979, Carroll Rosenbloom decided to go for an afternoon swim in front of his house on Florida's Atlantic coast. Accounts of the day state that the surf was particularly rough and within a few moments the owner of the Los Angeles Rams was in desperate trouble. Screaming for help, Rosenbloom struggled to keep his head above water and, despite the efforts of a passerby to save him, the man who had beaten Hugh Culverhouse to the punch in acquiring the Rams drowned.[19] The death of the 72-year-old Rosenbloom shocked the NFL.

The events surrounding the drowning of Carroll Rosenbloom have been disputed for more than 30 years by friends and family. Rosenbloom was a savvy man who had lived on the water for many years. Never a strong swimmer, he would often use the pool at his home for laps, eschewing the Atlantic. Some found it highly irregular

Hugh Culverhouse wielded considerable power and influence in the NFL during his reign as Buccaneers owner from 1974 until his death in 1994. As chair of the Finance Committee and the NFL Management Council, very little NFL business was transacted without Culverhouse's input and approval. Culverhouse was known as vice commissioner by some of his fellow owners (*Tampa Tribune*).

that he would have chosen to swim alone in such rough conditions. One of those who remains skeptical is his son Steve.

"There were circumstances that I have never been comfortable with because I knew my father, and I knew his habits, and I knew his great respect for the ocean," Rosenbloom said in a 2009 interview. "What I saw the next day looking at that ocean, and I was told it was just the same as the day before, he would not have gone in that water by himself. I am just not comfortable with it. Now at the end of the day it could have been an unfortunate accident, but I haven't been able to come to grips with it."[20]

Rosenbloom is adamant about not being portrayed as viewing his father as the victim of foul play. He also made it clear that he is not making any claims of who would have committed such an act.

"I'm not going to point any fingers because it would be irresponsible," Rosenbloom said. "I don't have any information one way or the other. I'm just talking as a son that lost a father. I haven't been able to come to grips with that. If you lost your father in an accident you couldn't come to grips with, you would carry the same thing. I can't just say, 'Yes, that is the way it went.'"[21]

If Steve Rosenbloom was shocked by the manner in which his father passed away, he was mortified by the ensuing estate battle that would see him jettisoned from the Rams organization, his stepmother, Georgia, named owner and Hugh Culverhouse granted unofficial control of the franchise.

Hugh Culverhouse and Carroll Rosenbloom developed a good working relationship in the aftermath of their battle over the Rams. Culverhouse counted the Los Angeles owner as one of his best clients, and the two men communicated frequently. One of the duties Culverhouse was assigned by Rosenbloom was to act as executor of the Rams owner's estate should he pass away. Shortly after Rosenbloom's tragic death, the first phone call made by Carroll's wife, Georgia, was to Hugh Culverhouse.[22]

As executor of Carroll Rosenbloom's estate, Culverhouse was right in the middle of one of the stranger controversies in NFL history. Rosenbloom left the majority of stock in the team to his widow, Georgia. As vice-president of the Rams, Steve Rosenbloom would remain responsible for the day-to-day operations of the team. It seemed a logical set-up. Georgia, a 52-year-old former lounge singer and TV weathergirl, had no practical business experience save for the marriage and divorce industry (Rosenbloom had been her sixth husband). Steve, Carroll's son from his previous marriage, had been working for the Rams for many years and would attend ownership meetings in his father's absence. In Steve Rosenbloom's opinion, it appeared that Carroll wanted his widow provided with a steady source of income and his son to run the team in the manner the elder Rosenbloom had established.[23] Like many plans, however, Carroll's went awry.

Georgia and Steve did not see eye to eye on the operations of the Rams. In Georgia's opinion, she was the final authority of the team due to her status as majority stockholder. Steve felt that his stepmother was in over her head and that she should back away and let him run the franchise he built with his father. Unfortunately for Steve, his stepmother didn't seek his advice or allow him liberty in the operation. Instead she turned to the man whom her late husband entrusted with his estate, Hugh Culverhouse.

The level of influence he carried with Georgia Rosenbloom made her stepson uncomfortable. Steve Rosenbloom believes to this day that Culverhouse was an accidental executor, named to the position by Carroll Rosenbloom on a temporary basis in a side business deal. Steve Rosenbloom feels the Tampa Bay owner overstepped his bounds when an opportunity to enrich himself was presented.

"I don't think my father expected it [the will] to go to that point," Steve Rosenbloom said. "I know he had people do wills for him before, lawyers around the club. He had no interest in using that will. This thing is sort of a mystery because those weren't the original executors, and I can see him drafting something appointing Culverhouse because he wanted to get something else done through Hugh.[24]

"My father died tragically and before he could change anything," Rosenbloom continued. "I know when he took off for the trip, he and I talked and he said, 'When I get back I am going to sit everybody down in the family and tell them how I want things and why, and we'll get everything taken care of.' But of course he never came back from that trip.

"I don't think he would trust Hugh to do the right thing."[25]

Culverhouse communicated often with Rosenbloom's widow and the two became close professionally and personally. Steve Rosenbloom continued to run the football team in the manner he felt his father would have wanted. At the same time, Georgia Rosenbloom was making decisions under the advisement of counselors and friends, one of whom was Hugh Culverhouse. With two strong-willed people pulling in opposite directions, something had to give.

The internal battle poisoned what little relationship Steve had with his stepmother. By the time training camp opened in the summer of 1979, the two were no longer speaking, and the younger Rosenbloom was desperately trying to fulfill his duties as manager of the Rams' day-to-day operations, just as his father had wished. His job was made difficult by what he felt was unnecessary interference from Georgia Rosenbloom.

"I was persona non grata," Rosenbloom said. "It appeared the whole deal about the Rams was to remove any vestige of Carroll and the way he ran the team. They were going to do it completely different."[26]

This shocked Steve Rosenbloom, because his father and he had built one of the best franchises in football. Since 1972 the Rams had been a perennial Super Bowl contender, making the playoffs on several occasions.

"We had spent the last seven or eight years putting the right people in the right places," Rosenbloom said. "That operation was so well oiled that he and I could have gone to Europe on an extended vacation and the organization wouldn't miss a beat because we had great people in there. Georgia dismantled the organization.[27]

"It was a messy situation," Rosenbloom said. "I was there for five, six months, and I tried to help her, but she got advice from all the wrong people. She had a full staff of very competent people in all areas and all she had to do was come over once in a while and say hello and things would have run itself and she would have been better off."[28]

When Steve Rosenbloom re-assigned Rams general manager Don Klosterman, one of Georgia Rosenbloom's allies and confidants, she decided to exercise the authority she believed the will of her late husband granted to her.

Steve Rosenbloom recalled late one evening after practice being summoned to Georgia's California home for a meeting. The young Rosenbloom had an uneasy feeling about what was coming. When he walked in the room and saw Georgia with one of her lawyers, he knew his uneasy feeling had merit.

"The lawyer suggested it would be best if I resign," Rosenbloom said. "I said, 'No. I'm not going to resign. You can fire me.'"[29]

Termination of his services was quick to follow. While the termination was Georgia's idea, Steve was dumbfounded that she never uttered a word during the entire meeting, instead relying on her lawyer to dismiss Steve.

"She didn't say a word the entire time. She just sat there," Rosenbloom recalled. "I said, 'This is the land of soap operas and the media will love this. It will go on and on and take on a life of its own.'"[30]

Relieved of his duties, Rosenbloom drove back to Rams camp to say good-bye to the players. Rosenbloom claims that when he arrived at camp it appeared his stepmother had attempted to prevent even that.

"When I got there a few players were in my room waiting for me," Rosenbloom said. "They said that [head coach] Ray Malavasi got a call from Georgia and told him to give the players the night off. The players got wind of it and stayed around.[31]

"I told them I had been fired and there's nobody left now that can help you guys anymore," Rosenbloom explained. "Things aren't going to be the way they have been under Carroll and me. I feel terrible about it but there is nothing I can do. There is a lot of talent in this room, and you guys can win. You must put this crap behind you and do this for yourselves. You have the talent and ability to go to the Super Bowl."[32]

On the day he was terminated by his stepmother, Steve Rosenbloom had made two assertions. One assertion was that the Rams had the talent to make the Super Bowl. The other was that the Rams were going to be a Los Angeles soap opera under the direction of his stepmother. In 1979 and beyond, both assertions proved accurate. Interestingly, Hugh Culverhouse and the Tampa Bay Buccaneers had a role in both.

On January 6, 1980, the Tampa Bay Buccaneers' impossible dream of a season came up one victory short of a Super Bowl appearance. Just a little over two years removed from a 26-game losing streak, head coach John McKay had led the Bucs to the NFC Championship Game. The Rams defeated the Buccaneers 9–0 in a fiercely contested defensive struggle. The Rams, having fought through the distraction of the death of their owner, the termination of their vice-president in an internecine battle, and the accompanying media coverage, had achieved what Carroll Rosenbloom had long worked for—a Super Bowl berth.

In hindsight it is only appropriate that the Rams' road to the Super Bowl went through Tampa Bay. After all, their owner was making decisions based on the recommendations of the Buccaneers owner. In essence, the two teams battling for the NFC Championship on that unusually cold day in Tampa were under the control of Hugh Culverhouse. The Tampa Bay owner may have been rooting for his Bucs, but he had more than a passing interest in the fortune of the Rams.

During the remainder of 1979, Culverhouse worked diligently for Georgia Rosenbloom in overseeing Carroll's estate, interpreting Carroll's last will and testament, guiding the estate through probate, and getting a handle on the estate's financial picture, including the most prominent possession in the family, the Los Angeles Rams football club. In performing these duties, Culverhouse regularly consulted with Rosenbloom on the day to day operations of the Rams franchise, a role that would grow in prominence and influence in the years to come.

In addition to becoming a key advisor to Georgia Rosenbloom in the boardroom, Culverhouse was a major factor in the new Rams owner's personal life. In July of 1980, just a little over a year after the death of her husband, Georgia Rosenbloom became Georgia Frontiere. Her wedding to Emmy-winning composer Dominic Frontiere was conducted by Culverhouse in his role as a notary public in his former hometown of Jacksonville, Florida.[33]

While some people were shocked that the former Mrs. Rosenbloom married so quickly, her ex-stepson was happy about it.

"I am indebted to Dominic Frontiere for marrying her because she took his name!" Rosenbloom said. "I think she brought him home within a week or so after returning from Florida [after Carroll Rosenbloom's funeral]."[34]

While the younger Rosenbloom's assertion may be a bit of an overstatement, Dominic Frontiere quickly became embroiled in controversy.

In one of the more infamous cases of greed and duplicity, Dominic Frontiere would be imprisoned for scalping tickets to the Rams' Super Bowl game against the Pittsburgh Steelers following Los Angeles' victory over the Bucs. The tickets were temporarily in possession of Hugh Culverhouse's Tampa Bay Buccaneers in the week before the NFC Championship Game.

"The NFL had all of the Super Bowl tickets locked up in the vault in our stadium that day," said former Buccaneers public relations director Rick Odioso. "But they went back to Los Angeles with the Rams."[35]

The tickets went back to Los Angeles, but not all of them went to the Rams. A good deal of them wound up in the Frontiere-Rosenbloom home, and hundreds of thousands of dollars ended up in their bank account. As the host team to Super Bowl XIV, the Rams were allotted 10,000 tickets by the NFL to do with as they wished. As winners of the NFC title, the Rams were allotted an additional 17,000. With a face value of $30 apiece, the tickets would fetch the Rams organization $810,000 if sold through proper channels. However, Frontiere had a different idea.

Frontiere chose to scalp roughly 7,500 tickets while distributing the remaining supply to fans. On his 1980 tax return, the first he and Georgia would file as man and wife, Dominic Frontiere claimed that he gave the majority of the tickets away, taking a deduction of $116,335. In reality, Frontiere scalped the tickets for well above face value, refusing to take less than $125 per ticket, and cleared roughly $500,000.[36]

It is important to note that in California at the time, selling tickets for more than face value was legal as long as the scalping activity did not take place at the sporting venue. While greedy, Frontiere's activity didn't cross the line into illegal dealing until he filed a false tax return. The tax return got the attention of the IRS, Culverhouse's former employer, and Frontiere made things worse when he lied during an interview.

After several years of suspicion and investigation, the federal government indicted Frontiere in 1986. With nowhere to turn, Frontiere pleaded guilty to two counts of filing false income tax returns and willfully making false statements to the IRS. Georgia Frontiere's name was also on the tax return that led to her husband's conviction. However, she was adamant that she was not involved in the scalping and while viewed suspiciously by the media, Georgia Frontiere was not charged. Whether or not Frontiere gained any advice on his plea from Culverhouse is unknown. One thing was certain: despite their Super Bowl appearance, the Rams had fallen from being one of the most respected franchises to a national punchline in the years since Rosenbloom's death.

The soap opera aspect of the Rams only intensified in the weeks and months after the Rams defeated Tampa Bay. One of the services provided by Culverhouse was an attempt to dissolve the trust that left the Rams stock to Rosenbloom's children so Georgia would be free to acquire total control.

"Everybody was out for their own pound of flesh," Steve Rosenbloom recalled. "If it meant cheating Carroll's kids, so be it. They tried to get us to sign some papers that would have given them our percentages."[37]

The younger Rosenbloom is irked to this day by the maneuvering of his stepmother and Hugh Culverhouse. Steve Rosenbloom sought legal counsel to protect his siblings and him.

"Hugh's retort was, 'There is Steve looking out for himself again,'" Rosenbloom recalled Culverhouse telling him at the start of the legal wrangling. "It wouldn't have been necessary if as an executor he handled it in the true sense. I didn't consider him an executor; I considered him an executioner."[38]

Eventually the children were bought out by their stepmother, giving Georgia 100 percent ownership of the Rams. While she was in complete control, it was rumored that she was not the one calling the shots. As the weeks went on it became apparent that Culverhouse had been assisting Georgia Rosenbloom in running the business side of the Los Angeles Rams, arguably running two NFL franchises at one time. Seven years after losing out on the Rams to Carroll Rosenbloom, Culverhouse was at the top of the franchise's organizational chart in an unofficial capacity.

While admitting that Culverhouse's ascension in the Rams organization was completely coincidental, the result of a tragedy, Steve Rosenbloom surmises that the irony was not lost on the Tampa Bay owner.

"I think going back to when he thought he was going to be the new owner, maybe in the back of his mind he never forgave my father even though it got resolved in the end," Rosenbloom said. "Now he is in the catbird seat to help himself because Georgia wasn't smart enough to know the football business or any business in general. He could run that ship all by himself."[39]

What vexes Steve Rosenbloom is the obvious conflict of interest present when the owner of one NFL franchise has any kind of say in how another NFL franchise is run.

"The fact that he had a hand in the Rams organization at all was a disgrace," Rosenbloom said. "I was gone by then but that could only happen if he was invited in. He had no business being in the Rams' books or anything else. That didn't have anything to do with being an executor. There is no reason for him to delve into the books. I think she ended up paying him much, much more than she needed to, and that raises a whole bunch of different questions."[40]

Rosenbloom wasn't alone in his pointing out the ethical dilemma of the Hugh Culverhouse–Georgia Rosenbloom business relationship. According to the David Harris book *The League*, various newspapers were trying to ascertain who was running the Rams, and more and more the answer appeared to be Culverhouse.

As the personal relationship between Frontiere and Culverhouse grew, so did the business relationship. By the summer of 1981, it was reported in many Los Angeles papers that Culverhouse was the unofficial president of the Rams. "It is now quite apparent that Hugh Culverhouse is playing a prominent role with the Rams," read a story in the *Los Angeles Herald Examiner.* "Georgia Frontiere doesn't dare make a major move without consulting him."[41]

According to a high-ranking Rams official who was quoted in *The League*, Culverhouse was in complete control of the Los Angeles franchise. "Georgia thinks Hugh Culverhouse is the smartest man on the face of the earth," the source said. "Maybe so, but he's also very cheap. This may be the direction we're heading in."[42] The same source claimed that after Culverhouse spent a good deal of time studying the Rams' books, the travel arrangements became noticeably more Spartan. "In St. Louis, we stayed in a rundown old hotel whose best days were in the 1940's and 1950's because it was $20 a head cheaper than the other options," the source said.

Quipped an unidentified Rams player, "Next week we'll probably stay at the Y."[43]

If any of the owners in the National Football League had a problem with Culverhouse's actions regarding the Rams, it was kept very low-key. Commissioner Pete Rozelle viewed Culverhouse's actions as merely taking care of a very messy estate situation. Rozelle was quoted as saying, "There was no conflict of interest as far as I was concerned. He [Culverhouse] wanted to settle the estate and get out of that role as soon as possible."[44]

Culverhouse had provided the NFL with a necessary service. The Buccaneers owner had stepped in when one of the most powerful men in the league passed away and oversaw the transition of power (no matter how messy or controversial) of one of the league's elite teams in the second largest media market in the nation.

Over the next decade and a half the Rams would be a roller coaster team, just as Steve Rosenbloom feared. A theatrical woman, Frontiere would greet players in the locker room with pecks on the cheek following victories. She was a vocal believer in astrology and drew up charts for some of her players. At one point she even attempted to have the team wear magic crystals around their necks to help improve performance during a losing streak.

Despite the eccentricity of their owner, for a short term in the mid to late 1980s the Rams were a solid team. Relying almost exclusively on the running game provided by future Hall of Fame tailback Eric Dickerson, the Rams made the playoffs but didn't advance to any more Super Bowls. By the time the 1990s began, the Rams were a moribund franchise that lost connection with their fans. Looking for greener pastures, Georgia Frontiere shocked the NFL when she relocated the Rams to her hometown of St. Louis in 1995. While she does deserve credit for being owner of the Rams when they finally won a Super Bowl in January of 2000, Frontiere's legacy will be the odd regime she oversaw in the 1980s. When she passed away in 2008 most obituaries gave equal time to the Super Bowl and the controversial manner in which she took control of the team.

Steve Rosenbloom believes the failure of the Rams to make a go of it in the second largest media market in the United States is a testament to the dysfunctional organizational structure created by his stepmother at the advice of Culverhouse.

"She dismantled the organization, screwed up the rapport with the players and was intensely disliked by the people who worked there," Rosenbloom said. "Then she goes the opposite way, going from on of the top three markets to one of the smallest markets."[45]

More than 30 years after he left the Rams, Steve Rosenbloom has come to peace with all that transpired in the aftermath of his father's death.

"I don't wish to come across as bitter, because I am not," Rosenbloom said in the summer of 2009. "I don't blame Hugh Culverhouse for her mistakes; she's the one that asked. I do believe that Hugh had a conflict of interest from the very beginning. It's not a painful thing. I took a stand and took it as far as I could. Hugh Culverhouse didn't appreciate it because he wanted to get his hands in there. Mr. Conflict of Interest."[46]

It wasn't just the Rams' ownership controversy that involved ethically questionable relationships between Culverhouse and his fellow owners. There would be others during the 1980s as he cleaned up messy situations for the National Football League time and time again.

Granting personal loans of hundreds of thousands of dollars to business leaders had long been Culverhouse's modus operandi. Whenever a business mogul faced liquidity issues, they knew that Culverhouse was the man with a plan to bail them out. In the mid-1980s, a troubling times for airlines, he personally secured a loan of $1 million to help prop up struggling Provincetown-Boston Airline (known as PBA). When asked why he would put himself on the line for a near bankrupt airline, Culverhouse explained that there were three reasons he did any kind of deal.

"I like to work. I like people and enjoy solving problems ... I enjoy making money," Culverhouse told the press.[47]

In the case of Provincetown-Boston Airline the man he liked was airline owner John Van Arsdale, Sr., Culverhouse's golfing buddy, and while not without risk, the upside to the deal was Culverhouse gained control of an airline and added it to his vast holdings.

Stephen Story, Culverhouse's point man in his business deals, said the PBA loan presented a great deal of risk but turned out to be a boon.

"We were very lucky in that transaction," Story recalled. "He called me on a Thursday, and said he had a friend in Naples that needed help. He said he had agreed to loan him a million dollars and asked if I could get down there by nine the next morning and cut the best deal I could. We just took a kind of blanket lien on their assets, but the numbers they gave us really weren't real. Hugh had a victory lap with Mr. Van Arsdale and then 90 days later I'm signaling bankruptcy. Fortunately, the bank that was the primary lender missed an airplane in the collateralization package so we ended up getting paid in full on that."[48]

Culverhouse's willingness to gamble on loans in exchange for ownership stakes and investment opportunities translated well to the NFL. A number of owners were in financial trouble and Culverhouse gladly traded loans not for just financial reward, but the chance to build on his power base at NFL headquarters.

In 1980, the same time he was advising the Rams, Culverhouse personally loaned Philadelphia Eagles owner Leonard Tose $400,000.[49] Tose, a notorious gambler at Atlantic City casinos, had lost hundreds of thousands of dollars at the blackjack table and had leveraged the team dangerously close to the limit Culverhouse had successfully lobbied for.

"He helped Leonard," said Stephen Story. "But he got paid back."[50]

Tose paid Culverhouse back with interest, but soon ran afoul of the casinos again. Fortunately, Culverhouse was there to provide relief again.

In 1983 Culverhouse personally guaranteed a $3 million loan for Tose that the Eagles owner was able to successfully pay back. While he didn't grant the loan, he did collect a fee for his services to Tose.[51]

While Culverhouse's role in the Rams was questionable, his financial assistance to Tose was in total violation of the NFL constitution which prohibited such loans. However, the NFL allowed both transactions to take place and didn't sanction Culverhouse, who controlled so much of the NFL ledger.

"If it is a violation, it would amount to a technical violation that didn't cause harm to anyone," NFL counsel Jay Moyer was quoted as saying in *The League*.[52] Once again, the NFL allowed Culverhouse's conflict of interest to stand because it was necessary for the NFL to navigate through a messy situation.

When Culverhouse helped broker the deal that saw Tose sell the Eagles to Norman Braman in 1986, the Tampa Bay owner gained even more stature.

"We represented Norman Braman's buying out of Leonard's interest in the Eagles too," said Stephen Story. "Hugh was always interested in helping any other owner in the league if they wanted to sell or whatnot. He moved in good circles. He had an understanding of the league that a lot of people didn't. I think he was one of the first to really understand the economics.[53] I think he had more of a vision of what was happening in the league and where it was going than a lot of the other owners did," Story said. "He and Pete Rozelle were extremely close. I think Pete respected his insight in those areas and Hugh could help Pete get a consensus from the owners to go in different directions."[54]

In the early 1980s, Culverhouse was named to the most powerful committee in the league, the NFL Management Council. His financial talents and business acumen had been necessary to navigate the league through some delicate situations. Now he was in the NFL's inner circle. From this position of influence two of his most notorious personal characteristics, stubbornness and frugality, placed him in the middle of an epic work stoppage, one that would change the fortunes of his franchise for the rest of his life.

CHAPTER FOUR

Strike One

WAR WAS ON THE HORIZON and a sense of dread enveloped the NFL when 1982 dawned. A decade of labor strife was coming to a head, and the first regular season work stoppage in league history was a very distinct possibility. Professional football had never been as popular or profitable as it was at this moment. Unfortunately for many of the league's players, the popularity and profitability of the NFL as a whole was not reflected in their personal bank accounts.

Almost from the day the first player accepted a paycheck, the rank and file members of NFL rosters felt underpaid and limited in their freedom to ply their trade. Wages were kept artificially low due to a league-wide reserve system. The major tenet of the reserve system dictated that a player who wanted to become a free agent was obligated to play one additional year at the option of his ball club, otherwise known as an option year. The player entering an option year was subject to a 10 percent decrease in his pay. Needless to say, not many players wished to exercise this clause, opting instead to sign a multi-year contract with their current employer if they were fortunate enough to do so. Those that dared to brave free-agency faced a market in which the owners were motivated to not offer contracts by the Rozelle Rule.

The Rozelle Rule stated that any team signing a player who played out his option had to pay compensation to the player's former club. The compensation was determined by Pete Rozelle himself and often involved high draft choices.[1] The Rozelle Rule encouraged collusion among the owners to not sign free agents to contracts. The resulting lack of individual bargaining power kept football player salaries the lowest of the four major professional sports.

Starting in the early 1970s, the neophyte National Football League Players Association (NFLPA) began to fight for player rights in a very public manner. Leading the charge was NFLPA executive director Ed Garvey. Garvey, a skilled rabble-rouser, orchestrated a mass walk-out in 1974.[2] The 40-day strike during training camp didn't win many concessions from the owners, but it did start the two entities on a collision course that led to a protracted battle in 1982.

Having witnessed first hand the impact the Rozelle Rule and the reserve system had on salaries, the NFLPA was determined to fight for a say in how the NFL was run. With the current collective bargaining agreement (CBA) between owners and players expiring in 1982, Ed Garvey felt the time had finally come to wage all out war on the NFL. In February Garvey had boldly outlined his proposal for increasing player salaries. The union demanded that 55 percent of the NFL's gross revenues be set aside for the players. This would increase the average salary of an NFL player from $95,000 to almost $200,000.[3]

The NFL balked, claiming there was no possible way an owner could afford to run a franchise under such conditions. The NFL argument was somewhat undercut when the new television contract was announced in early 1982. The NFL's five-year, $2.1 billion contract with ABC, CBS and NBC guaranteed each franchise $14 million in income without the necessity of selling a single ticket or hot dog.[4] This did not go unnoticed by the NFLPA, and they increased the volume of their arguments.

Not only did the NFLPA demand salary increases, it also wanted an active role in doling out the money. Garvey argued that the 55 percent of gross revenues be placed into a general fund and of that money, 70 percent would go toward salaries with a minimum annual salary for rookies and a step-increase based on years of service.[5] The salary structure would be administered by the NFLPA, leaving the owners out of the equation.

In early 1982 500 NFL players gathered in Albuquerque, New Mexico, for a summit with their union. Garvey laid out in detail his plank and the phrase "55% of the gross" almost became a rallying cry. While not universally embraced among all union members, the 55 percent of the gross plank was accepted and battle lines drawn. An attendee of that summit was Buccaneers defensive lineman Dave Stalls. Now known as Dave DeForest-Stalls, the lineman had come to Tampa Bay after starting his career as a Dallas Cowboy. Having the chance to play for the flagship franchise of the NFL in Dallas and the upstart Buccaneers, Stalls was in a good position to articulate the exact principle the players would fight for in 1982.

"The term that came to me immediately was equity," DeForest-Stalls said in an interview for this book. "I think it became so clear to players that when you are able to operate a business that is an effective monopoly within a free enterprise system, that is just a license to steal.[6]

"They [the NFL] had just signed their first $2.1 billion contract," DeForest-Stalls continued. "That was back in the time when we didn't use the term billion ever. When they signed that contract with the networks and we looked at what they paid out to us, it was unbelievable. It was an approved, sanctioned monopoly, and I think the amount of money we were receiving, and the inequity of most of that money going to unproven players, we were just looking for some balance in that equity."[7]

While the new television contract gave an inkling of how much revenue a franchise generated, a lawsuit joined by an NFL maverick provided everyone with specific numbers. This revelation put Hugh Culverhouse front and center in the battle between the players and owners, and when drawn into a battle, the former pugilist fought to win.

In 1980 Oakland Raiders owner Al Davis joined a lawsuit against the National Football League. The suit claimed the NFL violated anti-trust laws in refusing Al Davis the right to relocate his franchise to the city of Los Angeles. As a result of the trial, all 28 NFL franchises were required to open their ledgers for judicial purposes. The NFLPA, heading into a contract negotiation year, fired off a public relations salvo by releasing the financial information to the media. With the books opened to public scrutiny, eye-popping revelations were made. Perhaps the most stunning was the amount of money Hugh Culverhouse was receiving from the small market Tampa Bay Buccaneers.

In 1981 the Buccaneers rated as the 5th highest grossing franchise in all of the National Football League. With revenue of $17.04 million, the Buccaneers were in exclusive company with the likes of the New York franchises and the Dallas Cowboys.[8] Unfortunately for the Tampa Bay players, that revenue did not translate into competitive wages.

With an average salary of $76,761, the Buccaneers were 21st out of 28 clubs.[9] The disparity was staggering and with the television money from the latest contract set to start rolling in, 1982's disparity would only become greater. Tampa Bay players, perhaps more so than any other roster, bristled with righteous indignation at the inequity between the revenue they generated and the percentage of that money dedicated to salaries.

"Back then it seemed like good money when we were playing," said Dave DeForest-Stalls. But, according to the former lineman, when one factored in the lack of guaranteed contracts, the relatively meager funds allocated for Tampa Bay player salaries were insulting.[10]

"The book *Meat on the Hoof* was such an appropriate title; we were just cattle," DeForest-Stalls said. "Any contract we had could be over the next day; it was a one-way contract. It could be because of injury or just because someone is better, you could be gone the next day."[11]

The NFL owners viewed the release of 1981's revenue and salary figures as an act of bad faith by the NFLPA. The owners claimed the NFLPA had violated an agreement not to make those figures public.[12] While there may have been an agreement, none of the owners should have been surprised by Garvey's action. Once referred to as a "bomb-thrower" by CBS's Brent Musberger,[13] Garvey prided himself on being a burr under the saddle of the NFL. What Garvey lacked in polish, he more than made up for in attitude and showmanship.

Unfortunately for Garvey, the public relations battle he won by releasing the revenue figures roused Hugh Culverhouse to action and put a target directly on the back of the NFLPA executive director. Garvey soon learned that when Culverhouse had an opponent in his sights, he had no compunction about pulling the trigger. According to Hugh Jr., the Bucs owner would make it his mission to crush Garvey and the NFLPA.

"My father had a hard-on for the union," he said. "He hated Ed Garvey. Hated, hated, hated him."[14]

Culverhouse and the rest of the Management Council knew that Garvey had a critical weakness: he did not enjoy overwhelming support among the rank and file of the players union. Despite all of Garvey's vitriolic rhetoric and pronouncements, the players had not won any major concessions from the NFL owners during his tenure. If anything, they had taken a step backwards.

In 1975 former Baltimore Colts tight end John Mackey won a lawsuit against the NFL in which he had claimed the Rozelle Rule violated anti-trust law. The NFL appealed, but while the case was under review a handful of players that were in the option year of their contracts were able to become true free agents, including running back John Riggins who jumped from the New York Jets to the Washington Redskins without any draft choice compensation being paid.

Later an appellate court ruled that if the Rozelle Rule was agreed to in a collective bargaining agreement, it would not violate anti-trust law. Garvey bargained away this temporary free agency for recognition of the union and other cash considerations in 1977.[15] This angered many of his constituents and left Garvey's position vulnerable if he couldn't score a quick victory in 1982.

As a member of the NFL Management Council, Culverhouse would be among a small cadre of owners that would be charged with crafting the league's negotiating strategy. Realizing that Garvey was on tenuous ground, Culverhouse and the owners elected to make the NFLPA chief the sole focus of their campaign. The battle plan which emerged could have been a boxing strategy from Culverhouse's days at the University of Alabama: stand toe to toe with your foe, shake off as best you can any early punches, count on your stamina and training to carry you through to the later rounds and when your opponent finally shows a hint of fatigue, go for the knockout.

In this case however, he wouldn't be in the ring. The NFL had decided years earlier not to allow owners to take a public negotiating position during what was expected to be a protracted battle. Instead they elected to hire a chief negotiator to go up against Garvey. It is no surprise that in a war in which Culverhouse had a lead role it would be one of his lieutenants leading the charge. Philadelphia Eagles owner Leonard Tose claimed that Culverhouse introduced a business acquaintance by the name of Jack Donlan to the Management Council.[16] The name Jack Donlan would fill the NFLPA with angst for years to come, just the thing Culverhouse wanted.

Jack Donlan was a bona fide all-star when it came to labor negotiations. As a chief negotiator in the airline industry, most recently with National Airlines, Donlan had worked on more than 40 labor contracts, some much more contentious than others. Donlan had been involved in strike negotiations four times, including a year long walkout by the Machinists Union.[17] When Donlan came before the Management Council for an interview, he came with the reputation as a negotiating mercenary. If the owners wanted a man to go all out on their behalf, they couldn't have done any better. An anonymous opponent of Donlan told *Sports Illustrated* in 1982, "Jack is a tough negotiator. Basically what he does is uphold his boss' wishes. The NFL owners couldn't have found a better man. If they want to try to break the players, Donlan is the tool to do it."[18]

At the time fellow owners credited Culverhouse with bringing Donlan to their attention. Donlan doesn't remember who notified him of the job opportunity first, but does remember Culverhouse conducting a background check on him.

"Chuck Sullivan [New England Patriots owner] was the chairman of the Management Council at the time," Donlan said in an interview for this book. "I know after the fact that Hugh Culverhouse went over to the airport in Tampa and talked to a number of people. National flew into Tampa and one of their union heads worked out of Tampa. Hugh went and talked to them to get their take on who I was."[19]

After initial meetings with Chuck Sullivan, the entire Management Council and finally Pete Rozelle, Donlan was hired as chief negotiator. Today Donlan scoffs at the notion that he was brought in to break the union. As Donlan tells it, his role was to be a vessel for passing information from the negotiating table to the Management Council and vice versa. Donlan claims he served at the pleasure of the Management Council, the group that made all final decisions.

"The Management Council was made up of six owners, or owner types," Donlan explains. "They were the committee and so I answered to them. The six owners of the Management Council communicated with the other owners so you had pretty good representation."[20]

It didn't take very long for Donlan to learn that 1982 was going to be a tough contract, mainly because Ed Garvey was viewing it more as a battle than a negotiation. "The Players Association and the league had entered into a fairly acrimonious bargaining situation," Donlan recalls. "There was a lot of anger and, as I understood it, Ed Garvey had basically promised the league that they were going to get a strike in their next round of negotiations."[21]

Realizing that there was a very good chance for a strike, Donlan prepared himself for the negotiations. While he was busy polling owners to learn which issues they particularly wanted addressed, Hugh Culverhouse went about provisioning the league against the ramifications of a long delay in the season. The amount of work Culverhouse did on behalf of his fellow owners impressed Donlan greatly.

"Culverhouse was on both the Management Council and the also on the Finance Committee back in 1982," Donlan remembered. "You had a lot of respect for him from a financial standpoint. Part of getting ready for negotiations is that you have to make sure all of your people can withstand a work stoppage if it comes about. A lot of expenses continue without regard to if you have games. If you are renting a stadium, you still have to pay rent. Hugh Culverhouse was very helpful in establishing a line of credit that we could borrow on if needed. Because he had a lot of respect within the financial community, we got a very favorable rate. The members could stay solvent during the period of the strike."[22]

While Culverhouse and Donlan worked to prepare the owners for a likely strike, Tampa Bay Buccaneers players prepared as well. One of their first steps was to vote for a player representative, a fellow member of the roster who would be responsible for attending union meetings, bringing information back to his teammates and voting on union matters. The Bucs players chose their All-Pro defensive end and team leader Lee Roy Selmon to be their head representative. As assistant representative the Bucs players chose another defensive lineman, much less known than Selmon.[23] However, as the strike deadline approached, the assistant's relative anonymity would disappear, and he would find himself in direct confrontation with Culverhouse in one of the most intriguing owner-player skirmishes of the 1982 walkout.

Dave Stalls had arrived in Tampa in 1980 in a trade with the Dallas Cowboys. A part-time starter, Stalls had been a solid if unspectacular contributor to the Bucs' 1981 NFC Central Division championship. Looking back on his election as alternate player rep, the now Dave DeForest-Stalls claims his more outgoing personality combined with Selmon's status as team leader provided the Bucs with model representation.

"It definitely made sense for Lee Roy to be head representative and me the assistant representative," DeForest-Stalls said. "We worked so well together, because Lee Roy is a quiet leader type, leads by example, asks a lot of questions, listens a lot. I was a little more active. I was out in front of responding to media inquiries."[24]

Willingness to answer any question elevated DeForest-Stalls to the role of team spokesman in the eyes of the media. DeForest-Stalls laughingly recalled that by all rights Selmon should have been the spokesman, but the All-Pro was too crafty to fall into that trap. "Reporters kept talking to me because I was an idiot and kept answering them," he said. "That is where Lee Roy is so skilled at being polite and not answering a damn thing! I just ended up becoming spokesman because I was trying to answer people's questions."[25]

By becoming an unwitting spokesman, DeForest-Stalls also became a target of Hugh Culverhouse. As the season approached, almost daily quotes

Buccaneers defensive lineman Dave Stalls participates in a loosely organized team practice during the 1982 players strike. In his role as a representative of the striking National Football League Players Association (NFLPA), Stalls would go toe to toe with Hugh Culverhouse both in person and in the press. Notice the NFLPA cap Stalls is wearing during the game of catch (*Tampa Tribune*).

and photographs of DeForest-Stalls made the local papers. The media attention did not go unnoticed by Culverhouse, who subtly reminded DeForest-Stalls that the owner of the Buccaneers was a leader in the charge to defeat the union.

"One of the main newspapers had a photo of me when I answered some questions," DeForest-Stalls said. "So answering the questions meant putting me in contrast to Hugh Culverhouse. Within like 48 hours of that article and picture, first the training group made the comment, 'Nice picture,' and somebody from the front office said, 'Nice picture, Dave.'[26]

"Now I'm paranoid as hell," DeForest-Stalls continued. "Then twice

Hugh Culverhouse says, 'Nice picture, Dave.' He was biting and sarcastic. 'Really nice picture, Dave, you need to save that picture and article.' Twice within 24 hours he said that to me. He was basically saying, 'I read that article. I know what you said and you're mine.' That's Hugh Culverhouse. He didn't necessarily come out and say, 'I'm going to take your legs out from under you.' He was just making it clear that he was the person in power."[27]

The reason for DeForest-Stalls' paranoia was Culverhouse's growing reputation among the players union for cutthroat dealing. His tax practice client list was well known, as was his growing influence in the power structure of the league office.

"We knew that he was in the Management Council," DeForest-Stalls said. "We knew that he was a very skilled attorney. The success of Culverhouse was the fact that his outer persona, the good-old Southern gentleman, never gave you an indication that he was intelligent, conniving and powerful. He was a behind-the-scenes guy, an arm twister. He was just this very gentlemanly man whose knife goes in very slow but effectively."[28]

The exchange between Culverhouse and DeForest-Stalls in the hallway of One Buccaneer Place was private. As the strike wound on, those confrontations would become much more public.

By the time training camp rolled around, negotiations had been going on for almost half a year with little to show except hard feelings and a sense that the 1982 football season was at risk. Jack Donlan was particularly perplexed because he got the impression that Ed Garvey and the players union representatives were not up to the task at hand. The union was struggling to communicate their basic demands and instead of providing detailed economic proposals only offered vague percentages.

"Truthfully, I thought they looked at this more like a high school debate than a negotiation," Donlan said. "Usually the parties exchange opening proposals. These are things we would like to see in the contract and then you negotiate from where we are to get to those positions and bargain back and forth. It was a very long time before we ever got any proposals from the union.[29]

"They just had this, 'We want 55 percent,'" Donlan continued. "The number was just very vague until you could find out what it included. That was my sense. It didn't seem like any other negotiation I had been involved in. We had difficulty getting them to really identify the things they wanted. People are usually very specific. You can put a pencil to things and tell exactly what they want and what it would cost."[30]

While Donlan was perplexed by the union, the player representatives were equally frustrated by the owners' unwillingness to sit at the table. Hugh Culverhouse and the Management Council were calling the shots, but they were nowhere to be found during negotiations, instead funneling their opinions through Donlan.

"We had our people at the table, but they had hired help at the table," said Dave DeForest-Stalls. "We weren't getting an accurate picture of what their decision-makers were thinking. It was the Management Council that was going to make the final decision"[31]

In explaining the role of the owners in negotiating, Pete Rozelle stated that management's position was identical to the NFLPA. "Just as the players have a paid negotiator in Ed Garvey, the owners have their paid negotiator in Jack Donlan," the NFL commissioner said plainly.[32]

Culverhouse rarely spoke to the media, honoring a self-imposed gag order. The rest of the owners on the Management Council acted likewise. The implication was clear: the contract was going to be a battle between Jack Donlan acting on behalf of the owners and Ed Garvey acting on behalf of the players. Considering the labor background of both men, the owners had the clear talent-advantage and some of the players suspected as much.

Players around the NFL headed to training camp not knowing if there would be a season or not. Reported fissures in the NFLPA's solidarity were becoming apparent. NFL superstars such as Joe Montana resigned from the players union citing discomfort with the union's strategy and a lack of confidence in Ed Garvey.[33]

On the Buccaneers many players, including quarterback Doug Williams, had reservations about walking away from their livelihood behind the leadership of Ed Garvey. In an interview with the local media Williams was quoted as saying, "Ed Garvey is going to lead the strike, but Ed Garvey's check is still going to be coming from somewhere. I've got a mortgage every month. I have a car note to pay. I'm going to play. That's the way I look at it. Ed Garvey will pay his note regardless."[34] Williams wasn't alone but as the team's offensive leader he was in the spotlight.

Buccaneers linebacker Scot Brantley was another Buccaneers player not convinced the threatened strike was in the league's best interest. While not as vocal as Williams, Brantley summed up his feeling about the summer and fall of 1982 recently.

"Percentage of the gross?" Brantley asked in a quizzical tone during an interview for this book. "You play football because it is a fun game. You don't play because it is a business. You don't play because you make a lot of money. You play because you enjoy the game, the camaraderie in the locker room, the friendships, the relationships you have with the coaches."[35]

The public displays of friction within the ranks had to buoy Culverhouse's spirits. The NFL plan was working just as it was envisioned. Meanwhile, with player support fracturing even before training camp, Ed Garvey and his representatives had to fight a battle on multiple fronts. On one front was Jack Donlan and on the other was public perception, and neither battle was going well. Adding to the players' frustration was what they perceived to be Donlan's condescending attitude towards them.

"The degree of contempt and disrespect was unbelievable," recalled Dave DeForest-Stalls. "I have never been at a table where a group of men considered me and my peers with so little respect. They thought we were idiots. I had never experienced that before. They were not going to entertain that our opinions had any validity whatsoever. 'We are in control of the game, the media and the entire industry, and there is not a damn thing you can do about it.'"[36]

Sensing their grip on negotiations slipping away, the NFLPA orchestrated a symbolic display of solidarity in the most public venue possible, an NFL game. Naturally, one of the leading figures necessary for that event was Buccaneers lineman Dave DeForest-Stalls.

Incongruent and conflicting feelings abounded during the opening weekend of the 1982 NFL pre-season. In the days leading up to the games, several members of the NFLPA communicated surreptitiously and planned an act they hoped would prove to the owners and the public that while there might be some fissures in their membership, the solidarity of the ranks was strong.

The act was a coordinated pre-game handshake at mid-field right before opening kick-off. Two complete sets of rosters strolling to mid-field, comprising approximately 50 to 60 men on a side (factoring in the extra roster spaces made available for the pre-season). The scene would involve men who would soon be battling for playing time and their professional career during the game momentarily setting aside their personal quest to show solidarity with their opponents. This seemingly simple act by today's standards was revolutionary at the time. According to Dave DeForest-Stalls, the handshake would set the tradition of professional football on its ear.

"Part of this has to do with old school football," DeForest-Stalls said. "Old school football is the week prior to the game one of the things you do, even if you have to make stuff up, you just have to hate the guy across from you. You have to hate him, you have to want to kill him; you have to want to murder him. There is no way you can even smile at a player before a game, because you want to kill him."[37]

As a player's representative, Dave DeForest-Stalls was in charge of communicating with the reps from the Philadelphia Eagles, the Buccaneers' opponent during the pre-season opener.

"The idea came out of our national office," DeForest-Stalls said. "I don't know whose idea it was. We tried to do it across the league."[38]

The first handshake took place during a Thursday night game between the Kansas City Chiefs and Cincinnati Bengals at Arrowhead Stadium in Kansas City. The next night in the Houston Astrodome, members of the Houston Oilers and New Orleans Saints shook hands before their game. By the time the slate of Saturday games arrived, including the Bucs' opener, league officials were warning that any future displays would result in fines for all participants. The fines would be for violating a NFL rule prohibiting "fraternization or disruptive activities during a game."[39] This was no small matter for players who were already trying to save money for a possible work stoppage and those uncertain of a roster spot.

The choreographed handshake was a large public relations gamble on the part of the players association. There had been dissension in the ranks as evidenced by several players resigning from the union. In locker rooms across the league, heated discussions were taking place about whether a strike was a good idea. If a significant portion of a roster refused to walk to midfield, the owners would be able to crow to the media that if the players couldn't agree to shake hands, how could they possibly be able to administer a salary structure?

In addition to the public relations aspect, the handshake also made very public targets of the players. By requiring every player on the roster to walk to mid-field, the handshake put players who were not guaranteed a roster spot in the position of visibly committing an act in defiance of a league edict. One of those players was Dave DeForest-Stalls.

Adding to DeForest-Stalls' sense of apprehension was the fact that the man who many viewed as vice commissioner of the NFL, Culverhouse, would be sitting in his owner's box high atop Tampa Stadium when the handshake took place. Already in the sights of Mr. C, DeForest-Stalls certainly didn't want to be left standing alone at mid-field.

"You want to talk about a world of emotion and fear just about a handshake, for God's sake," DeForest-Stalls said. "What would be the repercussions of meeting at mid-field? For the players to do anything, especially publicly, that would say you [the owners] don't control everything. We do. We are going to walk out to the field and shake hands for three seconds and walk back."[40]

When pre-game warm-ups ended and the fans started to settle into their seats, members of the Tampa Bay Buccaneers and Philadelphia Eagles stood on their respective sidelines facing each other from across the way. Then in a very subdued manner, the players started to walk towards each other as though they were meeting a neighbor while picking up the morning paper. DeForest-Stalls admitted the players only seemed subdued; they were actually quite emotional on the inside.

"The first time we didn't know if all the players from our side and their side were going to do it," DeForest-Stalls said. "Until we headed out there we didn't know if the whole team would come, but they did."[41]

"I was probably never more proud of our core group of leaders," he continued. "It wasn't until we were halfway out that we looked out of the corner of our eyes and saw that everybody came out."[42]

After walking roughly 20 to 25 yards to meet, the Eagles and Bucs shook hands, smiled, slapped shoulders and then just as quickly turned and walked back to their respective sidelines.

"That was the most magnificent time," DeForest-Stalls continued. "As the players walked back, every single player gained an immense amount of self-respect, just the fact we were able to come out and shake their hand when the owners and everybody else was saying you better not."[43]

Once the game began, Dave DeForest-Stalls and his Buccaneers teammates quickly got down to the business of routing the Eagles 35–7. DeForest-Stalls had a very good game, earning public commendation from head coach John McKay which probably spared him from Culverhouse's wrath. It was quite a heady evening for DeForest-Stalls: the handshake he helped organize went off better than expected, he played well enough to make a claim on a roster spot, and he got to stick it a little bit to Hugh Culverhouse.

The NFL backed down on its threats of fines and the players continued their solidarity handshakes for the remainder of the pre-season. While the players gained a symbolic victory, DeForest-Stalls and many other players were disappointed that the majority of the media sided with the owners.

"The reporters, especially the columnists, showed themselves for what they were, being in the pockets of the owners," DeForest-Stalls said. "They just railed against us like we had spit on the U.S. Constitution. It was just a handshake, for God's sake! How is this hurting the game of football? It was just really amazing."[44]

The handshake had accomplished what DeForest-Stalls and the rest of the NFLPA had hoped. Despite lingering disputes among themselves, the players as a whole felt underappreciated by the owners. While many did not agree with the strike, the players were willing to fight for pay commensurate to other professional athletes. It appeared the strike Ed Garvey promised was on the way.

Culverhouse and fellow members of the Management Council were about to get the battle of attrition they planned for. Thanks to the loan he had arranged, the owners knew they could just wait the players out.

As August melted into September the regular season beckoned. Negotiations had become an on-again, off-again affair between Ed Garvey and Jack Donlan. Although Culverhouse and the rest of the Management Council maintained their stance of not participating in negotiations, their influence was felt.

An early move of the Management Council was to consider playing the regular season with a group of replacements should the regular players walk out. In preparation for this, the Buccaneers invited the most players to their training camp since their inaugural season of 1976. The thought was that any player who didn't make the active roster would be in good physical shape and have a grasp of the team's offensive and defensive schemes and therefore be ready to pick up and play football at a moment's notice.

The Buccaneers denied the extra players were brought in as strike insurance, but personnel man Phil Krueger did tell the *Lakeland Ledger* if the NFL decided to use replacement players he would be ready.

"I'll do whatever the Management Council tells me to do," Krueger said of Culverhouse's committee. "We have not contacted anybody yet, but that's not to say we wouldn't. We've got everything ready to go. I have a list of players right here on my desk. All we need is for somebody to tell us something."[45]

At NFL headquarters however, Commissioner Pete Rozelle adamantly opposed using replacement players, so the idea was shelved. One positive of the plan was the threat of being replaced did dampen the union's idea of striking random pre-season games.

With replacing strikers ruled out, the Management Council elected to simply stop making offers and force the union to put up or shut up. The final offer before the players' deadline was to raise salary levels to $1.6 billion over five years.[46] The owners felt they had made some concessions, with the $1.6 billion representing 48 percent of gross revenues to player costs. The players' reaction was a refusal to agree by Ed Garvey. The 48 percent offer, which according to Jack Donlan included salaries and benefits, was met by the union's continued demand for 55 percent of the gross. Donlan was especially frustrated by the fact the union didn't specifically break down the 55 percent into categories.

"In exploring it with them, they wouldn't identify what things were included in that percentage and what things were excluded. They wanted 55 percent of the gross which was not a common way to negotiate back then," Donlan said. "If you have 55 percent and that's everything, that probably isn't any more than what we were paying if you accounted all the costs involved with players. But when you talked to them, they said that percentage doesn't include pensions or that doesn't include insurance."[47]

As the impasse continued, Donlan could sense that Garvey was more interested in showing off to the players and media than securing a deal.

"They almost had a war cry, 'We are the game!' Ed is very quick-witted and he has a quip for everything," Donlan said. "He has a lot of one-liners. Things could remain light but there is a big difference between that and negotiating. It wasn't a matter of getting in the last word or one-upmanship, it was a matter of explaining what the issue is, how you'd like to see it altered, the reason behind it and how it would affect you."[48]

With the regular season days away, the Management Council chose to deal with a strike by simply waiting the players out. The battle plan was for trench warfare and to allow financial attrition to be the determining factor.

In this battle, the NFL had the largest weapon thanks to the maneuvering of Culverhouse. The line of credit he had arranged for the NFL would be put to the test. Unfortunately for the players, they didn't have the same access to funds. In the weeks leading to training camp the NFLPA did advise the players to start saving money in the event of a strike. Players were told to save game checks and to budget for a work stoppage which, if necessary, would occur following the second week of the season.[49]

While Dave DeForest-Stalls and Lee Roy Selmon had done a solid job of preparing their teammates, not every roster was so well-prepared. In lieu of the fact that the NFLPA had a negligible strike fund, the players voted to walk out the Tuesday following the second week of games so that each player would receive three full paychecks.

Dave DeForest-Stalls admitted the vote to walk out was not easy, but it ultimately passed because teammates acted on behalf of the greater good. "It was very difficult, no question," DeForest-Stalls said. "When you look at the starters and more high profile leaders or more talented players, there was definitely some who voted what's best for the team. There were many of them who strongly said even if it is best for me to go in, there is no way. If my offensive line isn't getting what they need, how in the heck can I go in? I depend on them."[50]

Following two weeks of play, the NFL players walked out the minute the Monday night game between the Green Bay Packers and New York Giants concluded. What ensued was a 57-day battle of wills that ended only when one side finally blinked. Naturally, the battle's most important men would be related to the Tampa Bay Buccaneers.

For the first time in the history of the National Football League autumn Sundays were devoid of professional football. Instead of physical confrontations on gridirons from coast to coast, NFL combat took place in conference rooms and in front of microphones. After almost a full year of negotiations, Donlan and Garvey still could not come to terms on how much revenue to dedicate to salaries.

Jack Donlan said the issue was still the union's demand that 55 percent go all to salaries, while the owners felt the percentage should include all player costs. "There might be a way to get what they want another way," Donlan said, but Garvey just wouldn't budge.[51] Donlan explained it was simple question of mathematics: if 55 percent went to salaries only there would be no money left over for other expenses and the owners were not interested in spending more than 75 percent to 80 percent on personnel costs.

"[The owner's offer] include all things that are players' costs," Donlan said for this book. "That amount includes pension, insurance, career counseling, a lot of things. As you ground away, they would say, 'That's not included, this is not included,' and the number got out of hand. We passed 55 percent on the fly."[52]

When Donlan would make an offer it was up to player representatives to communicate the offer to the rest of their teammates. This is how Dave DeForest-Stalls spent the majority of his time during the strike as assistant representative with Lee Roy Selmon.

"We traded time in New York and Washington in bargaining sessions," the former defensive lineman said. "It was truly like any elected position. You are truly a conduit. The phone calls with our national office, going to informational meetings and bringing that back to our constituents and getting feedback from them, and bringing that feedback back."[53]

In addition to the travel, DeForest-Stalls still acted as an unofficial spokesman for the NFLPA and created a firestorm when he claimed that Culverhouse once told him the owner was in favor of a wage scale but the NFL couldn't afford the 55 percent plank. The defensive lineman said that during an informal conversation with Culverhouse the owner admitted that he wanted a wage scale because he was tired of negotiating contracts. DeForest-Stalls was quoted as saying, "He agreed that he would love to get to where salaries are based on performance, not potential."[54]

Donlan adamantly denied the allegation at the time, as did several other owners. Interestingly, Culverhouse refused to comment continuing his self-imposed silence during the negotiations. This silence infuriated DeForest-Stalls, who argued that the real man in charge, Culverhouse, should be at the table. "If Donlan can't budge on meal money and fines for being overweight, how in the hell can we negotiate on wages?" DeForest-Stalls argued to the press.[55]

DeForest-Stalls continued to stand by his comments almost 30 years later. "That was a huge, huge thing," DeForest-Stalls said of Culverhouse's comments. "If at any time an employer says we can't afford it, that means the books have to be opened up to prove it. Nobody at the bargaining table ever said we couldn't afford it."[56]

While DeForest-Stalls battled in the negotiating room, Lee Roy Selmon got ready to play in a momentous football game.

As a method to raise money the NFLPA scheduled a series of football exhibitions known as P.A.S.S. games. Short for Players All-Star Season, the P.A.S.S. games were to be played in cities across the country in an attempt to provide striking players with income. Backed by media mogul Ted Turner, the original idea was to create 28 teams which would play on Sundays during the strike. The games would be televised by Turner's fledgling cable network, WTBS. NFL owners filed suit and by the time the case was decided in the players' favor, only six teams were formed. The teams represented the NFL's six divisions with teams for the AFC East, Central and West and NFC East,

Central and West. Several Buccaneers took part including Kevin House, James Owens, Larry Swider, Cedric Brown, Neal Colzie and Charley Hannah. The best known Buccaneer to participate was Lee Roy Selmon.

With only six teams there was not room for every player interested in playing, so the NFLPA tried to stock the rosters with as many name players as possible. In addition to Lee Roy Selmon, future Hall of Fame players Harry Carson, John Riggins and Ron Yary volunteered to play. Dave DeForest-Stalls had interest in playing but admitted many years later he was not highly sought after. "There was much more demand for star players, and I was never a star," DeForest-Stalls said. "Who's Dave Stalls? But, Lee Roy Selmon? Yeah, let's get Lee Roy in this!"[57]

Little money was promised to the players and pay would be based on performance, $3,000 going to each member of the winning team and $2,500 to each member of the losing team. The participants risked a great deal by playing in these non-sanctioned games. A serious injury in an NFLPA game could mean not just the end of a career, but the player could be responsible for a great deal of medical expense even with the insurance policy purchased by the NFLPA. As far as Dave DeForest-Stalls is concerned, the fact Lee Roy Selmon was willing to risk a stellar career for his fellow players illustrated Selmon's stature as the Bucs' true leader.

"That really spoke to me highly of Lee Roy Selmon because what he risked in that game was huge," DeForest-Stalls said. "Not only his name, but his future finances and his well-being. There wasn't a lot of insurance. At least in the NFL there was some protection, but not in those games. I take my hat off to him."[58]

The first of the P.A.S.S. games took place at Washington, D.C.'s RFK Stadium. Rusty from almost a full month of inactivity and trying to avoid injury, the action the players put forth was far from top caliber. However, the game was a competitive back and forth affair that saw several lead changes. Naturally, given the team's amazing ability to be at the forefront of big stories, a Tampa Bay Buccaneer made the key play to save the game. Late in the fourth quarter the NFC All-Stars took a 23–22 lead on a 45-yard field goal by Redskins kicker Mark Moseley. The AFC All-Stars moved the ball steadily down the field until Lee Roy Selmon broke through the line of scrimmage and forced a poorly thrown ball by Dolphins quarterback Don Strock that sealed the NFC's victory.

The next night at the Los Angeles Memorial Coliseum, a second set of AFC and NFC All-Stars played another P.A.S.S game with the AFC winning 31–27 in another see-saw battle.

The players had proven that they could play the game even without the owners, but the victory proved pyrrhic. The players learned that while football was a popular sport, the NFL brand was critically important. A non-sanctioned professional game without the ever-present shield logo just didn't appeal to the fans. While the games were televised by WTBS, the ratings were abysmal. Worse than the ratings, only a total of 8,000 fans attended the games, 5,000 in D.C and 3,000 in Los Angeles. With a capacity of over 100,000, the Coliseum looked particularly empty.[59] The $15.00 admission tickets were a detriment when one considered that not enough big name players took part. In fact, the NFLPA had such a difficult time filling rosters that several players, including Tampa Bay running back James Owens, flew to Los Angeles to play in the second P.A.S.S. game moments after playing in Washington, D.C. Due to the lack of interest the P.A.S.S. experiment ended after just one weekend.

With putting on a season of their own games no longer an option, the players continued to slug it out in the boardroom. Neither side was willing to give any ground as the talks slogged on. Although the players were rapidly depleting their funds, the owners were also starting to feel the pain of lost television revenue and gate receipts. As the calendar turned to November, Culverhouse finally took to the airwaves and proved his influence over the NFL. His presentation effectively ended the strike in one swift media-covered event.

Culverhouse had remained silent for almost all of 1982 when it came to commenting on the labor talks. As a key member of both the Finance Committee and Management Council, he had a level of power that was second to none. Chuck Sullivan may have been the head of the Management Council, but given Culverhouse's control of the league's purse strings he was the one to put dollar amounts on the negotiating table.

The fact that he had remained silent during the talks gave him an advantage by putting the players on edge. Continually frustrated by having to deal with an intermediary in Donlan and coming to the realization that Ed Garvey was not going to deliver the goods, the players union was showing signs of fracture. Reports of players contacting their home clubs for permission to come in for workouts circulated.

"We got a lot of information that the players wanted to come back," remembers Jack Donlan. "They were going to the clubs. We got message after message about players wanting to return, and they had no place to go. At the time the union was telling them, 'Don't worry. We're going to make up all the games.' But after awhile you are looking at April so that wasn't going to happen."[60]

In Tampa, quarterback Doug Williams was of the opinion that if the Bucs took a vote, the vast majority of players, 40 out of 49, would vote to come back to work under the latest management offer. In an interview Williams, who had opposed the strike from the beginning, said it was ludicrous for the players to continue the walkout considering how much money they made. "It's amazing," Williams told *The Evening Independent*. "They're laying people off everyday around the country and we chose to walk away from thousands of dollars. We chose to walk away when people who are out of work paid to see us play. Can you imagine that?"[61]

While Williams was one of the few vocal dissidents, there were many other players that just wanted to play and felt the union had overreached. This gave Culverhouse the opening he was looking for. Realizing there was a chance to both win the strike battle and effectively crush Ed Garvey the owner finally broke his silence on November 8. Armed with charts, graphs and other presentation materials, Culverhouse spoke with the manner and tone of a lawyer making his closing argument to a jury. The gist of his argument: Ed Garvey is the impediment preventing the National Football League season from resuming.

"The gag rule, as you can see, is off today," Culverhouse joked with the assembled reporters. "The season is in dire jeopardy today.[62]

"Our negotiations with the National Football League Players Association have reached a dead end," the owner continued. "We have made our best offer yet, one which would guarantee each player an average of more than $200,000 a year in wages and benefits over four years and the player's leadership has rejected it without presenting it to the rank and file."[63] Just in case there was any doubt who Culverhouse was referring to as the "player's leadership," he clarified the point bluntly. "I think when Mr. Garvey wants a settlement, we'll have a settlement."[64]

He also called out Dave DeForest-Stalls, claiming that the defensive lineman was spreading misinformation and engaging in hyperbole, including a quote in which DeForest-Stalls claimed the owners were violating labor laws. "Dave Stalls," Culverhouse said, using the lineman's name at the time, "what you told the team that all 28 owners are going to jail is tommyrot."[65]

In closing, he called on the players to stand up and be counted, effectively circumventing the power Garvey had as union leader. "I would like to congratulate the union on their solidarity," Culverhouse said. "I'd like for them now to show the solidarity, the strength of it, to a true test of democracy and that is, have a secret ballot. If our team elects—if 51 percent or more of the players say they don't want the offer, I respect it and this is great. But I think it should stand the test."[66]

And with that he left the ball squarely and publicly in the players' court and effectively removed Ed Garvey from the equation. Teams began meeting and voting. Later that same day, the New Orleans Saints voted in favor of accepting the owners' terms. The next day the Los Angeles Rams, Dallas Cowboys, and Houston Oilers likewise agreed to return to the fields. Within a week of Culverhouse's presentation, the strike was over and an abbreviated nine game schedule announced. The defeat was a crushing blow to Garvey and the NFLPA.

Dave DeForest-Stalls said the union and its representatives were put firmly behind the eight ball not only because of Culverhouse's direct appeal to the players, but because the NFL parlayed the appeal into a rumor that a settlement had been reached and Garvey was preventing agreement when there was in fact no deal at all. The teams were merely voting to accept the proposal, not agree to terms.

"The NFL did a brilliant job of announcing that there was a deal when there wasn't a deal," DeForest-Stalls said. "The momentum that created, just lying to the media, hundreds of times they lied to them during the strike, and the media was just so gullible. Our constituents thought there was a deal and are ready to go back in and we couldn't recover from it."[67]

The fact that Culverhouse came out so strongly in favor of the owners' offer just weeks after allegedly telling his franchise's two player reps that he was in favor of a salary scale was not lost on DeForest-Stalls. Arguing in favor of something that contradicted a previous statement was just the owner's style, says the former defensive lineman. "He's a very, very smooth operator," DeForest-Stalls said. "He just knows how to manipulate a situation. He probably just told us what we wanted to hear."[68]

The endgame for Garvey was not pleasant. Jack Donlan said that when they met for the final time, Ed Garvey was opposed to signing the deal. "You could tell it [the end] was coming because there was so much heat and pressure," Donlan said. "We banged it out. The fact of the matter is that Garvey didn't want to sign it."[69]

But the deal was finally done and Culverhouse and his fellow owners could warm themselves over the fact that they had withstood the most unified attack on their power base in league history. The man Culverhouse introduced to Management Council had not just defeated Ed Garvey, but eviscerated him. Garvey would soon resign as union chief and be replaced by former Oakland Raiders offensive lineman Gene Upshaw.

The great irony of the 1982 players strike is that the settlement the players finally agreed to was the same proposal offered days before the walkout: $1.6 billion over four years.[70] Culverhouse had not had to cough up one extra nickel, but there was plenty of collateral damage to go around his franchise.

Former general manager Phil Krueger said of the impact of the walkout, "That strike hurt everybody."[71]

The strike hurt everybody, that is, except Culverhouse and Donlan.

Culverhouse parlayed the 1982 strike into another promotion for himself, moving from a member of the Management Council to chair of the Management Council shortly after the strike ended. As chair, he more than any other owner or league official, including Pete Rozelle, would wield absolute power.

One of his first errands as chair was to talk to Jack Donlan about continuing to work for the NFL.

"We had come out of the 1982 strike and all the money issues had been resolved because of his dealings," Donlan recalled. "I had signed a three-year agreement in mid–1980, so after the 1982 negotiations my contract was running out. He and I had a long conversation about whether or not I would renew my contract."[72]

Donlan did agree to a new deal that would see him through the expiration of the hotly contested CBA in 1987. It also led to a profitable friendship with Culverhouse that would last for years to come.

Unfortunately, for another Culverhouse friend, the ramifications of the 1982 strike would lead to a somber and melancholy end to a legendary coaching career.

The fallout from the strike at One Buccaneer Place was not felt immediately; it would be parsed out over a period of two years. The week leading up to their return to the field brought a sense of optimism back to the team's headquarters. Linebacker Scot Brantley recalled the players were so overjoyed to be back at work that the atmosphere was akin to college football.

The first game of the post-strike season was against the Dallas Cowboys at Texas Stadium. With only three days to prepare, the players and coaches went forward with a "what the hell" attitude.

"We put in a skeleton defense and a skeleton offense," said Brantley. "We flew to Dallas, and we played our asses off and we had a ball. I know we got beat [14–9], but I did not feel like I had missed a day. We were all over their ass."[73]

The Buccaneers rebounded from their 0–3 start to make the playoffs for the third time in four years, losing again to the Cowboys in the first round. Despite the sour finish, the team's resilience in bouncing back from a dreadful start, both on and off the field, gave the impression that big days were ahead for the Tampa Bay Buccaneers.

However, upon closer inspection, problems were brewing as a result of Culverhouse's active participation in the destruction of Ed Garvey and the union. Culverhouse's son sums up the feeling this way: "The union got nothing," he said. "My father was happy, but his players were humiliated and they showed it."[74]

A sample of the players' changed attitude was in their perception of head coach John McKay. An iconoclastic coach, McKay had crafted a reputation as a chief executive who delegated the majority of the weekly coaching duties to his assistants. This led to few verbal exchanges with his players. While this style did not differentiate McKay greatly from his peers, the hands-off approach left him vulnerable to the interpretations of others in the weeks after the strike.

"McKay had a unique relationship with his team, and this comes from a guy who played for Tom Landry, Al Davis and Tom Flores," said Dave DeForest-Stalls. "John McKay had a real mixed relationship with the players because we rarely saw him at practice. He let his assistants run practice. That being said, it was really hard for us to tell where McKay was with this [the strike]."[75]

One hint of McKay's loyalty was evident when the coach made the mistake of organizing telephone calls to players and asking if they would have any interest in returning to the team headquarters during the strike to practice. Not only did this violate the NFL's rule on not practicing during the strike, it was a violation of the National Labor Relations Board. Many players, including DeForest-Stalls, didn't believe that McKay made the mistake honestly, but instead was acting on behalf of Culverhouse in an attempt to divide and conquer the Buccaneers roster. "I have a hard time believing the coaches would do this on their own," the lineman told the press at the time, implying Culverhouse was behind it.[76]

Even if McKay's calls were completely unrelated to Culverhouse, they only acted to heighten the perception that he was the owner's man. McKay's close personal friendship with Culverhouse put him at odds with the players. It was well known that the two dined together and golfed together. Culverhouse even was an interested participant in the legal education of McKay's younger son Richard, who would go on to one day be the Buccaneers general manager. To the players there was no way McKay could be sympathetic to their side while maintaining a close personal relationship with their chief antagonist. This caused the coach's credibility with the players to wane.

"The strike killed him [McKay]," says Hugh Jr. "He sided with Dad and he shouldn't have done it. John went against his players, and they were never his again."[77]

Further alienating McKay was his use of humor. Once his weapon for keeping the focus on him and off his players during the formative years of the franchise, the off the cuff remarks caught players still smarting from the strike the wrong way.

"When we did see him, a lot of what he would say was sarcastic," said DeForest-Stalls. "His humor was sarcastic, but his humor was often at the expense of a player. That was not the most endearing behavior for a leader."[78]

Whatever McKay's loyalties, the head coach was unduly hamstrung by more than just a morale problem. A disturbing pattern of personnel decisions was about to culminate in the loss of his field general. As with all decisions made by Culverhouse, this particular decision would come down to frugality and be necessary to set the stage for the most sociologically important Super Bowl start in NFL history.

CHAPTER FIVE

The Curse of Doug Williams

THE BUCCANEERS MADE NFL HISTORY when they chose Doug Williams with the 17th pick in the first round of the 1978 draft. An All-American and Heisman Trophy finalist at Grambling, Williams possessed all the physical attributes scouts of the time looked for in a quarterback except one: race.

For years the NFL had taken collegiate African American quarterbacks and moved them to other positions citing the conventional wisdom that players of color lacked the necessities to be an effective field general. While pioneers such as Marlin Briscoe, James Harris and Joe Gilliam had proven the notion wrong, there had still not been much movement in the direction of racial equality at football's most visible position when Doug Williams entered the draft.

By selecting Doug Williams with a first round draft choice, the Buccaneers did more than select their franchise quarterback; they became the first team in the NFL to select an African American franchise quarterback, a distinction not lost on Williams. In a 2005 interview, Williams admitted his selection gave him an opportunity many others had fought for and he appreciated it greatly.

"I think to be drafted number one and given the opportunity to play quarterback is more correct," Williams said, putting his place in history in context. "There were guys like Marlin Briscoe who came before me but weren't given the same opportunity. I was fortunate at a later date to get the chance mainly because of a guy like John McKay to whom race did not matter."[1]

McKay's track record in the area of race spoke for itself. During the 1960s McKay was one of the few Division I coaches to start African Americans at the quarterback position. One of McKay's most successful signal callers was Jimmy Jones, an African American quarterback who led the Trojans from 1969 to 1971 and won the 1970 Rose Bowl. Of all the victories Jones and the Trojans achieved none was more important than a 1970 encounter with the Alabama Crimson Tide. McKay's all African American backfield of Jones, running back Clarence Davis and fullback Sam Cunningham ran roughshod over the all-white Crimson Tide. The 42–21 victory by USC had far-reaching societal implications. The defeat to USC convinced Crimson Tide boosters to allow legendary coach Paul "Bear" Bryant to finally integrate the team.[2]

McKay didn't change his attitude on race when moving to the NFL. In fact while Williams' selection was historic, he was actually the second African American chosen to play quarterback by the Bucs. During their inaugural 1976 season, Parnell Dickinson had started one game and played in seven others. The Bucs' seventh-round draft choice from Mississippi Valley State, Dickinson was a raw talent hampered by injuries. Dickinson was released in 1977, but his opportunity to earn the quarterback position illustrated that McKay's color-blindness had followed him from USC.

While John McKay had no qualms about starting an African American at quarterback, his primary concern as a football coach was to win football games. In order to do that McKay needed the best players available. The historic selection of Williams was also an example of the collaborative personnel system with which the head coach and the personnel department worked in the 1970s.

Doug Williams had an impressive collegiate resume, but there were questions about how valid his statistics were based on the level of competition the young quarterback faced while at Grambling. Former Buccaneers director of player personnel Ken Herock liked Williams but wasn't sure he would be worth the first overall draft pick, which the Bucs held as a result of their 2–12 record in 1977.

Wanting to learn more about Williams, Herock dispatched a young Buccaneers assistant coach to the Louisiana school with a mandate. "We had a guy on our staff named Joe Gibbs," Herock recalled. "I said, 'Joe, I want you to go down to Grambling and I want you to stay with Doug Williams for one whole week. Wherever he goes, you go. He goes to class, you go to class. He goes to dinner, you go to dinner. Just don't sleep with him. I want you to be with him for as long as you can for one week.'[3]

"Joe comes back after a week and we ask him, 'What do you think?'" Herock continued. "Gibbs says, 'All I can tell you is he can do it. He is a number one draft pick and will be a good quarterback.'"[4]

There was no question Williams would be an upgrade over the current stable of quarterbacks on the Buccaneers roster. "We needed a quarterback, there was no doubt about that," Herock said.[5]

A hire by Ron Wolf, Ken Herock filled a similar role in 1978 to the one Wolf had filled in 1976 and 1977, and enjoyed the same relationship with John McKay in regards to acquiring personnel.

"I was involved in everything there," Herock said. "In actuality, John McKay was the power broker, but if you had his ear, you could pretty much direct him into what you wanted to do."[6]

What Herock really wanted to do was draft Doug Williams, but he couldn't see doing so with the first selection in the draft, not when Heisman Trophy winning tailback Earl Campbell of Texas was universally considered to be the best player in the draft. Herock worked the phones to find a trade partner willing to ante up an attractive package of players and picks for the Bucs' top selection and found one in Houston. The Oilers, long a moribund franchise, were eager to draft local hero Earl Campbell. Houston agreed to send Tampa Bay four draft choices, including the 17th choice in the first round, and second-year tight end Jimmie Giles in exchange for the right to select Earl Campbell.

Herock believes that one move transformed the Bucs from laughingstock to title contender while upgrading the team's talent pool exponentially.

"My biggest move was probably Doug Williams because that involved a gigantic trade," Herock said. "We traded the rights to Earl Campbell to the Houston Oilers and in return got Doug Williams, a Pro Bowl tight end in Jimmie Giles and a running back that was sort of a throw-in named Jerry Eckwood. That helped get us in the playoffs: a good quarterback, an All-Pro tight end and a good running game."[7]

The new players paid dividends immediately. By the midway point of his rookie season, Williams and the Buccaneers were 4–4 and in the middle of the NFC Central Division race. A broken jaw sidelined Williams for the majority of the second half of 1978, but the next year he picked up right where he left off.

In 1979 Williams helped lead the Bucs to a 5–0 start on the way to a 10–6 record and the team's first divisional championship. By no means was Williams a one man show. In 1979 the Tampa Bay defense finished number one in almost every meaningful defensive statistic and running back Ricky Bell, benefiting from having Eckwood and Williams as his backfield mates, enjoyed his greatest year as a professional, rushing for more than 1,200 yards and scoring nine touchdowns. Those performances were critical to the Bucs being in the playoff race, but it was the leadership and clutch play of Williams that put Tampa Bay over the top in 1979.

In four of the team's road games in 1979, Williams had rallied the team to victories after trailing at the beginning of the fourth quarter, including wins in the waning moments at Chicago and Detroit. Those victories typified the style of football John McKay advocated. McKay's approach to winning a football game was to suffocate the opponent with a defense built on speed, forcing the opposing offense to commit mistakes. Conversely, McKay's offensive approach was to bludgeon the opponent with a bruising running game and occasionally catch the run-conscious defense off guard with a long pass to a tight end over the middle of the field or down the sideline to a split end. If this approach didn't build a lead by the fourth quarter, it would then be the job of a John McKay coached quarterback to bail the team out.

Doug Williams may have best described John McKay's style during a 2005 interview. "We weren't a very complicated offense," Williams said. "If you knew Coach McKay it was pitch right, pitch left, slam it up the middle. When we passed it was try to find one of the receivers deep and if not, scramble until you find someone open."[8]

Williams' five years as the quarterback in a John McKay offense resulted in mediocre statistics. Between 1978 and 1982 Williams completed 895 of 1,890 passes (a 47 percent completion percentage) for 12,648 yards, 73 touchdowns and 73 interceptions. Those statistics didn't matter compared to the victories Williams engineered. In 1979, Williams was the youngest quarterback in NFL history to lead a team to a division championship and playoff victory.

In 1981 Williams led the Buccaneers to a second NFC Central Division championship. Mixed in with the nine victories the Buccaneers earned that season was a fourth quarter come-from-behind victory over the Atlanta Falcons. A 71-yard touchdown pass from Williams to Kevin House secured a 24–23 victory at Tampa Stadium. But Williams saved his best for the next season.

In 1982, the Buccaneers' record stood at 2–4 with only three weeks left in the strike-shortened season. One loss in the final three games would eliminate the Buccaneers from the playoff tournament. Williams guided the Bucs to a narrow 24–23 victory over the Buffalo Bills in a game where Lee Roy Selmon forced a fumble that prevented the Bills from attempting a game-winning field goal. The next week the Buccaneers trailed the Detroit Lions 21–6 midway through the third quarter. With the season on his shoulders, Williams led three scoring drives in the last 20 minutes of the game including one that led to a 27-yard field goal by kicker Bill Capece with just 25 seconds remaining in the game.

If overcoming a fifteen point deficit in one half had appeared daunting, Williams faced an even stiffer challenge the next week. Against the Chicago Bears in a winner-goes-on, loser-goes-home contest, Williams found his team trailing by seventeen points, 23–6, midway through the third quarter. For the second time in as many weeks, Williams put the team on his shoulders and carried them to victory. Throwing 49 passes, almost unheard of in a John McKay offense, Williams gained 367 yards and hit tight end Jimmie Giles for two touchdown passes and moved the Bucs in position for Bill Capece's game-tying 40-yard field goal with 26 seconds remaining.

In overtime Williams got some much needed help from running back James Wilder. Wilder's 47-yard run put the Bucs in position for a game-winning field goal. For the second time in as many weeks Bill Capece, a rookie from Florida State, kicked a game-winning field goal, this one from 33 yards for a 26–23 victory that put the Bucs in the playoffs. Future Hall of Fame defensive end Dan Hampton said after the game that there was a clear difference between the Bears and the Buccaneers and that difference was Doug Williams.

"He's grown up and matured a lot in three years," Hampton told the media. "He makes things happen for the Bucs. He's their leader by far."[9]

In 1981 and 1982 the Bucs were bounced out of the playoffs by the Dallas Cowboys in lopsided contests, but Williams appeared to be a player the Bucs could build around for years to come. However, when Williams' contract expired in 1983, he discovered an opponent more daunting than the Dallas defense: the fiscal conservatism of Hugh Culverhouse.

Despite winning two of the past three NFC Central Division championships, not much was expected of the Tampa Bay Buccaneers in 1982. As the major sporting magazines' NFL preview issues hit the stands, a theme regarding Tampa Bay became apparent: mediocrity. The range of predictions had the Buccaneers finishing in the same 9–7 range as the year before where others, including *Sports Illustrated* expected the team to finish with a losing record. Longtime *SI* football writer Paul Zimmerman explained his prediction of a 7–9 record with an interesting question: "Writers have selected six yearly MVP's since the club was formed, and half of them have been traded away. Why? Why do superstars seem to go sour after a few years there?"[10]

Zimmerman's question was posed in late summer of 1982. As 1982 turned to 1983 the answer became unmistakably clear: money.

The Tampa Bay Buccaneers were the most visible commodity in Culverhouse's portfolio, but far from his only interest. He had relocated his law practice to Tampa so that he could oversee the Bucs, the NFL and his clientele from a centralized location. An avid deal-maker, he scoured his surroundings, holding countless conversations with acquaintances and colleagues, always on the lookout for the next investment that would grow his fortune.

Stephen Story, an associate at Mr. C's firm, and later a partner, acted as the owner's point man on many of his deals. In fact, Story was so integral to Mr. C's operations that he actually worked out of the team headquarters even though he wasn't an employee of the Buccaneers.

"I moved to Tampa in 1980," Story recalled. "I worked the first nine months at One Buc Place. I used that as an office until we found space that fitted our needs."[11]

Story was amazed at Culverhouse's ability to manage a NFL franchise while at the same time working multiple deals simultaneously. In Story's opinion, business was a game to Culverhouse and the owner had an insatiable desire to play to win. An unfortunate side effect of that was that Culverhouse was often cash poor.

"Part of it is that he was such a gambler and he leveraged himself all the years I was with him," Story said. "He probably never enjoyed a day in his life where he had real strong positive cash flow because every time he would get some he would go further in debt doing another deal."[12]

Unlike his fellow owners who ran their teams into debt, only to be saved from themselves by Culverhouse's intervention, the Buccaneers owner saw the revenue potential in a franchise. As was proven in the lead-up to the NFL strike of 1982, Culverhouse had crafted one of the most profitable NFL franchises in existence and used those funds to balance his non-football related books with the help of Stephen Story. Story viewed his role as one of gatekeeper, the man who kept Culverhouse informed of the financial reality of his situation so the owner could make the most fiscally responsible decisions possible.

"That is where I probably came in as a balancing act," Story said. "I would have to do that quite often on transactions. He would see an opportunity—and it may have been a fine opportunity—but the risk it put the rest of his assets in wasn't worth it even if it turned out to be successful."[13]

One of those risks was paying too much for NFL personnel and in the early 1980s, the Buccaneers began shedding payroll and in the process ceased to be a viable on-field threat for the next decade.

The 1981 and 1982 Tampa Bay playoff teams' rosters looked dramatically different than they had in 1979. Key contributors such as David Lewis, Dewey Selmon, Jeris White and Jerry Eckwood had been cut or traded away. The result of those personnel moves not only lowered the Bucs payroll, they also systematically made the Bucs a young, inexperienced team. The only saving grace was Ken Herock's ability to spot young talent combined with John McKay's coaching methods which kept the Bucs winning while Culverhouse's profits piled up. Herock explained this personnel philosophy was untenable, and he tried his best to bring that to the attention of his boss.

"Mr. Culverhouse wasn't meddlesome," Herock said in giving the owner's side of the conversation. "He said, 'Ken I don't worry because you are always going to get me good players.' But you know it isn't the way it always happens. You go through streaks of not having good players. He had that much confidence in me. Thanks for the compliment Mr. C, but it is not that easy."[14]

An example of Herock's success at avoiding the repercussions of cutting payroll was the trade of popular offensive lineman Charley Hannah.

"We had a guy named Charley Hannah whose contract was coming up," Herock recalled. "We have to sign Charley and it comes down to like a $25,000 difference and my thing is, 'Hey, let's sign him. He's a starting right tackle, and you don't find them everyplace.' We had just signed a new coach and this coach tells McKay, 'This guy [Hannah] is just an ordinary player, and we can replace him no problem.'[15]

"They [McKay and Culverhouse] always thought I was going to find them," Herock recounted with a hint of sarcasm. "It's easy for me to find them. 'Go find them, Ken.' They just don't pull starting tackles out of the blue like that. Fortunately, I was able to replace Hannah with a guy named Ron Heller. I hate to say it, but I was good enough to do those things. We were losing players but still were able to win and they're thinking, 'Hell, Ken will get the players.'"[16]

Herock's fears about not being able to continue landing top talent soon became realized. The Bucs' amazing streak of solid drafts ran dry as highly selected players like Ray Snell and Booker Reese failed to pan out. Also, trades of 1st and 2nd round picks for Wally Chambers and Norris Thomas respectively were too expensive for the production returned. The system that had been so successful in the beginning fell apart under the mandate to pare spending to keep the books tight. When Doug Williams' contract came up for renewal, the Bucs' organizational philosophy couldn't cope.

Success has many fathers, but failure is an orphan. In no case is that more apparent than the decision to not re-sign Doug Williams. The primary parties involved all have a compelling version of the story and all agree on one thing: they wanted Doug Williams to remain a Buccaneer.

"I wanted to sign Doug Williams," said Ken Herock. "We should have never lost him. But for some reason at that time Mr. C, who was the ultimate judge, didn't sign him. He was hearing that we could win without him, but we couldn't win without him."[17]

John McKay wanted Doug Williams, telling John Underwood of *Sports Illustrated*, "He [Williams] is becoming—not there yet, but on the way—one of the better quarterbacks in the game." McKay was so sold on Williams that he fired quarterbacks coach Bill Nelson because he worried the two men didn't get along.[18]

Williams wanted to remain a Buc, telling Underwood in the same article that "I'd be lying if I said I didn't want to stay in Tampa."[19] However, Williams felt that he was vastly underpaid for the production he had provided the Buccaneers and felt the time had come for the Buccaneers to pay him in line with his peers. Anything less would be insulting to him.

Despite all parties agreeing that the best place for Doug Williams to continue his career was in Tampa Bay, it never happened.

This one personnel move more than any other has come to identify the

Culverhouse era, yet it is also the most misunderstood. The owner was branded a racist over the failure to ink a deal, but there is little evidence to support that claim. He was labeled a cheapskate unwilling to sign any player to a top-flight contract, but the men who worked directly under Culverhouse contend that was false as well.

The perception of Culverhouse as a racist was at odds with his hiring of John McKay. McKay had a reputation as a racial progressive, and Culverhouse was enamored with the coach. He had also been supportive of the massive trade that brought Doug Williams to Tampa Bay in the first place, a high draft choice that no other NFL team had been willing to make. The racist reputation came not just from the pitched battle over money with Doug Williams, but from Culverhouse's inability to master the art of public relations. His son puts it succinctly.

"My father was not a good public speaker," Hugh Jr. admits. "He had an innate way to be offensive. He would use motherfucker as a noun, adjective, pronoun and verb all in one sentence. Dad just saw what needed to be done, but he wasn't tactful."[20]

That lack of PR savvy also made it easy to characterize Culverhouse as a modern day Ebeneezer Scrooge. From the day he purchased the Buccaneers, he gave off an air of tight-fisted money management that belied his true nature. An early interview provided a fair warning of how he viewed spending money, a view obscured by the Bucs' early success. When commenting on his private jet, Culverhouse told a reporter, "You gotta buy 'em used like I did. Only rich people can buy 'em new. If you worry about nickels—be cost conscious—then you get along just fine. I haven't bought a new suit in two or three years."[21]

The irony is that despite his public perception, he was far from cheap. Stephen Story argues that cheap was an ill-chosen word with which to define Hugh Culverhouse. "It's funny that people have that perception of him, but it is far from the truth," Story claims. "He was as big a tipper as there ever was."[22]

Culverhouse believed in spending money to make money but was adamant that not one cent more than necessary be spent. By adhering to that philosophy, he had been able to parlay a handful of shrewd investments into an empire that included the Tampa Bay Buccaneers. The franchise, in turn, acted as a revenue stream to fund larger business deals. When it came time to re-sign his franchise quarterback, he wanted to do so with as little impact on his cash flow as possible.

One of the men hamstrung by Culverhouse's desire was Phil Krueger, who was the lead man in contract negotiations for the Bucs.

"Mr. Culverhouse was very good with a dollar," Krueger said. "The only advice he gave me [in contract negotiations] was, 'Don't make friends with my money. Otherwise, that's my only advice.' I held that as a maxim."[23]

Krueger took that advice to heart and made Culverhouse's initial offer. From the moment the first offer was made, chaos and mystery reigned.

"That is a terrible story," Krueger said when asked to comment on the Bucs' exchanges with Williams and the colossal misunderstandings, resentment and bitterness that unfolded as a result.[24]

In his autobiography, *Quarterblack*, Williams wrote that the Bucs offered a contract worth $400,000 a year.[25] Phil Krueger and the Bucs maintained in the press that the offer was for $600,000 a year and included an opportunity to join Culverhouse in a Tampa area land deal worth hundreds of thousands of dollars.[26]

Krueger maintains to this day that Williams' agent, Jimmy Walsh, was demanding a contract that was out of line with the salaries comparable quarterbacks in the league were earning.

"He [Williams] has his side of the story, and we have a side too," Krueger said. "He had an agent that wanted to make him the highest-paid quarterback in the league. He was a good quarterback, but wasn't the number one. We did offer him the same contract as that of Minnesota quarterback Tommy Kramer, but they wanted more money. I was limited in the amount of money that I could spend. Mr. Culverhouse was very tight with his money. Mr. Culverhouse did not want to be the highest paying club in the league."[27]

Krueger relayed Jimmy Walsh's demands to Culverhouse. "I told Mr. Culverhouse it was going to be difficult because the agent wanted the highest paid quarterback for his ego," Krueger said.[28] Culverhouse elected to not make a counter-offer and instead instructed Krueger to express that the original offer was the best Williams could expect.

Williams wasn't happy to be dealing with Krueger, writing in his autobiography that he and his agent, Jimmy Walsh, wanted to deal with Culverhouse. However, Culverhouse did not wish to deal with Walsh, so Williams reluctantly dealt with Krueger, a man he didn't much care for because he felt he had been low-balled on his rookie contract. Former public relations director Rick Odioso recalled that Williams' personal feelings for Krueger were a difficult obstacle to overcome.

"The Doug Williams deal floundered mainly because the Buccaneers let Krueger do the negotiations, and Doug Williams did not trust him and did not like him," Odioso said.[29] In fairness to Krueger though, Odioso added that the Bucs' negotiator was only following orders from further on up. "Whether it was all Kruger's fault or not..." Odioso said in an open-ended comment, adding that neither side communicated well. "Doug was very hard to pin down."[30]

Soon the negotiations became public fodder with the Bucs claiming to have offered Williams $600,000 a year and the quarterback adamantly denying any such thing, claiming the Bucs' only offer was $400,000 a year. The Bucs countered saying that Jimmy Walsh, Williams' agent, was demanding $800,000 a year in an attempt to make Williams the highest paid quarterback in the NFL.[31]

No matter whether the dollar amount was $400,000, $600,000 or $800,000, the difference between the two sides was still relatively small when compared to other quarterbacks around the NFL. The fact that the two sides were so entrenched, especially someone with Culverhouse's resources, puzzled many in One Buccaneer Place, players and executives alike.

"That was a big squabble over a minimal amount of money," recalled Williams' teammate, linebacker Scot Brantley. "You think of that kind of squabble today, you'd be talking about the third assistant to the equipment staff."[32]

Personnel man Ken Herock agreed, "Doug was holding out for a few dollars and at the time it wasn't a lot of money. We could have done that deal easy, and it wouldn't have hurt the franchise."[33]

In an attempt to explain his father's recalcitrance, Hugh Jr. opined that his father was a bit overconfident following his role in the defeat of the NFLPA and may have overplayed his hand in taking a hard line against Williams.

"Let's put it in time context," he explains. "You've just had the strike, you feel the power of having just crushed the union, and now, 'What do you mean this guy wants more money than I'm offering?'"[34]

To make matters worse, during the heat of negotiations Williams' young bride, Janice, died of a brain tumor. Overwhelmed with grief, Williams was incensed when Culverhouse made what the young quarterback deemed a token appearance at Janice's funeral.

"I remember Culverhouse showing up, and it was so much like a mafia movie," Williams wrote in *Quarterblack*. "They came there in one of those long black limousines, and as soon as it was over, they got right back in their limo and drove out of there. I mean they got out of there as quickly as they could. They never said anything to me. They showed no sympathy."[35]

Coping with the loss of his wife and angered by what he viewed as an unseemly display at the funeral, Williams' negotiating position hardened considerably. Once one of Culverhouse's most loyal players—Williams had been against the strike—the quarterback declared publicly that he would settle for nothing less than a contract commensurate with those of his peers.

With both sides locked in, Krueger knew the impasse was unlikely to be resolved without Culverhouse's direct involvement. He told the owner so and much to Krueger's relief, Culverhouse agreed to meet with Williams personally in an attempt to finally close the deal.

"Mr. Culverhouse said, 'Phil, have Doug come down here tomorrow and talk with me,'" Krueger said. "I knew damn well he [Culverhouse] was going to give Williams the contract and he was going to be the hero. I told Doug, 'Tomorrow morning, you meet Mr. C and talk over the contract. You're going to get the contract. He doesn't want any agent there. He just wants you and him talking and you're going to get the contract.'"[36]

Krueger continued, "Doug went to his agent and told him what I told him. The agent told Doug not to come in because Mr. C is a strong and powerful man and you'll be killed. So the next morning Mr. C was in bright and early. He's at his desk waiting. Doug comes in and says, 'I'm not going to talk to Mr. C.'"[37]

The lines had hardened and the franchise was left in the lurch. An attempt to be proactive by the Bucs' coaching and personnel staff would prove to be an inadvertent disaster.

While Williams and Culverhouse battled, John McKay and the rest of the Buccaneers were left to ponder the rapidly approaching season. If Williams didn't re-sign, or at least engaged in a protracted holdout, McKay would be facing a season with Jerry Golsteyn as his starting quarterback. Golsteyn, a veteran journeyman with minimal starting experience, had attempted one pass in all of 1982 as Williams' back-up. Realizing that he needed a viable quarterback in case Golsteyn didn't pan out, McKay recalled a player that started for him in an obscure collegiate all-star game.

In 1979 McKay coached the Pac-10 All-Stars in the Challenge Bowl, a short-lived post-season all-star game that pitted the best players of the Pac 10 Conference against the best from the Big Eight. The game, played in Seattle's Kingdome, was more impressive for the coaching match-up. McKay went head to head with former Oklahoma coach Bud Wilkinson, at the time head coach of the St. Louis Cardinals. McKay's side featured a strong-armed senior from Washington State named Jack Thompson. Nicknamed "The Throwin' Samoan," Thompson won MVP honors in the Challenge Bowl and was drafted in the first round by the Cincinnati Bengals.

Thompson didn't earn much playing time in Cincinnati as Bengals quarterback Ken Anderson was in the midst of a late career renaissance having led the Bengals to a Super Bowl appearance in 1981. Thompson was on the market and McKay, perhaps a bit desperate, was willing to pay almost anything to get him.

Ken Herock recalled that when he did his due diligence on Thompson, the reviews came back as mostly negative.

"When Doug doesn't accept the deal, Coach McKay said he had this 'Throwin' Samoan' in some college all-star game and Cincinnati is trying to trade him," Herock recalled. "McKay said, 'If Doug doesn't want to sign, we should trade for the 'Throwin' Samoan.' Well that was probably the biggest disagreement we had when I was there. The guy can't play. But John thought he could coach him and make him a successful player."[38]

Phil Krueger seconded Herock's recollection of McKay's interest and Thompson's ability.

"They wanted a quarterback, and McKay had had Thompson at some kind of all-star game," Krueger concurred. "Thompson did quite well in the game and Cincinnati offered him. He didn't pan out. Nice kid, but he didn't pan out."[39]

McKay ultimately got his man, but it cost the Buccaneers their first round draft choice in the 1984 draft. Making matters worse, Thompson's contract called for an annual salary of $200,000 a year which was the difference between what Williams said he wanted and the Bucs were willing to pay. When Williams' agent, Jimmy Walsh, called the Bucs to say that for $200,000 Williams would re-sign, he was told the Bucs couldn't afford it. Williams wrote in his autobiography that when he spoke to Krueger shortly afterwards, he was told the Bucs' offer was now $375,000 per season.[40] Feeling as though he had no other choice, Williams signed a five-year, $3 million deal with the Oklahoma Outlaws in the rival United States Football League.

Krueger denies that the offer was lower, claiming Culverhouse was prepared to give Williams the raise he demanded. "To be honest with you, Mr. C was going to give him the money he wanted plus a side deal," Krueger said. "But Doug never went in there. Doug took the money in the USFL and seemed to think that we bad mouthed him."[41]

No matter what happened behind closed doors, one thing was clear. When Doug Williams left neither he nor the Tampa Bay Buccaneers were ever the same again.

Williams maintained his reputation as a rifle-armed quarterback during his stint in the USFL. Williams had solid seasons, throwing for more than 3,000 yards in 1984 and 1985. Rusty from almost two years away from the game, Williams threw 21 interceptions in 1984 but rebounded in 1985 to be one of the highest-rated quarterbacks in the upstart league. In neither season, however, did the Outlaws have a winning record. When the league went belly-up in 1986, Williams found himself without a football home for the first time in his career.

For the better part of the 1986 off-season, Williams sat at home and waited for the phone to ring. And waited. And waited. And waited.

Writing in his autobiography, Williams was certain that the reason no NFL team was willing to talk to him was because Hugh Culverhouse and Phil Krueger were making every effort to blackball him. "I wouldn't be surprised if Krueger called other coaches and general managers to persuade them not to sign me," Williams wrote in *Quarterblack*. "That's just the type of person that Phil Krueger is. And I'm sure Hugh Culverhouse would have done the same thing. He probably told Krueger to do it."[42]

Phil Krueger denies that he made any attempt to blackball Williams, stating that not many teams were interested in acquiring Williams, to whom the Buccaneers still held negotiating rights. "There weren't any other people knocking down the door to get him after his appearance in the USFL," Krueger said. "I didn't have anybody calling me."[43] As further proof of his innocence in blackballing Williams, Krueger points out that if he had it in for Williams, the young quarterback would have never been signed by the one man that did call, Redskins head coach Joe Gibbs. "If that was true he would have never signed with Joe Gibbs," Krueger said. "Joe Gibbs and I were like brothers."[44]

The relationship between Gibbs and Krueger stretched back to their days as assistant coaches under John McKay at USC in the late 1960s. The two shared living space and traveled on recruiting trips. In 1978 the two were reunited in Tampa Bay as Joe Gibbs served as the Bucs' offensive coordinator and Krueger worked with special teams.

Since his one season as Tampa Bay offensive coordinator in 1978, Joe Gibbs had become an elite NFL head coach, restoring the luster to the long dormant Washington Redskins. Triumphant in Super Bowl XVII and as two-time NFL Coach of the Year, Gibbs and San Francisco coach Bill Walsh were considered the deans of NFL coaching in the mid–1980s.

In 1985 Redskin quarterback Joe Theismann had suffered a horrific leg injury in a Monday night game against the New York Giants. The broken leg proved career-ending, and Gibbs was in need of a veteran to compete with second-year pro Jay Schroeder. In August Gibbs agreed to send a fifth-round draft pick to Tampa Bay in exchange for Williams.

"The deal actually worked for him," Krueger said of Williams.[45]

That was an understatement.

Williams saw little playing time in 1986 as Jay Schroeder enjoyed a Pro Bowl season, throwing for more than 4,000 yards and leading the Redskins to the NFC Championship Game. In 1987 Schroeder was again named the starter, but an injury in the opener against Philadelphia gave Williams his first chance at meaningful NFL playing time in almost five years.

Williams played as if he had never left, tossing two touchdown passes in a 34–24 victory over the Eagles. The next week Williams started in Atlanta, throwing for three more touchdowns in a loss to the Falcons. Following a month long layoff due to a work stoppage, a healthy Schroeder returned to his starting position with Williams coming off the bench in relief appearances, securing an important victory over the Detroit Lions.

In the next to last game of the season, Schroeder posted pedestrian stats in a 23–21 loss to the Miami Dolphins. Throughout the 1987 season Schroeder had struggled to replicate his 1986 form, completing less than 50 percent of his passes and throwing almost as many interceptions as touchdowns. In the finale against Minnesota, Schroeder got off to an awful start, throwing two quick interceptions. Sensing his team needed a change Gibbs pulled Schroeder and sent Williams into the game. Williams didn't disappoint.

Williams steadied the Redskins and threw two long touchdowns in rallying Washington from 10 points behind to win 27–24 in overtime. The come-from-behind victory gave Gibbs something to think about. Ever since the days when he had shadowed Williams on the Grambling campus, the coach had sensed the quarterback had the innate ability to win. Williams won at Grambling. While under Gibbs' tutelage in Tampa, Williams had led Tampa Bay to playoff contention in his rookie year before suffering a season-ending injury. After Gibbs left, Williams continued to win in Tampa Bay becoming the youngest quarterback to win a championship. When Gibbs gave Williams playing time in Washington, the quarterback responded by leading the team to three dramatic victories. Playing a hunch, the former Buccaneers offensive coordinator gave Williams a chance to make NFL history.

"Doug has been making big plays," Gibbs told the media. "The opportunities he's had, he's come through for us. People are looking for specifics on why I am making a switch. You can't really point to anything. It's more of a gut feeling."[46]

Williams rewarded Gibbs' faith by guiding the Redskins past the Chicago Bears in the opening round of the playoffs. Trailing the Bears 14–0, Williams once again calmly led his team steadily from behind. Shaking off a fierce pass rush and the winds swirling throughout Soldier Field, Williams tossed one touchdown pass and helped secure a 21–17 win. The following week in a re-match against the Minnesota Vikings, Williams threw two touchdown passes to pace a tough 17–10 victory in the NFC Championship Game. That victory placed Williams once again under the spotlight of history.

Less than 10 years after the Tampa Bay Buccaneers made Doug Williams the first African American quarterback drafted in the first round to play the position, the former Buc was going to the be the first African American quarterback to start a Super Bowl game. The performance Williams enjoyed in Super Bowl XXII guaranteed that he would not be a mere footnote.

The week leading up to Super Bowl XXII was one of the longest of Williams' life as he was asked countless variations of the question, "How do you feel about being the first African American quarterback to start a Super Bowl?" The most infamous of those variations was, "How long have you been a black quarterback?" to which a chagrined Williams answered, "All my life."[47]

Questions of race aside, Williams was also asked about his time as quarterback of the Tampa Bay Buccaneers. Still smarting from his ignominious departure, Williams used the largest stage in football to let his former employer have it with both barrels.

"It makes you wonder whether you're in the money-making business or if you're playing football," Williams said of the personnel moves orchestrated by the Hugh Culverhouse owned Bucs in the years since the quarterback left. "They probably spend many a sleepless night wondering if they could have made that game [Super Bowl] with Doug Williams at quarterback."[48]

Upon first leaving the Bucs in 1983, Williams publicly stated that he hoped the Bucs would go 0–16. Asked the week of the Super Bowl if he still held a grudge, Williams admitted that he did, but was not alone. "When I said I wasn't pulling for the Tampa Bay Buccaneers to win, that was true, but then there were a lot of black Americans who were not pulling for them to win," Williams told Super Bowl reporters. "I look back and feel I had some wasted years."[49]

"Joe Namath said that the smartest thing a quarterback can do is find a good team to play for," Williams said when comparing the Redskins to the Buccaneers. "The philosophy in Tampa Bay was: just keep it close." In Washington, Williams said, the goal was to win championships.[50]

On Sunday, January 31, 1988, Williams and the Redskins did just that.

The first quarter of the Super Bowl was entirely forgettable for Doug Williams. The Broncos jumped out to a quick 10–0 lead and for a short time it appeared that Williams would be unable to continue playing after suffering a twisted knee. Williams limped to the sideline and was replaced by Jay Schroeder.

When the second quarter began, Williams limped back onto the field and into NFL history. In less than 15 minutes of playing time Williams led the Redskins to 35 points, throwing for 228 yards and 4 touchdown passes to pace a 42–10 Washington rout. The most amazing fact about the quarter was that it took Williams and the Redskin offense only 18 plays to accomplish their scoring flurry.

At the end of the game Williams' stat line read 18 completions in 30 attempts for 340 yards and 4 touchdowns. The performance earned Williams Super Bowl Most Valuable Player Award honors. To this day Williams continues to be the only African American quarterback to win a Super Bowl.

In addition to winning the MVP trophy, Williams permanently put to rest the notion that an African American quarterback was not capable of leading a team to a championship. When asked by NFL.com to reflect on his historic day during a 20th anniversary profile, Williams, a man who for years struggled to be accepted as a quarterback rather than a black quarterback, finally allowed himself to put his accomplishment in the context of the broader civil rights struggle.

"I can close my eyes and see it all like it was yesterday," Williams told

Thomas George of the NFL Network. "It just wasn't supposed to be carved out for a black man to do this. The Ku Klux Klan used to ride up and down the street in my hometown of Zachary, Louisiana. But that Super Bowl happened to me. And it makes me think of what Martin Luther King, Jr., said, 'I've been to the mountain top ... I've seen over on the other side.'"[51]

As a result of his trailblazing, Steve McNair and Donovan McNabb earned the opportunities that Williams had fought for. Drafted in the first round by the Houston Oilers and Philadelphia Eagles respectively, McNair and McNabb would both lead their teams to Super Bowl berths, becoming the second and third African Americans to do so. While neither won their games, McNair and McNabb both credited Williams for being a role model on their path to NFL stardom.

Could Doug Williams have made NFL history had he stayed as quarterback of the Tampa Bay Buccaneers? No honest answer can be given because it would be impossible to predict the vagaries of a football season. However, it is the opinion of many a former Buccaneer that Williams' continued employment would have greatly increased the chances of Tampa Bay continuing their winning ways.

Former linebacker Richard "Batman" Wood said that a combination of Doug Williams and Pro Bowl tailback James Wilder, who remains the Buccaneers' all-time leading rusher, would have made the Bucs' offense formidable.

"Wilder could catch the ball out of the backfield and he could run," Wood said. "He would have been in the top ten in rushing if Doug Williams had been here. Ten thousand yards would have been easy for him; 15,000 yards would have been easy for him."[52]

Hall of Fame defensive lineman Lee Roy Selmon admitted during the week of Super Bowl XXII that he agreed with many teammates who were haunted by the "What if?" question.

"I can certainly relate to that," Selmon told *St. Petersburg Times* reporter Bruce Lowitt shortly after Super Bowl XXII. "I wish I could've been there too. Doug's such a talent that you wonder what could've happened if he had still been here, if we had all stayed together."[53]

While it is debatable if Williams would have led the Bucs to a Super Bowl, one thing is certain. If not for Tampa Bay's failure to re-sign their quarterback, Doug Williams would not have been a Washington Redskin in 1987. Doug Williams' history making Super Bowl performance was the unintended consequence of Culverhouse's position on payroll. Another consequence was a history making streak in Tampa Bay, the kind the fans of the Buccaneers would like to forget.

While Doug Williams made Super Bowl history, the Tampa Bay Buccaneers made a different kind of impact in the story of the NFL. In 1983 the

Buccaneers, behind Jack Thompson, finished 2–14, the first of twelve straight seasons of posting double-digit losses. While the record was dismal, a closer look shows that Tampa Bay was competitive in almost every contest, losing nine games by a touchdown or less. In six of those nine games the Bucs had a chance to either tie, take the lead or run out the clock in the final quarter only to fall short. Given Williams' late game heroics over the previous years, it was apparent that the Bucs were missing more than just a quarterback, they were missing leadership.

"What the Bucs didn't take into account was that Doug was the leader of the team," said Rick Odioso. "There was a lot of respect for Doug, especially on the defensive side of the ball. I think a lot of them said, 'If Doug didn't get his, I'll never get mine.'"[54]

One of those players was linebacker Richard "Batman" Wood, who freely admitted that Williams' departure played on the psyche of the team. What had once been a close-knit family was now a rudderless group of individuals who didn't know where they stood anymore.

"That was a real controversy when he didn't sign," Wood said. "That kind of put a dent in our quest to repeat or even make it to the playoffs."[55]

"Here we are losing one of our best players on offense when all we needed was a little help," Wood continued. "Defensively we had a chance against anybody. All we needed was a little help on offense. All I know is contract hassles messed up our football team and our chances of going to the Super Bowl."[56]

Comparing Williams' negotiations with the team's larger reduction of payroll, Wood described an environment of uncertainty and mistrust at One Buccaneer Place.

"All of a sudden we start losing good players," Wood said. "Here we are coming off 0–26 to going in three years playing for a Super Bowl. We had some pretty good ball players; we just had a lot of wishy-washy things going on. When teams have a chance to win they do their best to keep their core players, and I don't think that was a priority. When you don't have a value system, when you're just aiming at a target but not the bulls-eye, you're going to have problems."[57]

Fellow linebacker Scot Brantley concurred with Wood and brought up the fabled curse of Doug Williams that allegedly enveloped the Bucs for more than a decade. "Everything after Doug was almost like a curse," Brantley said. "Some people said he buried a relic on the 50-yard line and put a hex on Tampa Stadium. We heard all kinds of rumors. It all had to do with Culverhouse."[58]

If Culverhouse was the target, the curse of Doug Williams seemed to afflict the men that followed Williams at the helm of the Buccaneers offense. The first victim was Jack Thompson. Thompson's stay in Tampa was mercifully short. Released in 1985, Thompson never played in the NFL again, but he did start the Bucs' historic revolving door of quarterbacks through the 1980s.

Former Tampa Bay public relations director Rick Odioso spoke in almost biblical terms of how the failure to re-sign Doug Williams begat one quarterback "savior" after another. "It was a pivotal event in franchise history," Odioso said of Williams's exit. "If it could have worked out they wouldn't have had to chase quarterbacks. They chased quarterbacks with Jack Thompson, Steve DeBerg, Steve Young, Vinny Testaverde, Chris Chandler, Craig Erickson, Trent Dilfer, etc. There were all those draft picks, effort and money to replace Doug for the next decade, and I'm not sure it ever happened."[59]

None of those quarterbacks had success while in Tampa Bay, but once they got out from under the curse of Doug Williams, they re-discovered their talent. With the exception of Thompson and Erickson, every man that quarterbacked the Tampa Bay Buccaneers led a team to a playoff appearance or better after leaving the Bucs. DeBerg and Testaverde led teams deep in the playoffs in the 1990s. Chris Chandler led the Atlanta Falcons to a Super Bowl appearance. Steve Young and Trent Dilfer joined Williams as former Tampa Bay quarterbacks who won a Super Bowl, Young with the San Francisco 49ers and Dilfer with the Baltimore Ravens.

The struggles on the field eventually led to John McKay's stepping down as coach following the 1984 season. He had guided the Bucs from their infamous growing pains to the brink of a championship only to be thwarted by the penuriousness of the franchise. At the press conference announcing his resignation, McKay looked tired and beaten.

"I'm sure it hurt a man like John McKay. God Almighty, you are the laughingstock of the world," said linebacker Richard Wood.[60]

Hugh Culverhouse, Jr., agrees. "Look at the timeline when McKay retired," he said. "His heart wasn't in it after that. He just didn't want to coach."[61]

For the remainder of his time as owner, Culverhouse never saw the Tampa Bay Buccaneers come close to a winning season. His bottom-line style of management kept the Buccaneers a supremely successful revenue stream, but the impact on the field was disastrous. Many well-respected football men would follow John McKay but would never come close to duplicating his success. The Buccaneers were now officially finished as contenders for anything but infamy.

Perhaps no one took a bigger beating over the Doug Williams contract fiasco than Phil Krueger. For years he was lambasted as "Freddy" Krueger, Culverhouse's henchman who held on to the franchise's purse string with an almost fanatically tight grip. Loyal to Culverhouse, Krueger is almost placid when talking about the most difficult days of his career and the impact it had on his public perception. "My job was to take pressure off of Culverhouse," Krueger said matter-of-factly in an interview for this book. "He didn't have to make a lot of statements to the press because he didn't like that. I just did what I was supposed to do. I think people assumed I had a lot more authority than I did. The final authority rested with the coach and owner."[62]

As for the perception that he was to blame for the failure to re-sign Williams, Krueger is blunt about setting the record straight. The former negotiator believes that Culverhouse, Williams, and the agent Jimmy Walsh all share equal blame for the failure to reach an agreement. Krueger believes Culverhouse could have and should have made a better initial offer, Jimmy Walsh shouldn't have had such an over-inflated sense of self and Williams should have been more realistic about the demands for his services around the league.

"If your hands are tied, if this is the amount of money I can offer, I can't offer any more," Krueger said. "If he didn't have an agent that influenced him so much, he would have gotten the money."[63]

"I haven't talked to him since then," Krueger said of Walsh. "Any agent I dealt with except that guy would tell you I was straight with them. I never tried to con anybody. Leigh Steinberg [a well-known NFL agent] and I signed a lot of guys."[64]

The man Krueger reported to also took a beating. Culverhouse was never given the benefit of the doubt after the Williams fiasco. As the losses piled up, fan attitudes became more and more entrenched against him, especially the African American fans. His son still feels that the negotiations fell apart because of money and pride, not race.

"The sad thing is that his agent asked for a pittance and unfortunately a trait of my dad was to dig in his heels and that was that," Hugh Jr. said. "At that point Doug felt he had no choice."[66]

"Considering Williams was suffering the loss of his wife, Janice, and was trying to bring up a young daughter at the same time, Culverhouse now looks particularly villainous," said Buccaneer historian Paul Stewart.[65]

Culverhouse's son has done the best he can to atone for his father's mistakes by donating generously to several colleges associated with Williams. Following his playing career, Williams embarked on a coaching career, becoming head coach at Morehouse College and Grambling. At those stops Hugh Jr. arranged financial gifts to the school's funds.

"If you look at Grambling, the largest donor is oddly a white man," Hugh Jr. said of his many gifts to the Louisiana school, including a $1 million donation to the Tigers football team in 2002.[67]

When asked if that was a form of penance, Hugh Jr. admitted it was. "That is atonement, sure," he said. "Williams is extraordinarily talented, and I followed him from college to college and donated every place he went."[68]

Eventually Doug Williams would return to Tampa Bay, joining the Buccaneers front office in 2004. Despite coming back to where his professional football career began, Williams never forgot the events that precipitated his departure. In a 2005 interview Williams admitted that while he was happy to be back in Tampa Bay, he had no intention of letting Hugh Culverhouse off the hook, standing by what he wrote in *Quarterblack*. "I have no reason to retract anything that has been said in that book about that situation," Williams said.[69]

One of the reasons Culverhouse may have felt confident in taking a hard line stance against Williams during the contract negotiations was his belief that his quarterback had nowhere else to go. Free agency was out of the question for Williams unless he wanted to sit out a year and gamble that another team would be willing to pay a high draft pick in exchange for his services under the Rozelle Rule.

However, there was an option for Williams and many NFL players who felt underpaid. In 1983 the United States Football League had formed, playing football in the spring and early summer. The Oklahoma Outlaws' multi-million-dollar offer to Doug Williams had cost Culverhouse leverage against his quarterback, but it was another USFL franchise that tormented the Buccaneers owner and would cause him to make the downfall of the USFL a personal crusade.

Culverhouse had a war on his hands, and the key battleground would prove to be Tampa Stadium.

CHAPTER SIX

Battling with Bandit-Ball

THE CONTENTIOUS CONTRACT negotiation between Hugh Culverhouse and Doug Williams was the biggest Buccaneers story in the spring and summer of 1983, but it was far from the biggest football story in Tampa Bay. In February of that year, a professional football team founded by a respected showman and co-owned by a Hollywood legend took to the field and captured the hearts and imagination of Tampa's sporting public. In doing so, they also captured something that Hugh Culverhouse had started to take for granted, Tampa's sports dollar.

Over the course of the next three years, the NFL and a rival league would engage in a protracted war for talent and market share. From his position at the apex of football history, Culverhouse would have a ringside seat for the bout. As he battled an imaginative local rival, his lieutenants in the league office would engage in a wider ranging battle with the upstarts. Ironically, his business model with the Buccaneers was the necessary catalyst for the most successful franchise in the short-lived, upstart league.

The United States Football League was formed in the spring of 1982 with franchises in 12 cities. Professional football had positioned itself as the country's most popular spectator sport in the 1970s, and the USFL originally staked its reputation on the belief that America's love affair with gridiron action could support two separate leagues. However, football history was littered with failed attempts at creating a second league. The World Football League had been the last to attempt competition in the 1970s, failing after just over one season of play. With a proposed 18 game schedule stretching from mid–February until early June, the USFL's design intended to capitalize on the popularity of the pro game without engaging in head-to-head compe-

tition with the wealthier NFL. A playing schedule during what had traditionally been football off-season would present many challenges, chief among
them, marketing. Selling football during baseball season would require showmanship. Fortunately, the USFL had one of the most personable and competent individuals in sports running their Tampa Bay franchise.

Canadian businessman John Bassett came to Tampa Bay with a reputation as a true sportsman. In many ways Bassett was the antithesis to Hugh
Culverhouse. While they shared a love for competition and real estate—Bassett owned major Floridian holdings in Panama City and Longboat Key—
the two could not have been more different in their approach to business,
sports or life. In his early 40's, Bassett was equal parts charisma and energy.
Bassett's fashion sense was anything but corporate, telling *Sports Illustrated*,
"I only wear a suit and tie when I go to the bank. My hair is short when I'm
raising money and long when I'm spending it."[1]

Where Culverhouse had been brought up in humble surroundings, Bassett was the scion of a wealthy family, known in some circles as the Canadian
Rockefellers. The family wealth was spent on sports, and Bassett had been
brought up in an environment of sports and publicity. Bassett's grandfather
had been the owner of the *Montreal Gazette* newspaper, and his father was
a minority stakeholder in the famous Maple Leaf Gardens hockey arena and
for a time owned the Toronto Argonauts of the Canadian Football League.
The youngest Bassett had made an athletic name for himself as a tennis
player. Bassett played the sport well enough to earn a spot on the Canadian
Davis Cup team. Upon graduation Bassett cut his teeth as an entertainment
promoter and newspaper writer, learning the importance of giving both the
fan and the press what they wanted: entertainment and access.

Bassett's first foray into professional sports was as a partner in the purchase of the Ottawa Nationals of the World Hockey Association, a rival to
the more established National Hockey League. The Ottawa franchise was
shifted to Toronto and eventually Birmingham, Alabama, and re-christened
the Bulls. Not satisfied with a role as part-owner of a hockey franchise, Bassett also became an initial investor in the newly formed World Football
League in 1974 and quickly made headlines.

The World Football League lacked any kind of credibility except for
that which Bassett provided. Arguably the best financed owner, Bassett made
a splash when he signed Miami Dolphins stars Larry Csonka, Jim Kiick and
Paul Warfield to play for his Memphis Southmen. Those deals effectively
ended the Miami Dolphins dynasty and brought Bassett to the attention of
the NFL. Unfortunately, the signings did nothing to help the WFL as too many
franchises couldn't match Bassett's wherewithal in providing the needed
funds to operate a team. In less than a year and a half, the WFL was out of
business leaving Bassett out of football.

Having had a taste of professional football, Bassett turned his sights on acquiring an NFL franchise. Before Tampa Bay and Seattle had been awarded franchises in 1974, Memphis, Tennessee, had been a serious contender for an expansion franchise. With several WFL players still under contract, Bassett gave a presentation to NFL officials petitioning for the absorption of his Memphis franchise into the league. Citing that he had a "ready-made team" in a city the NFL coveted,[2] Bassett made an interesting case that ultimately fell on deaf ears. Pete Rozelle turned Bassett down, forcing Bassett to abandon the Memphis plan. Instead, Bassett entered into discussions to purchase the San Diego Chargers, but Gene Klein, who had expressed interest in selling his club, experienced a change of heart and pulled the club off the market.

Stifled in his attempts to join the NFL, Bassett tried to keep his hockey team viable in the rapidly failing WHA. In 1979 the hockey league went under and left Bassett out of sports until the USFL was formed in the early 1980s. This tumultuous time offers insight into why Bassett made such a splash when introducing the Bandits. Bassett had staked his own fortune into the WHA and WFL, spending his own money on the Bulls and Southmen respectively. Bassett even used the proceeds from the dissolution of the WHA to pay off his WFL debts, an act that earned him the respect of employees and creditors alike.[3] The hemorrhaging of capital Bassett suffered caused him to think seriously about what had gone wrong. In both cases, the WHA and WFL had attempted head-to-head competition with more established leagues to their own detriment.

Bassett wouldn't merely own the Tampa Bay Bandits; he would assume a leadership position in the USFL to rival that of Culverhouse in the NFL. Bassett was arguably the vice commissioner of the USFL, ranking only under true commissioner Chet Simmons in influence. Bassett knew the USFL needed more than a unique spring-summer schedule to survive. They needed a totally different style of play.

To that end Bassett unveiled Bandit-Ball.

"The NFL has a great big gray-flannel executive image," John Bassett told the assembled media during the early days of the Bandits. "Our image is dirt-kicking and down home. We're having a ball."[4]

The Bandits were officially introduced in August of 1982 at a press conference that was more of an open bar than an open question-and-answer session. Joining Bassett at the gathering was minority owner Burt Reynolds, at the time one of the most popular film stars in Hollywood. In addition to his film work, Reynolds was fondly remembered for his days as a Florida State Seminole tailback in the 1950s.

"I'm going to play linebacker. We're going to play Greenville Prison and Dom DeLuise is the coach," Reynolds cracked to reporters, making reference to his role in *The Longest Yard* and his corpulent co-star in many films.[5]

The team name was taken from Reynolds' profitable *Smokey and the Bandit* film franchise, although Bassett argued good-naturedly that the true origin of the name was from a family dog. "Don't tell Burt that," Bassett told reporters.[6]

Reynolds wasn't the only hint of show business at the gathering. An all you can eat buffet was provided along with a live band and very attractive women dressed as cowgirls guiding Reynolds from one reporter to another.

Bassett beamed. "I just wanted to be different," the proud owner said. "Where else have you seen a press conference for a sports team with Burt Reynolds, cowgirls, a band? I wanted it to be fun. I just wanted to have people mixing, rather than preaching."[7]

The owner continued, "This is the first time I've ever owned a sports franchise and not been the focus of attention."[8]

Having set up a football press conference unlike any other in history, Bassett next turned his attention to creating a team and marketing blitz unlike any seen in football. He succeeded on both counts, much to Culverhouse's chagrin.

No matter how much Hollywood influence Reynolds provided, Bassett knew that his team would never be marketable unless it won on the field. Bassett intended to build his team using local talent and was instrumental in convincing his fellow USFL owners to take a regional approach when constructing rosters. Having local players would sell tickets, Bassett surmised. The Tampa Bay area was a hotbed of college football and Bassett knew he could build a championship contender with Florida players. The owner also felt it would be best to have a Floridian football legend as coach and he could think of nobody better than Steve Spurrier, a man who had once helped Culverhouse sell tickets.

A Heisman Trophy winning quarterback at the University of Florida, Spurrier had spent most of his NFL career as a back-up with the San Francisco 49ers. When the Bucs stocked their roster, they acquired Spurrier for his name as much as for his experience. A legend in nearby Gainesville, Spurrier lent star appeal to an expansion team sorely lacking in it. Spurrier survived that inaugural season with his health and popularity intact. Even though the Bucs went 0–14, the local media thought well enough of Spurrier's effort to award him the Most Valuable Player award.

After his NFL career ended, Spurrier moved into coaching and gained a reputation as an offensive guru. In the relative obscurity of Durham, North Carolina, Spurrier coordinated Duke University's offense and helped establish the normally outmanned Blue Devils as an offensive force. In 1982 Duke's Spurrier-led offense finished as the fourth most prolific offense in the nation.

At 37 years old, Spurrier was very young to be given a head coaching job, but Bassett showed no qualms about his choice. Spurrier would put points on the scoreboard, and do so in an entertaining fashion. That was all that mattered to Bassett.

"I want my team to be interesting, exciting and fun," he told reporters. "We're not looking for any 7–6 ballgames."[9]

When asked if he had any concerns about Spurrier's lack of head coaching experience, Bassett replied, "I think he'll make a hell of a coach."[10]

Spurrier was also quotable. During his first press conference he outlined how he intended to play the game, a style that would involve not just plays too risky for the NFL, but in a style that would run counter to the three yards and a cloud of dust mentality that permeated the older league.

"We're going to throw the ball around," Spurrier said. "We're going to make it exciting for the fans. We want to have a team they can be proud of. We're going to have the kind of players who will get out into the community and we'll be accessible and available at all times."[11]

The last comment was a reminder of the status of the NFL, which had just returned to the field following the '82 strike the day before Spurrier was hired. Even though NFL games were back, fans that had felt betrayed were staying away. The timing of the NFL strike could not have come at a better time for Bassett's new football team. With the Buccaneers engaged in contract negotiations rather than football games, the Bandits were the fun football story in the fall of 1982, and they took full advantage. During the height of the strike as the Bucs walked the picket line, the Bandits broke ground on a new training facility, placed merchandise in area stores and started to sign players, including another University of Florida legend, quarterback John Reaves.

Looking back on the frenetic first months of the Bandits, Marketing Director Jim McVay noted it was almost unfair the advantage Bassett had on the Bucs.

"It was great for the USFL," McVay said in an interview for this book. "The NFL had been on strike; it was just an opportune time to launch a new league. It worked out beautifully, and there wasn't a better marketing guy in the world than John Bassett. He was a master marketer and promoter. He was sensitive about making sure fans got their money's worth. He was a lot of fun to be around."[12]

The focus on local talent paid off as the Bandits sold 300 season tickets alone on the day the NFL strike began and 10,000 by the end of October even without an official schedule of games.[13]

Those statistics and the method with which they were being created were noticed with grim irony by Culverhouse. Incensed that the Buccaneers' own home stadium would be the base of operations for the Bandits, he was

now forced to see the man who had once been his marquee quarterback introduced as the marquee head coach of a rival team. The owner had worked for
years to make the Buccaneers a Tampa football monopoly, going so far as
to battle Miami Dolphins owner Joe Robbie over televised games. For years
the NFL had mandated that if a home game did not sell out within 72 hours
of kick-off, the game could not be televised in the home market. This was
done in an attempt to protect ticket sales. However, Culverhouse went one
step further and instituted a secondary blackout where if the Bucs did not
sell out a home game, then neither the Bucs game or any Dolphins game
could be shown on Tampa television.[14] If he couldn't convince Dolphins fans
to watch his team, he would keep them from watching theirs. This led to a
feud with Robbie that ultimately culminated in the Bucs and Dolphins can-
celing their annual pre-season games.[15]

Comparing his father's situation with the Dolphins to what he encountered with the Bandits, Hugh Jr. is adamant that the USFL team got under
his father's skin immediately. "Tampa is one of the most rabid 'Gator Nation'
cities in the state, and their quarterback and head coach are former Gators,"
he said. "You couldn't throw dirt in the face of my dad more and it was the
smartest marketing thing."[16]

Bassett's marketing hits would keep on coming.

The billboards were a definite eye-catcher.

Rising high above the Tampa landscape, a Hollywood starlet in a football
uniform a few sizes too small smiled down at passersby accompanied by the
phrases "Special Thrills Coming this Year" and "All the Fun the Law Will
Allow."[17]

The starlet was Loni Anderson, the curvaceous female lead of the hit
CBS sitcom *WKRP in Cincinnati*. Wearing a mega-watt smile and little else
than the too tight football jersey and pants, Anderson's billboard was transformed into a promotional poster to be given out to fans throughout the
region. Anderson at the time was romantically linked to Burt Reynolds and
her image in a Tampa Bay uniform gave the Bandits a weapon the Bucs
lacked, sex appeal.

"That poster has been the best thing since popcorn," Bandits marketing
director Jim McVay told the media at the time. "The interest has been overwhelming. She is a very attractive woman. Maybe that poster is symbolic of
the type of fun we're going to have this year."[18]

Explaining the tie-in between football and the Hollywood starlet, McVay
said, "Football is at the heart and soul of our operation. Giving fans exciting,
professional football is the most important thing, but we want to offer fans
a total entertainment package."[19]

Shortly after the Anderson posters appeared, a new hit song hit the
Tampa Bay airwaves. "Bandit-Ball," a country-western themed fight song

written and performed by Jerry Reed, was another Bassett marketing hit. With Reed, co-star of Burt Reynolds in the Smokey and the Bandit movies, imploring "First and Ten, do it again, Bandit-Ball," the ditty quickly replaced the Bucs fight song, "Hey, Hey Tampa Bay the Bucs Know How to Shine," in the hearts and minds of Tampa football fans.

Bassett then scored two more marketing coups that shook up the Bucs. The first was the opening of a Tampa Bay Bandits merchandise store in November of 1982, just in time for the Christmas shopping spree. The store was located at Tampa Bay Center Mall directly across the street from Tampa Stadium. As the Bucs finished out the 1982 season, fans were streaming to the Bandits store to purchase glow in the dark Bandits shirts and other apparel. The lone horseman logo of the Bandits became so popular, that it quickly outpaced Bucco Bruce apparel sales.[20] A Bandits team store across the street from their home stadium may have made Buccaneers executives uncomfortable, but they could easily choose not to go in. Bassett's next move however was much harder to miss, and much more difficult not to see.

In February of 1983 Bassett personally arranged a state-wide television network to broadcast the Bandits pre-season opener against the Boston Breakers at the Tangerine Bowl in Orlando.[21] Bassett's decision to televise the game instead of blacking it out to boost ticket sales cost money in the short term, but the end result of the broadcast of Tampa Bay's 10–3 victory acted as a sales stimulus. Shortly after the game, the Bandits reported 20,000 season tickets had been sold.[22] Bassett's network also provided the Bandits the added cache of being the first USFL team to have a game televised, further entrenching the Bandits as the cornerstone franchise of the fledgling league.

When the day of the USFL season opener finally rolled around, many in the NFL were apprehensive about how the new competitor would fare. In most cities, NFL officials heaved a sigh of relief as average attendance figures were around 25,000. But Culverhouse knew he had a problem when the Bandits sold over 42,000 tickets to their opener. His response to the Bandits showed that for all his business acumen, public relations was his Achilles' heel and his mistakes would further the popularity gap between his team and Bassett's.

Culverhouse's initial reaction to the Bandits was to forbid any of his employees to engage in any semblance of fraternization. The ban was so total that former personnel man Ken Herock needed to request special dispensation to scout prospective players.

"He hated the USFL," Herock said. "We had a USFL team in town that was competing with us and they were pretty good. He hated that because they were getting attention and his Buccaneers weren't. He said, 'I don't want anybody associating or even going over to watch a game. I don't want anybody going to those games.' I went to a couple and told Mr. C., 'I need to scout them.' He said he understood and let me scout them."[23]

With the exception of Herock, Culverhouse showed that he meant what he said about not associating with the Bandits. When he learned that a game statistician, a contract employee of the Buccaneers, also worked Bandits games, the Bucs informed the man that his services would no longer be needed at Bucs games.[24] Later, Culverhouse learned that the local department store that made the uniforms for his cheerleaders, the Swash-Buc-lers, also made them for the Bandits cheerleaders. He promptly cancelled his account with that store.[25]

Joked linebacker Richard Wood, who saw his playing time cut significantly in 1983, "I had Bandits season tickets. Maybe that's why he didn't want to play me anymore."[26]

At first Culverhouse's prohibition appeared to be honored for the most part. Bandits linebacker Sankar Montoute recalled that he didn't see much of the Bucs players out and about. "There was some interaction, but generally, no. I don't think they appreciated the Bandits because of the popularity we enjoyed."[27]

His failure to re-sign Williams, and the decision by the quarterback to jump to the USFL, severely undermined the owner's ability to enforce his mandate. Within a matter of weeks Culverhouse not only lost the moral authority, but lost more personnel to the rival league. One of the most important names to leave was Ken Herock, the man who had been able to keep the Bucs' talent level competitive despite tight budget constraints.

"When the Williams deal didn't happen, I felt like I couldn't accomplish my job in Tampa," Herock said in 2009. "If this is the way it's going to go, I can't accomplish my job. I felt I got to get out of there."[28]

"I was approached by the USFL, and they offered me a lot of money," Herock continued. "I was thinking about taking the deal and pretty much had the contract wrapped up. Mr. Culverhouse got wind of it, and he was very upset. He felt I had betrayed him. I explained to him what happened, that I felt shunned aside and it was probably best for me to leave and he said, 'Okay, you're terminated.'"[29]

Phil Krueger recalled the situation similarly. "Ken interviewed with the new league, so Culverhouse let him go. It was kind of contentious the way Culverhouse let him go, but that is the way Culverhouse was."[30]

"We didn't speak for a couple of years," Herock said. "But eventually we talked again and became friends."[31]

The departure of Williams and Herock was a self-inflicted public relations disaster that Culverhouse was never able to recover from.

"Not a smart management move by the Buccos was it?" asked former Bandits marketing executive Jim McVay.[32]

When the 1983 USFL season ended, the Bandits stood with a record of 11–7. The Bandits failed to make the playoffs, but they more than surpassed the on-field success of the 2–14 Buccaneers. Quarterbacks John Reaves, Jimmy Jordan and Mike Kelley flourished in Spurrier's wide-open offense. The three combined for over 4,500 yards of passing with 27 touchdowns, ranking in the upper echelon of the USFL. The beneficiaries of those passers were receivers Danny Buggs and Eric Truvillion, who both posted 1,000 yard seasons. Complementing the passing attack was a solid running game that provided more than 1,500 yards on the year. Featuring Gary Anderson, Greg Boone and Sam Platt, the Bandits ground attack helped to keep opposing defense from keying on the quarterbacks.

Spurrier would employ a similar system less than a decade later at the University of Florida which revolutionized the Southeastern Conference. Bandits players recognized elements of their attack in what Spurrier would dub the "Fun 'N' Gun" at Gainesville.

"I wouldn't say it was the exact same offense as the 'Fun 'N' Gun,'" linebacker Sankar Montoute said. "It was a wide-open offense. We had really good skill players in Gary Anderson, Eric Truvillion, Greg Boone and John Reaves at quarterback."[33]

Burt Reynolds recalled Spurrier's style of football fondly, telling Mike Tollin in the ESPN documentary *Small Potatoes: Who Killed the USFL?*, "Bandit-Ball was unpredictable. It was totally spontaneous and wonderful. It was colorful."[34]

The free for all offense and winning record was more than enough for the Bandits to attract hard-core fans to Tampa Stadium in the spring. The Hollywood atmosphere and marketing genius of John Bassett also drew in the casual fans. Jim McVay recalled the thrilling environment of Tampa Stadium.

"The Bandits were exceptionally popular," McVay said. "We used to fly in Burt Reynolds. Burt Reynolds back then was more popular than Tom Cruise, Tom Hanks, Brad Pitt and George Clooney combined. He was by far number one at the box office with the *Smokey and the Bandit* stuff. This guy was huge and he was a football guy and a Florida guy. He would fly in loads of people: Ernest Borgnine, Esther Williams, Robby Benson, John Candy, Loni Anderson, Robert Urich, Charles Nelson Reilly and Dom DeLuise. People used to stand in front of the owner's box and just watch all these people come through. Those guys really created a buzz."[35]

In addition to the Hollywood stars, casual fans were drawn in by the array of eye-popping promotions. McVay remembers the promotions stretching the boundaries of what had always been a conservative sport. "We led the league in promotions, I guarantee that," McVay said. "Bikini contests, diamond ring giveaways, mortgage burnings, car giveaways, I mean it was the wildest thing you had ever seen."[36]

The hard work paid off. With average attendance of over 39,000 the Bandits were among the USFL leaders in that category. By comparison, the Bucs averaged 49,000 fans in 1983 but they saw a downward trend as the disastrous season wore on. A staggering 70,000 total no-shows over the last three home dates of the year was a preview of the struggle the Bucs would have in competing with the Bandits.

"The Bucs just weren't very popular back then," McVay said with understatement.[37]

Nineteen eighty-four and 1985 would be even worse for the Buccaneers. In 1984 the Bucs went 6–10 and bid farewell to John McKay. In 1985 the Bucs collapsed to 2–14 under head coach Leeman Bennett. By contrast, the Bandits, who put together a defense to complement their offense, posted records of 14–4 and 10–8, making the playoffs both years.

The difference in on-field success was illustrated by the box office appeal of both franchises. In 1984 the Bucs averaged attendance of 45,732 fans compared to 46,158 for the Bandits. In 1985 the Bandits pulled away from the Bucs with an average attendance of 45,220 to 38,753. A large statistic that especially hurt Buccaneers attendance was the large number of no-shows, people who purchased tickets but chose to stay home rather than watch what was rapidly becoming an uncompetitive and unimaginative product. In 1984 the Bucs had 31,000 no-shows for their final two games alone. In 1985, when the Bucs got off to a 0–9 start, over 60,000 no-shows were counted over the final five home contests.

The Buccaneers were still a highly profitable holding for Culverhouse. Network television money continued to flow through his coffers, but according to his son the Bandits were costing him money in ways that he never fully appreciated.

"Dad never understood marketing," Hugh Jr. said. "If you market a product you sell more memorabilia, you get higher prices. The Coca-Cola's can cost 25 cents more, the beer 50 cents more."[38] He pointed out that if the Bandits and Bucs had continued on their separate trajectories, the NFL team would have been soundly defeated.

"You don't make money in entertainment by being cheap," Hugh Jr. continues. "You market a product that people want. In the NFL you're fucked if you think you're going to make money by being chintzy on expenses. You maximize stadium revenue because you don't have to share that with visiting teams. So you take the Tampa Bay Bandits vs. the Tampa Bay Buccaneers and you have two different products. One you really enjoy and one you endure."[39]

Fortunately for Culverhouse, a shift in the USFL's business philosophy would save him from himself.

The Doug Williams defection also blazed a path for other disaffected

Bucs to follow. The rival league offered NFL players the leverage denied by the Rozelle Rule. With 12 new teams unfettered by concerns over reserve clauses, NFL players were more than happy to make the jump to the USFL. Not only was the move financially rewarding, in some cases it was personally fulfilling.

One of those players was former Buccaneers player rep Dave Stalls. After his Buccaneers career ended in 1983, the now Dave DeForest-Stalls signed a contract with the USFL's Denver Gold and upon arrival was pleasantly shocked by how refreshing their approach to the game and its fans were.

"The Denver Gold were absolutely wonderful," DeForest-Stalls said. "What was interesting about the Denver Gold was that we saw so many families in the stands. We're talking about blue-collar families that were able to bring their kids. That was such an honor to see blue-collar families back at the games because it had got to the point [in the NFL] where you couldn't afford it, especially in Dallas where you had to inherit tickets. It was really cool to play in front of the fans in Denver."[40]

In addition to Williams and DeForest-Stalls, many NFL players jumped to the USFL when their contracts expired. Brian Sipe, Gary Barbaro, Richard "Batman" Wood, Coy Bacon and Joe Cribbs were just some NFL All-Pros who either extended their careers or gained pay raises by switching leagues. DeForest-Stalls claims the entire NFL workforce almost joined the USFL during the height of the NFL players strike.

"We almost did a deal with the USFL during the strike to move our entire personnel over to the USFL," DeForest-Stalls said. "An executive of the USFL was my former agent, Steve Erhardt. We were talking and we had a really interesting meeting in New York. We had some serious possibilities to make it happen, but it just didn't work out that way."[41]

Lee Roy Selmon, the face of the franchise, even went so far as to say that he would consider a career in the USFL if that was his only option given the prolonged work stoppage.

"I'd consider it if it didn't cause any legal problems," Selmon told the *Lakeland Ledger*. "I haven't given it much thought up to now, but if the season was cancelled and I was free of any legal obligations, I'd have to think about it. You only have so many years you can play. It would be an option."[42]

The thought of Lee Roy Selmon in Bandits red and silver had to send a chill down Hugh Culverhouse's spine.

In addition to NFL players making the jump, the USFL was successfully recruiting college football stars to shun the NFL and sign contracts to play for USFL teams. The first big coup was University of Georgia tailback Herschel Walker, who agreed to terms with the New Jersey Generals. A Heisman Trophy winner, Walker was ineligible for the NFL draft because he was a junior and the NFL at the time did not draft anyone who was not a senior. Walker's decision to sign opened the floodgates and soon other major college stars followed.

A 1984 *Sports Illustrated* article previewing the NFL Draft opined that the annual allocation of college talent was almost moot because a significant percentage of the blue-chip talent had already been signed by the USFL. "Of the top 100 prospects, 32 are signed by the USFL," author Paul Zimmerman wrote. "This includes Herschel Walker, Mike Rozier, Steve Young and Reggie White."[43]

When Doug Flutie of Boston College also agreed to terms with the USFL, it made the third consecutive year college football's Heisman Trophy winner opted for the rival league, joining Herschel Walker and Mike Rozier. These signing coups came at a heavy cost to the fledging USFL, however, and John Bassett tried to sound an alarm.

"It would be insane to get into a bidding war," Bassett cautioned.[44]

Unfortunately, Bassett's message of fiscal responsibility was drowned out by the latest USFL phenomenon: Donald Trump.

When Trump purchased the New Jersey Generals after the 1983 season, he set about making a splash by signing quarterback Brian Sipe and Heisman Trophy winner Doug Flutie to join Herschel Walker in his million dollar backfield. Not wanting to be left behind, many USFL owners overextended themselves to try and match Trump player for player. In order to raise revenue, the USFL owners did something foolish. They expanded too rapidly.

In 1983 the USFL expanded from 12 teams to 18 teams with the revenue generated from the expansion fees being split among the original groups. With that money, many owners signed more free agents to exorbitant contracts, including Steve Young's infamous 40-year, $40 million deal with the Los Angeles Express. The revenue generated from the pyramid scheme of selling franchises was quickly depleted, but it served to win the short-term public relations battle.

The NFL chose not to panic in the face of these signings; instead they crafted a patient strategy. The NFL had been in a battle for talent in the 1960s with the American Football League. From 1964 to 1966 the two leagues were forced to spend exorbitant sums on signing bonuses to collegians and were forced to raid each others rosters. The leading reason for the merger between the NFL and AFL had been the mutual conclusion by the two leagues that they could no longer afford the inflated salary structure caused by their battle. With the USFL raiding NFL rosters and collegiate campuses for stars, the NFL owners elected to follow the advice of the man Culverhouse had hired to do battle with the NFL Players Association.

With the strike over, Jack Donlan authored a memo explaining a possible strategy for countering the flurry of activity at USFL headquarters. Upon studying the finances of the USFL, it became apparent that the salary structure was lopsided. Star players such as Young, Walker and Flutie had inked multi-million dollar deals while the vast majority of players received much more modest wages. Dave DeForest-Stalls stated his Denver salary was in the "$70,000 to $80,000 range." With a meager television contract, the USFL didn't have the resources to fight the NFL on all fronts, and Donlan made that known to his bosses. Known as the Donlan Memo, his missive encouraged NFL owners to focus on raising the salaries of mid-level caliber players in order to artificially inflate the salaries of all players. By doing so, the NFL would make it difficult for the USFL to sign college players because they would exhaust their resources on keeping their current players from switching leagues.

"With low-salaried players making up the vast majority of USFL rosters it seems to me we can force the USFL to increase salaries of existing players or run the risk of losing them," Donlan reasoned in his memo. "Each dollar spent on current players is one they cannot spend on a draft choice."[45]

The plan was simple but effective, helped along by the reckless spending encouraged by Donald Trump and other like-minded USFL owners. There was one man in the USFL camp who could see what the NFL was doing, but by the time 1985 arrived John Bassett had a much more pressing battle which kept him from saving his league and beloved team.

To portray John Bassett as a man who didn't want to spend money on payroll would be inaccurate. The veteran owner just wanted to make sure that the USFL didn't overextend itself, making the same mistakes that doomed the WFL and WHA. When Steve Spurrier came to Bassett during the Bandits' first year and stated he needed a more versatile tailback to make his offense work, the owner was open-minded and cooperative. "John Bassett asked me who we needed," Spurrier told the *Lakeland Ledger*. "I said we needed a guy like Gary Anderson, so John went out and got him."[46]

Gary Anderson would indeed be a difference maker for the Bandits, rushing for over 1,000 yards in his two full seasons in Tampa. In order to get Anderson though, Bassett had to outbid the San Diego Chargers, which held Anderson's NFL rights. In the end Bassett won out, giving Anderson $1.375 million over four years, but the experience reinforced the owner's belief that making a habit of attempting to outbid the NFL would doom the USFL.

Bassett trumpeted his belief in staying out of direct conflict with the NFL to any USFL owner that would listen, and he engaged in heated discussions with Trump and the other USFL owners who wanted warfare.

"The two combatants that happened most were Trump and Bassett," former USFL commissioner Chet Simmons said in *Small Potatoes: Who Killed the USFL?* "They were trying to make their own point about what should happen to the league. They were both intractable. John was always logical because of his background and Trump was illogical."[47]

Working against the Trump business model of engaging in a salary war was the fact that spring football was not as profitable as autumn football. Sports fans had grown accustomed to football in the fall for decades and achieving a level of comfort with the thought of spring football was going to take some getting used to. John Bassett knew this when the league started, telling the press: "We know there are fans out there. The question is whether they want to watch football in April, May, June and July. Initially, I'm sure they'll be skeptical. But when we start signing quality players, they'll come out to watch us."[48]

As far as Bassett was concerned, the USFL just needed time to grow and in time, it would be able to stand toe to toe with the NFL. Bassett's marketing director, Jim McVay, agreed with that assessment. "John's vision was that we could be a stand-alone professional sports league in the spring."[49]

That interpretation was seconded by New Jersey Generals president and Donald Trump employee Jimmy Gould in the ESPN documentary *Who Killed the USFL?* "I think John's business model was to stay in the spring, build your audience, build your following, and then perhaps at a later date it would be recognized as a primary league," Gould said in the documentary.[50]

But Gould's boss, Donald Trump, didn't see it that way, telling the media, "My attitude has always been that the spring is a wasteland. If God wanted football in the spring, He wouldn't have created baseball."[51]

Trump believed the best way to generate revenue as a football league was to move the playing schedule to the fall. In Trump's mind the USFL shouldn't just compete with the NFL for players, they should compete with the NFL for audience. Burt Reynolds told documentary film maker Mike Tollin that Trump was able to find allies for this plan at USFL owner meetings. "Everybody was so in awe of this man that had made so much money and taken such chances," Reynolds said of Trump. "Half of them were willing to give it a try."[52]

One of those not willing to give the fall a try was John Bassett, and he once again made his feelings known to Trump both privately and in the media. Former USFL marketing director Dom Camera said in an interview with Tollin that Bassett was one of the few owners willing to confront Trump on this issue and at first, the flamboyant Trump backed down. "Donald was a marketing genius," Camera told the filmmaker. "But he would never take on John Bassett. He could control everyone else, but he couldn't control Basset."[53]

The Bandits owner also took to the airwaves, telling ABC play-by-play man Keith Jackson during a USFL telecast that there was no reason to move the USFL to the fall because the league had the perfect niche. "I think we have the players," Bassett said. "I think we have the product and I believe we have the season."[54]

Unfortunately for Bassett just as the battle over the fate of the USFL heated up, his ability to fight for his side was taken away by a dreaded adversary: cancer. Bassett had undergone surgery to remove skin cancer in the mid–1970s, but in 1984 doctors discovered two tumors in his brain. At first, Bassett attempted to battle both the cancer and Trump, but he ultimately succumbed to both

Bolstering Bassett's contention that a move to the fall was folly was the announcement by ABC and ESPN that they would not televise USFL games in direct competition with the NFL. Secondly, the USFL strategy of paying top dollar for players resulted in the insolvency of multiple franchises. The San Antonio Gunslingers, Portland Breakers, Los Angeles Express, Chicago Blitz, Oakland Invaders and Houston Gamblers all announced they would cease operations following the 1985 season.

Trump and other USFL owners weren't dissuaded by Bassett's arguments or the collapse of franchises. Their hope was to take enough business away from the NFL to make a merger possible. If a few USFL teams could be absorbed by the NFL, Trump and the other owners would see the value of their franchises skyrocket. There was precedent on Trump's side. In the 1940s the NFL had absorbed the Cleveland Browns, Baltimore Colts and San Francisco 49ers of the All-American Football Conference. In the 1960s every American Football League team joined the NFL in a historic merger. Trump and his allies believed the USFL's move to the fall would result in the same acquisition.

In mid-1985, Trump's view held sway as the USFL voted to move to the fall with only Tampa Bay and Denver voting against it. Bassett had owned the most financially secure WFL franchise and knew full well the NFL was in no mood to merge ever again, but his arguments fell on deaf ears. Realizing that he had been defeated, Bassett announced that as far as he was concerned the Tampa Bay Bandits would no longer play in the USFL. Instead, the Bandits would be part of a new sports league Bassett would spearhead composed of spring football, golf, tennis and indoor soccer.

"This decision is being made because our fans have told us what they want," Bassett said shortly after pulling his franchise out of the USFL. "They want the Tampa Bay Bandits to play in Tampa Stadium in the spring and that's what they'll get. This is our team, our fans and our time of the year and that's when we are playing."[55]

The final USFL game for the Bandits occurred in June of 1985. Tampa Bay lost to the Oakland Invaders 30–27 in the first round of the playoffs. Sadly it would be the last time Tampa Bay fans saw the Bandits play. It would also be Bassett's final time with his team.

On May 15, 1986, John Bassett lost his battle with brain cancer and died at the age of 47. Dubbed the "Pied Piper of the USFL," Bassett left a lasting legacy in Tampa Bay. Bassett's dream of a professional multi-sport league died with him, so the Bandits never again took the field. However, almost 30 years after their final game, the Bandits live on in the memory of Tampa Bay fans.

"I still see Bandit license plates all over the place," said Jim McVay on the USFL team's memorabilia that is still popular to this day.[56]

Bassett's team did what no other USFL franchise could: stand toe to toe with their local NFL competitor. Now, on the same day the charismatic owner passed away, Donald Trump and the USFL entered into a legal battle to force a merger of the few remaining upstart franchises with the more established NFL. Naturally, the iron will of Hugh Culverhouse would be the necessary ingredient that prevented any merger talk from gaining traction.

At the time many NFL owners felt the expedient thing to do would be to absorb Trump's New Jersey Generals to buy his silence and loyalty. Hugh Culverhouse, however, was never a man to sacrifice money for expedience. In late 1985, he took it upon himself to state unequivocally that as chair of the NFL Management Council, he would not countenance any talk of mergers. "I have very strong convictions about this," he said. "There will be no merger between the USFL and the NFL. The stories about settlement negotiations and a merger that are coming out of USFL cities are hogwash, just hogwash."[57]

Culverhouse had been seething over the USFL for three years, watching as the Bandits surpassed his Buccaneers. Bassett's untimely death and Donald Trump's questionable strategy had given Culverhouse a second chance at reasserting his dominance in Tampa Bay sports. Presented with the opportunity to crush the USFL once and for all, he would not be stopped. Through sheer force of will, he would demonstrate the level of power he wielded in the NFL.

Donald Trump and the USFL filed an anti-trust lawsuit against the NFL contending that the elder league engaged in monopolistic practices that prevented the USFL from operating as an effective sporting league. With the inaugural fall season of 1986 approaching, Donald Trump and the remaining USFL owners were faced with a quandary. ABC and ESPN would not televise their games in competition with the NFL. The stadiums which had both NFL and USFL teams as tenants were siding with the NFL. Without playing sites or television exposure, the USFL elected to suspend its plans to make the move to the fall and instead sued the NFL claiming that the elder league had coerced the television networks and stadium managers to break their USFL commitments. The USFL sought $1.69 billion in damages.

In the opening weeks of the trial, the USFL landed one successful body blow after another against the NFL. One of the first witnesses to testify was ABC commentator Howard Cosell. Cosell, an ardent supporter of the USFL, testified that Roone Arledge, head of ABC News and Sports, confided in him that "Pete Rozelle is all over me on the grounds that I'm sustaining the USFL with the spring contract."[58] The inference was that Rozelle was attempting to influence Arledge to cease his contract with the USFL, which the NFL quickly denied. While Cosell's testimony was hearsay, it appeared to have an impact on the jury.

Shortly after Cosell's testimony, the USFL lawyers presented Jack Donlan's memo as further proof the NFL was conspiring against the USFL. Jack Donlan was called to testify about the intent of his memo. In an interview for this book, Donlan explained that the memo was nothing more than a strategy for keeping salaries in order and not part of a grand anti-trust conspiracy. Donlan continues to view the entire USFL lawsuit strategy as an effort to avoid the consequences of their own financial irresponsibility. "When they [the USFL] were unsuccessful they turn around and file an anti trust suit," Donlan said. "We would have been successful but for...."[59]

"They called people from every walk of life, people in public relations or anything," Donlan said of the trial that lasted throughout the summer of 1986. "Their logic was to make them [NFL officials] explain what they had done. 'You did this because you were trying to undermine the USFL.'"[60]

The early consensus of the media was that the USFL was winning its case. Those comments unnerved some NFL owners, including Art Modell of the Cleveland Browns, who was quoted as saying, "I'd say we're about a touchdown and a safety behind."[61]

With the thought of having to pay out more than $1.6 billion in damages, many NFL owners began to deliberate about the soundness of absorbing a handful of USFL teams. Published reports showed that serious consideration was given to bringing into the fold Trump's New Jersey Generals in addition to the Baltimore Stars and Memphis Showboats. In exchange for the merger, Trump and the USFL would drop their lawsuit. Hugh Culverhouse wanted no part of that, his son recalled.

"Donald Trump thought his team would be one of those merged," Hugh Jr. said. "The USFL sued the NFL with the hopes of getting money for the owners of the teams that went bankrupt and getting a couple of teams to join the NFL. That was the settlement on the table.[62]

"A group of owners wanted to take the settlement and Dad just blew a cork and screamed and they all backed down," he continues. "I watched him absolutely manhandle a gaggle of NFL owners that wanted to settle the USFL trial. My father would not agree to any kind of settlement with the USFL. He wanted to take the trial to the bitter end. That ended up saving the league millions of dollars."[63]

While Pete Rozelle was commissioner and future NFL commissioner Paul Tagliabue was one of the lead lawyers, it was Culverhouse's behind-the-scenes arm twisting that sustained a unified front and prevented merger talks from becoming anything other than idle speculation.

"We never talked about specifics of the suit," said Rich McKay, who was becoming a more trusted confidant of the Buccaneers owner. "I would say I knew how important it was to him and how much time and energy he dedicated to it. I think any report that said he wasn't involved would not be accurate. I would just say that he wasn't approaching it from a lawyer's perspective. I think what he was involved in was formulating league responses and league decisions. I think that Commissioner Rozelle and Paul Tagliabue probably spent some time dealing with Mr. C in respect to those decisions."[64]

With the NFL refusing to settle the suit moved forward until at last the jury reached a verdict on July 29, 1986. The verdict both vindicated and doomed the USFL.

The jury found the NFL guilty of antitrust violations and deemed the elder league owed the USFL compensatory damages. The news shocked many owners, not least of all Culverhouse. However, before Donald Trump and the USFL could make plans to spend their $1.69 billion, the jury cut them off at the knees.

The jury found the NFL to be a natural monopoly, the result of decades of operating with little or no sustained competition. The jury found no cause to hold the NFL responsible for the fact that the USFL lost television contracts, players and stadium deals. Instead the jury stated the USFL lost those items due to their hasty decision to put on a fall schedule. Somewhere, John Bassett had to feel a sense of vindication that his argument for staying in the spring was being parroted by the jury.

The jury then further dampened the USFL's spirits by awarding the upstart league damages of only $1, tripled to $3 under antitrust law. That worked out to eleven cents per NFL team.

Culverhouse was overjoyed at the result, telling reporters, "We have said all along the USFL shot themselves in the foot."[65] If he realized the irony of stating the same argument as John Bassett, his former USFL adversary, in his quote to the press, he certainly didn't show it.

A quarter century later, many USFL alums also feel that the league shot itself in the foot. To this day they are convinced that if John Bassett had gotten his way, the league may still be around.

"Unfortunately, the league, like a lot of leagues, didn't work out because there was some excessive spending above revenues and some other things happened," said former Bandits PR executive Jim McVay. "If everybody could have followed a salary cap and done a better job managing and kept in the spring, we could still be viable right now. There are plenty of good football players and plenty of good coaches right now that would love to be a part of that league."[66]

Dave DeForest-Stalls concurred, "Bidding things up put the USFL out of business. If they had gone another year or two without bidding, they may have made a go of it. I don't know if it would have been around today, but it would have given the NFL a run for its money and probably by now would have been absorbed by the NFL in some way or fashion."[67]

Former Buccaneers linebacker Richard "Batman" Wood didn't think the level of play was on par with the NFL, but he felt the USFL, especially the Jacksonville Bulls, was a great alternative for fans. "I wouldn't say it was a bad league, because it was a good thing for the spring and the fans in Jacksonville. They were great and the stadium was full."[68]

The immediate emotion of USFL employees was a sense of desolation, particularly among the players who just saw their football careers come to a screeching halt.

"I feel cheated in that we won the lawsuit against them," Bandits linebacker Sankar Montoute recalled. "They [the jury] didn't know what the right award should be. It just wasn't meant to be for me. I'm not bitter about it, but had that gone differently I could have had a long and prosperous career.[69]

"I think we needed to get more established before going to the fall," Montoute continued. "It was a David vs. Goliath thing, only this time Goliath won."[70]

While Montoute's career ended with the USFL, many players and coaches had been given an opportunity to showcase their talent and the NFL was more than happy to hire them. As far as Jim McVay is concerned, that might be the lasting legacy of the USFL and John Bassett, the man who provided the league with show business.

"It sure did help a lot of guys get started in their careers," McVay said before reciting a litany of star players, coaches and executives that developed in the USFL. "Steve Spurrier, Steve Mariucci, Jim Mora, Carl Petersen, Bill Polian, Bruce Allen, Lee Corso, Herschel Walker, Doug Flutie, Steve Young, Jim Kelly, Gary Anderson, Nate Newton and Reggie White."[71]

Dozens of players were able to embark on NFL careers because of the experience they had gained in the USFL, but perhaps no one was left with a better NFL standing than Culverhouse. Although his team had suffered at the gate because of the Bandits, he now stood as the most powerful owner in the NFL because of his role in holding the line against merging with the rival league. Culverhouse even was viewed as more powerful than Pete Rozelle, who had seen his public image battered after multiple lawsuits and congressional appearances.

"There are some who said he was Geppetto and the commissioner was Pinocchio," Hugh Jr. said of his father's status in 1986.[72]

At the time Culverhouse was enjoying the greatest power of his life, his team was engaged in their worst streak of on-field failure since the expansion years. Shortly before his role in the historic USFL trial, his organizational philosophy short-circuited the opportunity to sign a Heisman Trophy winning tailback that may have been able to turn around the fortunes of the Tampa Bay Buccaneers. That failure proved necessary to launch a two-sport career by an athlete who would go on to become a national phenomenon.

CHAPTER SEVEN

Bo Knows No

HUGH CULVERHOUSE HAD SPENT a decade amassing a power base inside the National Football League's governing structure. In 1986 he ran both the NFL Management Council and Finance Committee. In addition to these roles, he was still acting as a financial advisor to a majority of owners and had his hands in multiple NFL issues including labor relations, civil actions and franchise ownership transitions. The Tampa Bay owner didn't view this staggering workload as a burden; he thought it was fun and told any who would listen that he was having the time of his life.

"He liked that [NFL business] so much more than the football team," Hugh Jr. recalls. "Running the league, running the finance committee, running the labor, the lawsuits, being the acting commissioner, so to speak. He liked that more by far. That to him was power."[1]

Stephen Story concurred, adding that Culverhouse felt the NFL provided him the chance to make a lasting impact that would help to burnish his legacy as something more than just an anonymous businessman. "Hugh was more global in his thought process," Story said. "That's why I think he enjoyed the NFL side at the league level because it gave him that opportunity versus his individual investments."[2]

The rigid, almost brutal thriftiness of Culverhouse had helped the NFL reap profits unparalleled in the history of sport. The Tampa Bay franchise, as one of 28 equal recipients of the NFL's bounty, continued to be a source of great revenue for Culverhouse despite the fact the team continued its precipitous decline. As loss after loss piled up, he grew frustrated, becoming determined to take a greater role in personnel decisions. Unfortunately, his desire to land marquee talent was undone by his equal desire to maintain the

Bucs as a revenue stream. These conflicting ideals would lead to many embarrassingly high-profile failures starting with the attempt to land the best running back prospect of 1986.

The 1985 Tampa Bay Buccaneers finished with a record of 2 wins and 14 losses, worst in the NFL and 13 games behind NFC Central Division champion Chicago. The Bucs' status as the worst team in the NFL guaranteed them the top choice in the April draft. That was good news for head coach Leeman Bennett. Bennett, who had succeeded John McKay as Bucs coach in 1985, was in the midst of a vast rebuilding project and the first overall selection was to be his cornerstone for turning around the franchise.

"We had to upgrade the personnel because the personnel had gotten to the point where there just wasn't any," Bennett said in an interview for this book. "We had two or three good players. One was Lee Roy Selmon, but he ended up having to retire [in 1985]. James Wilder was another but he had been used so often that he was on the edge of being overcome."[3]

The consensus was that the best available collegiate player was Bo Jackson, the Heisman Trophy-winning tailback from Auburn University. A six-foot, 220 pound ball of muscle, Jackson also possessed blazing speed and had turned in a senior season in which he rushed for over 1,700 yards, averaging more than 6 yards a carry. Blessed with size and speed, Jackson was impossible to stop. Former University of Alabama defensive back Paul Tripoli recalled that Jackson challenged your manhood any time you had to tackle him one on one.

"I played against him my junior and senior years," Tripoli recalled for this book. "Bo was hard to tackle. It was just a matter of physics. I was 195 pounds and as a defensive back you have to take a posture of getting down and going either way so you can't be an aggressive tackler. You had to take a beating if you are in a one-on-one tackling situation and if he decides to run over you. You had to tackle him low at the knees, you couldn't tackle up high or you are going to get embarrassed."[4]

At first appearance it seemed to be a no-brainer that the Bucs would draft Jackson. But during the Senior Bowl, some in the Bucs organization started to have doubts about the wisdom of drafting Jackson. Shortly after the Senior Bowl those Buccaneers employees would make their misgivings known. Much to the chagrin of his coaches and executives, Culverhouse would exercise his newly claimed personnel power and inadvertently launch a two-sport phenomenon at the expense of his team.

The Senior Bowl was held on January 18 at Ladd Memorial Stadium in Mobile, Alabama. As part of its tradition, the Senior Bowl pitted two teams of collegiate All-Stars against each other. One team was made up of All-Stars from northern schools and one from southern schools. Both teams would be coached by NFL staffs, one from the NFC and the other from the

Leeman Bennett oversees a team practice at One Buccaneer Place. Bennett succeeded original head coach John McKay in 1985 following a successful run with the Atlanta Falcons. Unfortunately for Bennett, he was not able to replicate his winning ways in Tampa, compiling a 4–28 record over two seasons (*Tampa Tribune*).

AFC. Bo Jackson's southern team was coached by Leeman Bennett and his Buccaneers staff. Many viewed this as the first of many games Jackson would play for Bennett. If it was to be a preview of coming attractions, it did not bode well.

The North defeated the South 31–17 in a lopsided contest. Jackson, who had been an unstoppable force for four years, looked merely pedestrian, rushing for only 48 yards. In one shocking series Jackson was stoned for no gain on back-to-back attempts from the goal line by future Miami Dolphins linebacker John Offerdahl. When the game was over, Jackson did not speak with the press, and his silence spoke volumes.

Some members of the Buccaneers staff left Mobile with a bad feeling about Jackson, not as a person or player, but as a draft prospect. Phil Krueger said he had a conversation with Jackson and learned that Bo was not all that thrilled about the possibility of becoming a Tampa Bay Buccaneer. "Bo had been at the Senior Bowl and some of the Buccaneer coaches were there, and he didn't have a good feeling about it," Krueger said. "He just told me he didn't feel comfortable. Bo wasn't nasty, he was just honest."[5]

In addition to believing that the Buccaneers just were not the team for him, Jackson was having second thoughts about whether professional football was the right sport for him as well.

Jackson left the Senior Bowl and returned to Auburn to focus on completing his senior year in school and enjoy returning to the baseball diamond. Jackson declined to be interviewed for this book, but wrote in his autobiography, *Bo Knows Bo*, that he had grown to endure football and found baseball to be his greatest athletic pleasure. "I didn't care much about football," Jackson wrote. "I did it mostly to pass the time after baseball season. I suppose you could say football was my hobby."[6]

Jackson was in fact a Major League prospect, having been drafted by the New York Yankees in 1982. Jackson turned down the Yankees because he wanted the chance to attend college. Following his junior year, Jackson was again drafted, this time by the California Angels. For the second time in three years, Jackson walked away because he knew he had a legitimate shot at winning the Heisman Trophy. But now with football season behind him, Jackson was back on the diamond and for the first time made it publicly known that the NFL shouldn't count on him. Shortly after the Senior Bowl, Jackson announced he was seriously considering a career in baseball instead of football.

As Jackson was contemplating whether or not he wanted a professional football or baseball career, the Tampa Bay Buccaneers began to craft their draft strategy. However, with the loss of Ron Wolf, Ken Herock and John McKay, there was no one strong voice to lead the way. Hugh Culverhouse, Jr., felt the situation was untenable and was the result of his father's stubborn refusal to assign a central executive as he had done with Ron Wolf. "Ron Wolf was excellent, but Dad could not deal with having a general manager," Hugh Jr. said. "One of the flaws of his character was that he could not delegate to a general manager and that ultimately haunted him."[7]

Having grown to control a large portion of the NFL, Culverhouse did not wish to cede authority or influence over his own franchise. Another layer of bureaucracy in personnel would be nothing more than an additional expense, and the owner felt if he was going to foot the bill for salaries, he might as well have the final say in acquisitions.

"Phil Krueger was the contract negotiator but was not a general manager," Hugh Jr. continues. "A general manager should have control. Unfortunately for my dad, he viewed that as his authority."[8]

Having the deciding vote meant there were many occasions in which Culverhouse overrode the opinions of the football men he hired. When it came time to decide whether or not to draft Bo Jackson, the owner ultimately won out, but his team lost.

As the draft drew closer, the Buccaneers started to receive offers for trading the rights to Jackson in exchange for multiple draft choices. There were reports that the Dallas Cowboys, Kansas City Chiefs and San Francisco 49ers were in the market to acquire the Bucs choice. Phil Krueger entertained these offers but never was able to consummate a trade because an unfortunate error cost the Bucs any kind of deal-making leverage and further alienated Jackson.

In March, the Buccaneers invited Jackson to meet one on one with Hugh Culverhouse and Leeman Bennett and take a pre-draft physical. Such meetings and physicals were standard in the NFL, and Culverhouse offered Jackson the use of his private jet to make the trip as he had done for numerous prospects in the past. The problem with this offer was that by accepting a free ride, Jackson violated a Southeastern Conference rule that prohibited accepting any type of financial gift or equivalent from a professional sports franchise. The moment Jackson stepped on the plane, the Auburn star unwittingly forfeited his baseball eligibility for the remainder of his senior season. Jackson was crushed by the news, telling reporters at the time, "I regret very much this has happened. Had I known it would jeopardize my eligibility, I would never have gone."[9]

Phil Krueger and the rest of the Buccaneers front office staff were mortified. They had flown recruits to town on multiple occasions but this time they had lost sight of the fact that Bo was still currently engaged in an amateur sport where all of their other draft prospects had completed their collegiate careers. Krueger claimed to the press that when he phoned the Southeastern Conference to inform them of the trip, no one brought up the possibility of the flight costing Jackson the rest of his collegiate baseball career. Instead Krueger was given a list of what he and the Bucs couldn't do, and according to Krueger the Bucs complied.

"The day prior to Bo's visit, I called the Southeastern Conference office to clarify aspects of his visit," Krueger told the media. "I informed the SEC official that we were bringing Bo to Tampa for a combine physical. And further, I asked for clarification as to what could take place during Bo's visit. I was told, 'No negotiations, no talk of money or contracts, no signing of a contract and no representation of Bo by an agent.' We strictly abided by all of these restrictions."[10]

Despite the Bucs protestations and appeals for leniency in Bo's case, the SEC stripped Jackson of his eligibility. In an attempt to make amends, Krueger went so far as to call Jackson an "innocent victim" and expressed that the Auburn player shouldn't be made to pay for this mistake. The plea fell on deaf ears.

Jackson's attitude towards the Buccaneers hardened over the incident. While at first Jackson referred to the flight as an "honest mistake," over time he became convinced that it was a set-up by Culverhouse in an attempt to sabotage his baseball career and take away the bargaining power offered by a competing athletic opportunity. Jackson posited a theory in his autobiography in which an early advisor of his surreptitiously worked with Culverhouse to sabotage his baseball career in an attempt to remove any bargaining leverage a prospective Major League contract would offer.

"I think I know what happened," Jackson wrote. "I don't know for sure, but I suspect my 'friend' made a deal with the Bucs—a you-get-Bo-to-come-down-to-Tampa-and-here's-what's-in-it-for-you deal. Then, after I made the trip, somebody—it could've been my 'friend' or somebody associated with the Bucs—called the SEC and told them about it. Somebody knew it was against SEC rules. Somebody knew I'd be declared ineligible. Somebody wanted me to be declared ineligible. Somebody thought I'd forget about baseball—I'd have to forget about baseball—and Culverhouse would have me."[11]

As Bo Jackson declined an interview request for this book, it is speculation if he still believes he was the victim of a Buccaneers conspiracy. To this day the Bucs proclaim there was no evil intent on their part and that it was just a simple case of not knowing all of the rules governing Bo's baseball eligibility. While the mistake was atrocious, it was honest.

"I think that was just ignorance on our part," said former Bucs public relations director Rick Odioso. "But I think Bo thought it was a set-up job to keep him from playing baseball. I don't think we were that smart though. It was just an honest mistake."[12]

No matter the intent, the flight on Culverhouse's jet only acted to increase Jackson's growing disenchantment with the team. In addition to the physical, Jackson had met with Culverhouse, Bennett and some of the current Buccaneers players on his visit. It is safe to assume based on the testimony of the parties involved that Jackson did not leave the Sunshine State with a burning desire to be a Buccaneer in general and a Culverhouse employee in particular.

During the trip to meet Culverhouse and Bennett, Jackson was also introduced to several Buccaneers players. One in particular, linebacker Scot Brantley, took a liking to Bo because the two of them shared a passion for bass fishing. Brantley agreed to take the prospect to some of the Tampa Bay area's best fishing spots and make Jackson feel at home.

"We went bass fishing," Brantley recalled. "I had permission to fish a lot of private lakes in the Tampa Bay area. That's what he wanted to do, and we had a ball. We caught a lot of fish and had a great time. He was a wonderful guy, I really liked Bo."[13]

When the day of fishing ended, Brantley and Jackson joined a group of teammates at a local restaurant for a meet and greet dinner. Depending on whose version of the story you choose to believe, that dinner was a seminal moment in the Bucs' attempts to land Jackson.

Some in the Buccaneers front office feel the players didn't exactly go out of their way to sell Tampa Bay as the place for Jackson to ply his football skills. While not accusing any players of skullduggery, former public relations director Rick Odioso intimates they may not have painted the prettiest picture of the franchise for Jackson. "One thing I heard was that Bo came in for a recruiting visit before the draft, and the Bucs sent him out with some of the current players on the roster, and they didn't do a good job of selling him on the team, if you get my drift," Odioso said.[14]

Scot Brantley argues it wasn't the players that couldn't sell the Bucs. It was the Bucs product itself that couldn't be sold. "If you think about it, in 1985 we went 2–14 under Leeman Bennett. What are you selling when you are 2–14?" Brantley asked rhetorically.[15]

Shortly after the meetings, Bo Jackson made it known through his representatives that he did not want to play for the Tampa Bay Buccaneers. In his autobiography, Jackson outlined a laundry list of reasons for not wanting to be a Culverhouse employee.

"I didn't want to play for him [Culverhouse]," Jackson wrote. "I didn't like what the Bucs had done to me, costing me my senior baseball season, and I didn't like Culverhouse's attitude toward me. And I didn't really want to play for a team as bad as Tampa Bay. I'd seen their offensive line. I didn't want to get beat up every week."[16]

Jackson's stated preference to not play for the Buccaneers was believed by Leeman Bennett. The head coach had had a front row seat for the first conversations between Culverhouse and Jackson and could see that there was no way the tailback was coming to Tampa. Bennett recalled that Culverhouse spent a good deal of time talking about the most recent Auburn–Alabama game, a thrilling last-second Crimson Tide victory. It was the second year in a row that Culverhouse's alma mater had defeated Jackson's school, and the tailback wasn't in the mood to relive what to him was a heartbreaking defeat.

"Hugh and I flew to Auburn to talk to Bo, and there was a lot of talk about Alabama," the head coach recalled. "I don't think Bo liked that conversation very much."[17]

The awkwardness for Bennett was only just beginning.

Heading into the draft both Leeman Bennett and Phil Krueger were adamant that the Bucs should take Jackson at his word and not make him the number one overall selection. As the head coach, Leeman Bennett was especially concerned that not signing Bo would do more than embarrass the franchise. A failure would hamstring the Bucs with the burden of a wasted number one draft choice. Bennett made the case to Culverhouse that if the Bucs drafted Bo, it would be extremely detrimental to the future of the club to not get him in camp. According to Bennett, the owner told him to relax.

"Hugh assured me that he could sign Bo. 'Don't worry about it, I will sign him,'" Bennett said. "Bo was clearly the best prospect in the draft, there was no question about that. At the same time, if you can't sign him there is no point in drafting him."[18]

So concerned was Bennett that he was busy drawing up contingency draft plans. "I don't remember so much who was number two on our draft board," the former coach said. "It might have been a defensive lineman."[19]

If the Bucs' back-up plan was indeed a defensive lineman, it most likely would have been Oklahoma's Tony Casillas, Alabama's Jon Hand or Oklahoma State's Leslie O'Neal, all of whom would be selected within the top eight selections. However, Bennett didn't dissuade Culverhouse and despite the concerns of Bennett and Krueger, the owner outvoted them 1 to 2 and in April the Bucs made Bo Jackson the first overall selection of the 1986 draft.

"Mr. Culverhouse was quite bull-headed about Bo," Krueger said.[20]

The reason Culverhouse overrode the desires of his coaching and personnel staffs were many and varied. First and foremost, the Bucs owner believed that he had the upper hand in the negotiations. Second, he truly believed he had the resources to convince Jackson to give up on baseball. Finally, the Alabama native was convinced that it was karma that a fellow Alabamian would be the savior the franchise needed.

Bo Jackson was the first Heisman Trophy winner in four years who would not have the USFL as a viable option. Unlike Herschel Walker, Doug Flutie and Mike Rozier, Jackson's only professional football option would be the NFL's Tampa Bay Buccaneers. In April of 1986, the USFL and NFL were just about to commence their final battle in a New York courtroom, and Culverhouse knew the rival league was about to go the way of the carrier pigeon and be relegated to extinction.

Without a rival such as the USFL to worry about, Culverhouse believed that Jackson's only other realistic opportunity was a professional baseball career. He studied past rookie baseball contracts and saw the majority were mere pittances compared to what a NFL rookie contract was worth. An average rookie in baseball earned a contract worth nearly half what an NFL top draft choice made and compounding the money disparity, the vast majority of baseball rookies had to earn their stripes in the minor leagues, playing in backwater towns and being forced to ride a bus to all games while staying in cheap hotels.

Even though Bo Jackson and his representatives had made it known that the running back was seriously considering a baseball career, the Tampa Bay owner was skeptical. An old hand at multi-million dollar negotiations, Culverhouse believed Jackson was simply attempting to leverage an interest in baseball to wring more money out of the Buccaneers.

"I think at the time Bo was drafted, there was a feeling that he was playing the baseball card just to drive up his price in football," Rick Odioso recalled, providing insight into what some at One Buccaneer Place, including Culverhouse, were thinking.[21]

Writing in his autobiography, Jackson stated that Culverhouse told him flat out he didn't believe the tailback was serious about a baseball career. Jackson wrote that Culverhouse claimed to have spoken with Major League Baseball scouts and learned that Jackson was a marginal prospect at best and that the real sport for him was football.[22] If Bo agreed to play with the Bucs, Culverhouse promised, he would become the highest-paid rookie in the National Football League.

Culverhouse later took his promise to the media, boasting to the assembled reporters on draft day that he intended to make Bo Jackson the richest rookie in the NFL. The boast was meant to impress upon Jackson that the Buccaneers were going to be the most lucrative option the running back could find.

"I was there the day when Mr. Culverhouse said he was going to make Bo Jackson the highest-paid rookie in the NFL," said Rick Odioso. "I think it's true that we didn't have a good reputation as a franchise. Mr. C made a big statement on draft day that he was going to make Bo the highest-paid rookie in NFL history."[23]

Unfortunately, what Culverhouse considered to be an eye-popping contract proved to be quite ordinary thanks to another rookie contract that off-season. Shortly before Culverhouse made his announcement, the Cleveland Browns announced the signing of University of Miami quarterback Bernie Kosar. Taken in the supplemental draft, the former Hurricane had inked a five-year, $5 million contract which made him the 4th highest paid player in the NFL at the time. The economics of the rookie salary structure had been significantly altered forever by the Kosar deal, and it made Culverhouse's offer pale in comparison.

"Somebody asked does that mean even higher than Bernie Kosar, who had been chosen in the supplemental draft," Odioso continued. "I don't think Mr. C took that into account. So the contract he had in mind for Bo was not as high as Kosar's initially and that kind of led Bo and his representatives to think that Mr. C was trying to put something over on them."[24]

The Bucs offer was $4 million over 5 years, a full million dollars under the Kosar deal. Jackson wrote that he found the first offer from Culverhouse insulting. When compared side by side with the Kosar deal, Culverhouse's overture to Jackson looked paltry and acted to further diminish the owner's reputation in the eyes of the Auburn tailback.

To complicate matters further, Jackson was being wooed heavily by the Kansas City Royals, the defending World Series champions. Faced with the choice between being battered and bruised in the backfield of the cellar-dwelling Bucs or roaming the outfield for the world champions, Jackson chose the latter, even though it was a less lucrative contract. In June Jackson agreed to terms with the Royals and reported to their minor league affiliate. Culverhouse and the Buccaneers were in a state of shock.

"I think Bo made the choice at that time to play baseball with the Royals because he saw his long-term health as an issue," Rick Odioso said.[25] Odioso and Krueger believe that while the contract the Bucs offered wasn't as rich as Kosar's, it was still a generous deal that would have more than fairly compensated a player of Jackson's caliber. The problem was that the Bucs' wooing of Jackson was plagued from the start by organizational mistakes and Culverhouse's inability to overcome his reputation for stinginess.

To this day the Bo Jackson rookie contract is the only one Phil Krueger couldn't close, and he can only sit back and view it 25 years later as an "I told you so" moment. "The only rookie I didn't sign was Bo Jackson," Krueger said.[26] "But I had told Mr. Culverhouse that I couldn't sign him."

What was particularly painful for Culverhouse was that unlike his hard line stance against Doug Williams, he had been willing to pay Bo Jackson more money than any other player in the history of the Tampa Bay Buccaneers. Culverhouse had learned from the loss of Williams that his team needed a star that both players and fans could rally around. He was certain he had found his man in Bo Jackson. Unfortunately, Culverhouse misread Jackson's desire to play baseball and vastly overestimated the power of money to overcome the ham-handed approach the Bucs had taken in courting the athlete. A courtship that cost Jackson his baseball eligibility was something that not even a vast amount of money could repair.

"Mr. Culverhouse thought that money could talk, and you could buy anything," Krueger said recently.[27]

It took many years for Culverhouse's son to come to grips with why his father had risked so much of his reputation to sign a player who publicly stated misgivings about playing for the Buccaneers. "We didn't understand the infatuation with Bo Jackson because the man said he didn't want to play for us," Hugh Jr. said.[28] But upon further reflection, the son realizes that his father saw an opportunity to not only hire a savior, but to hire a savior from his beloved home state to boot. "Bo Jackson went to Auburn, right?" he asked. "My dad's father went to Auburn. Bo Jackson is out of Alabama. My dad is from Alabama."[29]

A native Alabamian scoring touchdowns and leading the Buccaneers to victories would have no doubt been a dream come true for the proud Culverhouse. Instead the Buccaneers were left with a void in the backfield and on the draft board. The latter problem would continue to hamper the Bucs on the field for years to come as Culverhouse exerted further control over personnel decisions.

"We always seemed to be a few draft choices short of a load and then we didn't take advantage of the ones we had," recalled Rick Odioso. "We didn't have a first round pick in 1984 because of the Jack Thompson trade. The '84 pick was high because we went 2–14. You see teams that have extra picks, but we were missing every year. We would miss a two or a one or a three."[30]

In historical hindsight the Buccaneers could take small consolation out of one fact. Their inability to sign Jackson led to the phenomenon of the two-sport athlete.

Jackson spent the beginning of the 1986 season with the Royals Triple-A team in Memphis. Late in the season he was called up to the Royals and played in 25 games. Jackson batted .207 against Major League pitching, showing enough promise to stay with the Royals out of spring training in 1987. While Jackson was growing more comfortable in the majors, he was intrigued by what was transpiring at the 1987 NFL Draft. The Buccaneers held the negotiating rights to Jackson for one full year, but unless the Buccaneers selected him again in 1987, Jackson would become the property of any team that chose him.

The Los Angeles Raiders chose Jackson in the seventh round. The Raiders were owned by the legendary renegade Al Davis. A consummate iconoclast, Davis drafted Jackson with an eye towards making history. While Jackson had been adamant about wanting to make baseball his full-time career, Davis asked the outfielder if he would consider playing for the Raiders on a part-time basis,[31] after the baseball season ended.

Jackson's autobiography stated the athlete and his representatives sat down to discuss if such a thing was possible or practical.[32] After weeks of consultation with his representatives, Jackson announced that he would indeed pursue a two-sport career. When the baseball season ended in early October, Jackson reported to Los Angeles and took his position in the Raiders backfield. It didn't take him long to prove that he belonged.

In a nationally televised game on *Monday Night Football*, Jackson put on a tour de force performance against the Seattle Seahawks. In just 18 carries, Jackson ran for more than 200 yards including a touchdown sprint of 91 yards down the far sideline that left multiple Seattle defenders in his wake. In addition to his speed, Jackson showed on a touchdown still seen on highlight films to this day the power that made him the number one prospect the year before.

From the 2-yard line Jackson took a hand-off and met head to head with infamous Seahawks linebacker Brian Bosworth at the goal line. Bosworth had also been a collegiate superstar, answering to his given nickname "The Boz." However, when he attempted to tackle Jackson one on one, "The Boz" was proven to be a mere mortal. Jackson met Bosworth head-up, and ran over the stunned linebacker without seeming to expend much effort. The 2-yard touchdown came to be seen as Jackson's defining moment in the NFL. If Hugh Culverhouse was watching the game at home, he could only wonder at what might have been.

Jackson would go on to play for four years in the NFL and Major League Baseball, both at an amazingly high level. In baseball, Bo was voted to the All-Star game in 1989 and earned Most Valuable Player honors in that game.

In football, Jackson was a premier running back who came close to a 1,000 yard season in 1989 despite playing only half a season. Along the way, he would become one of America's top advertising pitchmen. A Nike ad featuring Bo playing sports such as tennis, golf and hockey was enormously popular and spawned the catchphrase "Bo knows." From late 1987 until 1990, Jackson was arguably the most recognized sports figure in the world.

Only a severely injured hip would prevent Jackson from attaining even further athletic accomplishment. In a January 1991 playoff game against the Cincinnati Bengals, Jackson was tackled from behind and landed awkwardly, dislocating the hip from its socket. His football career was over, but Jackson did manage to continue to play baseball, albeit not to the level that made him the Most Valuable Player of the 1989 All-Star Game. In order to return to the diamond, Jackson underwent a series

Hugh Culverhouse and Leeman Bennett address the press after 1986 number one draft choice Bo Jackson spurns the Bucs for a baseball career. Bennett had advised Culverhouse not to draft Jackson, citing Jackson's public proclamation that he did not want to play for Tampa Bay. Culverhouse overrode Bennett and by the end of 1986 Bennett would be terminated. In this photograph it appears that Bennett can see the handwriting on the wall (*Tampa Tribune*).

of grueling surgeries, including one to provide him with an artificial hip. Despite several obstacles, Jackson returned to baseball in 1993. For the courage and determination he showed in rejoining a big league roster, Jackson was named the American League's Comeback Player of the Year in 1993 when he was playing for the Chicago White Sox.

Jackson's ability to play baseball had provided him with a way of spurning the Buccaneers without costing him a single dime or ounce of fame. The two-sport career he embarked on provided a path for other like-minded athletes to follow. In addition to Jackson, Deion Sanders and Brian Jordan were just two of the better known names to play professional football and Major League Baseball simultaneously. This is the legacy that many former athletes feel Jackson will be remembered for, long after the "Bo knows" ads fade into obscurity.

"Before that there were no options between baseball and football," said Scot Brantley. "They didn't exist. If that existed when I came out of high school, I could have made more money signing with the Mets. Bo Jackson created two-sport deals where you could sign with one and play for the other. He had options."[33]

However, the physical price Jackson paid may have ultimately also served as a life lesson for others. Despite the high level of achievement Jackson enjoyed, his short-lived, injury-terminated career is also often cited as a reason why many athletes choose to focus on one professional sport.

"Maybe doing dual sports is not very conducive to the body because you are using different muscles for the two different sports," opined Brantley.[34]

Rick Odioso enjoyed watching Jackson play, but feels it is ironic that one of the reasons Bo refused to play for the Bucs was the concern that he would be highly susceptible to injury playing behind Tampa Bay's offensive line. "That's funny considering how his career was cut short because of an injury which I think came as a result of his body breaking down," Odioso said.[35]

No matter how one views the remarkable career of Bo Jackson, it is conceivable he would not have become the towering figure he became had he signed with Tampa Bay. Whether or not he would have been as productive a runner as he became in Los Angeles is open for conjecture. Given the struggles the Buccaneers continued to endure in the personnel field under Culverhouse, it is doubtful Jackson would have posted memorable numbers, but no one can say for sure. What can be said is that the failure of the Bucs to sign Jackson provided the talented athlete a necessary opportunity to play two professional sports, an opportunity that may never again be possible.

One of the unfortunate consequences of the Bucs' inability to sign Bo Jackson was that they headed into the 1986 season without the services of their number one draft choice. Without an upgrade of personnel, the Bucs floundered to a second consecutive 2–14 season. With a total of 4 wins and 28 losses in his two seasons as coach, Leeman Bennett knew he didn't have much of a record to defend when the 1986 season ended. However, he was convinced that he would be invited back for a third season because it was apparent his rebuilding plans had been scuttled by the failure to sign Jackson.

Sadly for Bennett, Culverhouse decided to clean house and terminated the coach shortly after Christmas. Bennett was stunned.

"I didn't really think he would let me go at that time because I thought we were at least headed in the right direction," Bennett confided recently. "Even though our record hadn't gotten any better. We were set back by not signing Bo Jackson. We needed personnel. We needed some personnel, and I thought it would take another year or two."[36]

Bennett's time in Tampa Bay was short and frustrating. The misguided attempt to sign Bo Jackson came to be considered one of the milestone moments of Bennett's tenure, despite the fact the coach was against drafting the tailback. Another sad trademark of the Bennett era was a string of uninspired blowouts including losses by scores such as 62–28, 31–7, 38–7, 45–13 and 48–14. These losses put into perspective just how much of a disparity there was between the Bucs and the NFL in terms of on-field success.

But one particular lopsided loss came to define the Bucs of Leeman Bennett more than any other. A severe storm in Wisconsin would provide the backdrop for the worst weather game of the 1980s. Tampa Bay had been necessary for so many other historically significant moments during Culverhouse's ownership it only stands to reason they would be the victim of the original Snow Bowl.

CHAPTER EIGHT

The Snow Bowl

IF THE TAMPA BAY BUCCANEERS had to be involved in a bad-weather game, they could not have picked a better venue than Lambeau Field. The small stadium in Green Bay, Wisconsin, had been the home of the most famous bad-weather game in the history of the National Football League.

On December 31, 1967, the Green Bay Packers defeated the Dallas Cowboys 21–17 in the NFL Championship Game. The last-second Packers victory propelled Green Bay to Super Bowl II and is known to this day as the Ice Bowl due to the frigid conditions under which the game was played. With a temperature of –13° F at kickoff, the Ice Bowl tested the endurance of all those who participated.

Playing half of their games in balmy Tampa Bay, the Buccaneers had not experienced much in the way of bad weather games when they rolled into Green Bay on the final day of November 1985.

The victorious 1979 season finale against the Kansas City Chiefs, the game that clinched the Buccaneers' first playoff berth, had been played in a torrential downpour. So much rain fell during Tampa Bay's 3–0 win that NFL Network placed it in their list of the Top Ten Bad Weather games of all time. A similar downpour occurred in a 1983 game against the Chicago Bears at Tampa Stadium, although in that contest the Bucs were swamped 27–0.

As for cold weather, the Bucs' worst experience to that point was a 1982 game against the New York Jets at Shea Stadium in Flushing Meadows. The Bucs shivered and slipped through snowy conditions and a temperature of 23° F. The frozen Bucs couldn't focus and fumbled the ball eight times, losing possession on three of them in a 32–17 loss. While the Bucs still had some veteran players left over from that 1982 defeat, nothing could have prepared them for the morning of December 1, 1985.

Leeman Bennett awoke to a ringing telephone bright and early on the day of the game. As was his custom, Bennett requested a wake-up call from the front desk early in the morning. During his coaching career, Bennett heard pleasantries from hotel switchboard operators across the United States, but this particular one will always be ingrained in his memory.

"In a lot of those northern cities, it's kind of interesting when they give you a wake up call," Bennett said. "The gal on the phone said, 'Good morning, Coach Bennett. It is two degrees above zero. We expect four inches of snow at game time and the wind chill factor will be minus fourteen. Have an enjoyable day.'"[1]

Once he recovered from his own shock, Bennett wondered what was going through the minds of his assistants and players as they received similar wake up calls throughout the hotel.

"When you are a warm weather franchise, that does play a factor in your mindset," Bennett stated.[2]

Unfortunately for Bennett and the Bucs, the hotel operator didn't provide completely accurate details. While the wind chill would drop below zero, she vastly under-reported the amount of snow that was going to fall throughout the day. None of the Bucs truly realized how bad things were going to be until they were well on their way to the stadium.

The official weather report stated that ten inches of snow had fallen overnight and that an additional twelve inches would fall throughout the day. The temperature would reach the mid–20s but with sustained winds of up to 30 miles per hour expected. The wind chill would be well below zero. Throughout the day, travel advisories would be issued and residents of Wisconsin were advised to stay home if at all possible, with the exception, it appeared, of the Tampa Bay Buccaneers and Green Bay Packers.

Scot Brantley was en route before many of his teammates had even received their wake up calls to take part in his pre-game ritual.

"That morning when we got up, Steve DeBerg and I were the first ones to breakfast, the first to have our bags packed, and we got a cab to go to the stadium," the former linebacker recalled.[3]

"That was one of the things I did every away game because I love the historic venues," Brantley continued. "Even though I played at Lambeau Field four or five times, you look at Lambeau Field and realize, 'I got to go.' I want to get there early, talk to the clubhouse manager, go out on the field. It was snowing like crazy that morning at 7:30 A.M."[4]

Once they were in the cab, Brantley and DeBerg were immediately transfixed by the news reports coming from the car radio. "When we were riding to the stadium we heard on the radio that the airport had been shut down,"

Brantley said. "They said, 'If you are going to the airport, don't waste your time. If you have tickets to the Bucs–Packers game, we suggest that you stay home due to blizzard conditions.' I was listening to this and thinking, 'Damn! If they shut down the airport how are we going to get out of here?'"[5]

When Brantley arrived at the stadium he immediately went to the locker room to continue with his pre-game ritual, but he was quickly coming to the conclusion that this would be no ordinary bad-weather game.

"We get to the locker room, get taped up and go outside and it is still snowing like crazy," Brantley explained. "I say hello to the guy that takes care of the field and I said, 'Just another typical day in Green Bay, huh?'"[6]

"He looked at me like he saw a ghost," Brantley said. "He looked me square in the eye and said, 'Scot, I've been working this field 34 years, and I have never seen a day like today.' I said to myself, 'Shit.' I just put on my jacket and walked back inside."[7]

The day turned out to be the worst snow day in the month of December in Green Bay since the 1880s and the worst conditions at Lambeau Field since the Ice Bowl of 1967. The 15 inches of snow that would fall during the game would be the most at a game since the 1960s, surpassing even the amount set the previous season at Denver when the Broncos defeated the Packers at Mile High Stadium in a Monday night contest. During the Monday night game the snow would taper off. On this day in Green Bay, there would be no letup, and the Buccaneer players would never forget the experience.

The snowstorm was a force of nature not yet encountered by the Buccaneers. The equipment staff prepared as much as possible, bringing out long underwear, SCUBA gloves and extra socks.[8] However, having flown from a balmy 80° Tampa, no amount of clothes could warm up the thin blood of the Bucs against sub-zero wind chill.

The Bucs did have a sideline heater, but with 45 men on the roster it would hardly radiate enough warmth to encompass the entire area. Throughout the game television cameras would capture Buccaneers players in orange ponchos packed tightly in front of the heater, stamping their feet and rubbing their hands in a futile effort to get comfortable.

Scot Brantley told reporters after the game the competition for heater space was more compelling than the battle on the field. Unfortunately for Brantley, a negative consequence of being a starting player was that you couldn't get close to the heaters.

"All the guys who weren't playing were crowded around them," Brantley said after the game. "You couldn't get close to them. I lost all the feeling in my toes after pre-game warm-ups. I couldn't feel the ground I was walking on."[9]

Ironically, the year before the Bucs played the Packers on the same field following a snowstorm. However, in that contest the field was far from frozen.

In 1984 the Buccaneers had lost to the Packers 27–14 in what was dubbed the Mud Bowl. Like the 1985 game, the Bucs witnessed snow the night before at their hotel. The next morning, however, the temperature had risen rapidly, and all that snow melted and turned the playing surface into a quagmire. By the end of the game, the Bucs all-white uniforms were plastered in dark black mud.

"[Equipment Manager] Frankie Pupello will tell you he had to throw away the uniforms because he washed and washed and washed them, but they never came clean," Scot Brantley recounted. "Everybody was solid black from that dirt in Lambeau Field."[10]

If only the Bucs could have played in mud again, it would have actually made their lives easier. The Packers, as the home team, had the option to choose the jersey colors the teams would wear. Green Bay elected to wear their dark green jerseys and gold pants. This left the Bucs with no choice but to wear their white jerseys. Combined with their white helmets, white pants, white socks and white shoes, the Buccaneers were almost invisible on the field during warm-ups. At first some of the Buccaneers, including Scot Brantley, thought the camouflage effect would give his defensive teammates an advantage over the Packers. Unfortunately, a severe disadvantage also became apparent.

"I'm thinking as a defensive player, 'Good, we're on the road, we're wearing white on white. They won't be able to see our ass,'" Brantley remembered. "Well, they didn't. But guess what? Our quarterback, Steve Young, couldn't see his receivers because they were all in white! White jerseys, white pants and white helmets. The Packers wore gold pants and dark green jerseys and you could see them stand out like crazy. But the Bucs were all in white in the white ass snow, and you couldn't find them!"[11]

Compounding the problem for Steve Young was the fact that this was just his second NFL start. After playing for two years in the USFL, Young had been drafted by the Bucs in the 1985 supplemental draft and looked to make the adjustment between the two leagues. The week before Young had led the Bucs to a 19–16 victory over the Detroit Lions in the much warmer environment of Tampa Stadium. But this week, when he dropped back to pass on the Bucs' first possession of the game, he couldn't see anything past the line of scrimmage.

Young was not alone in being affected by the whiteout. Tampa's wide receivers also had a hard time. When the receivers completed their routes and looked back towards the line of scrimmage, they discovered their quarterback was invisible to them, shielded by a wall of blinding snow.[12]

On the first play of the game, the Buccaneers attempted a sweep with tailback James Wilder following a wall of blockers. The play broke down quickly when both offensive tackler Ron Heller and tight end Jimmie Giles

Tampa Bay running back James Wilder is stopped for a loss by Green Bay Packers nose tackle Don Humphrey during the 1985 Snow Bowl. The Buccaneers
offense could muster only 65 total yards in the 21–0 loss (*Tampa Tribune*, courtesy
Tampa Bay Buccaneers).

slipped and fell down when attempting to make blocks. Sadly, the two-yard
gain would be one of the more productive plays for the Bucs offense on that
day.

Offensive guard Sean Farrell recalled that for many of the players the
number one focus was not to fall down. Executing the play came in a close
second. "I remember most of the day people were trying their best not to
fall down," Farrell said. "If you would fall down, depending on whom it was
you were dealing with on the other side, they'd be kind enough to push your
face into the snow or something silly like that."[13]

Farrell admitted that avoiding too much unnecessary contact with the
snow had been a concern going all the way back to the pre-game warm-ups.
Instead of lying down to do calisthenics and stretching, the players did what
they could while standing up. Also, instead of spreading out over the entire
field to do warm-ups by unit, the team stayed close together in the end zone.

"The field was covered with snow, so you had to try to get as warm as
possible without lying down," the former guard said. "You did mobile stretch-

ing, so it was pretty much abbreviated even to the extent where you were trying to run your drills in the end zone. You had no footing, so it wasn't the easiest thing in the world to get prepared for."[14]

It wasn't just the Bucs offense that was impacted. The Bucs defense altered their strategy to accommodate for poor footing. The Packers were not a highly successful team, but with a passing combination of Lynn Dickey and future Hall of Famer James Lofton, Green Bay had a well-respected and productive passing game. Featuring quick-hitting out routes and timing patterns, the Packers' attack was similar to the modern West Coast offense. To defend against such an attack, a defensive unit will usually try their best to disrupt the timing by jamming receivers at the line of scrimmage to throw off their routes or blitz a quarterback to disrupt his timing. With so much snow on the ground and the footing treacherous, the Buccaneers could not employ such a strategy. Instead the Bucs had to play well off the receivers for fear of losing their footing on an aggressive play and turning a short 5-yard pass into a much more devastating 50- to 60-yard play.

The Packers realized what the Bucs were doing and took advantage accordingly. Dickey, with almost no pressure from the Bucs' front seven, picked apart the Tampa Bay secondary, throwing for almost 300 yards despite the awful conditions. On their second possession, the Packers marched with ease down the field but Al Del Greco's field goal attempt was blocked by Tampa Bay's John Holt. Undaunted, the Packers marched down the field again the next time, and Dickey scored on a quarterback sneak from the goal line for a 7–0 lead. The seven points was all the Packers would need.

Throughout the remainder of the first half, the Buccaneers offense resembled Napoleon's army after being driven out of Moscow. Stymied by the elements, the Bucs never attempted to open up their attack. Instead, Tampa Bay ran between the tackles and only allowed Young to throw short screen passes to his backs and tight ends. By the end of the game, the wide receivers for the Buccaneers would catch a grand total of one pass for ten yards. At halftime the Bucs' total yardage was 43 yards compared to 236 for Green Bay. The Bucs also had accounted for only one first down in the 30 minutes of play to Green Bay's 14.

On more than one occasion the snow led to a Buccaneers miscue. On the Packers' scoring drive, linebacker Chris Washington was called for being offsides when he lined up beyond the line of scrimmage because he couldn't see the down marker. Washington wasn't the only Buccaneer with that struggle.

"The snow was packing in there and covering the field. It kept you from seeing the stripes. You can't tell where the sideline is half the time. It was wild," said Scot Brantley.[15]

Also, Leeman Bennett found it difficult to strategize during the game because he and his assistants were constantly double-checking to make sure they had enough men on the field.

"It was snowing so hard you had trouble seeing anybody on the other side of the field," Bennett admitted. "I can remember one time I thought we only had ten men on the field because we had on white uniforms, and it was snowing so hard. That was a miserable game there is no question about it."[16]

When the Bucs reluctantly returned to the sideline for the second half they gave the impression to many watching on television that they had given up. CBS commentators Jim Hill and John Dockery stated the Bucs looked as if they were more concerned with staying warm around the sideline heater than trying to win the game. In a refreshing bit of honesty, some of those players admitted as much, stating they sprinted towards the heaters after every series.[17]

"It was a big deal; nobody wanted to be out there," said Sean Farrell.[18]

While Farrell wanted to stay warm during his time on the sideline, he did admit to looking up into the crowd and being amazed at the number of fans who had defied the travel advisory to attend the game. Although the crowd of 19,856 was the smallest ever at Lambeau Field, Farrell thought there were 19,856 too many people there.

"I know we weren't very good, and I don't think at that point in time Green Bay was any good either," said Farrell of the match-up between 2–10 Tampa Bay and 5–7 Green Bay. "It was one of those situations where you sit there wondering, 'Why are we doing this?'"[19]

"It wasn't sold out, but it was well-attended," Farrell continued. "That was a takeaway for me, looking in the stands at the number of people that wore those enormous snowmobiling suits, ski suits and one-piece suits that look like the Michelin Man. Those people were happy, warm and content sitting in that snow. They were loud and harassing the daylights out of us. There are always snowballs at games like that."[20]

On the first drive of the second half, the Packers marched 59 yards in just four plays, scoring on a 35-yard run by Gerry Ellis. The 14–0 lead required Young to throw the ball more, but with his difficulty in finding his white-clad receivers in the snow, Young had to hold on to the ball for a little longer than normal, and this played into the hands of the Packers defensive line, particularly Alphonso Carreker. Carreker, a former star at Florida State, sacked Young four times on the day and hit the passer on many other occasions.

But with less than a minute left in the third quarter, the Bucs had a chance to put points on the board. A pass interference penalty on Green Bay's Tim Lewis had given the Bucs the ball at the Packers 20-yard line. With time winding down, Bennett sent kicker Donald Igwebuike onto the field to attempt a 33-yard field goal. Igwebuike, a native of Nigeria, was being exposed to snow for one of the few times in his life up to that point. A good-natured personality, Igwebuike had tried to have fun with the experience recalled Rick Odioso.

"'My kind of weather,' said Donald Igwebuike," recalled Odioso. "Donald was at the Holiday Inn Central in Green Bay looking out at what I think was his first snow-storm. I don't know if he saw snow at Clemson, but certainly not in Nigeria."[21]

Unfortunately for the Nigerian-born kicker, he would be left out in the cold due to a tactical error by Bennett. The Bucs failed to get the kick off before the clock ran out on the third quarter, forcing Igwebuike to walk 60 yards against the 25 MPH winds and driving snow to attempt his kick at the start of the final stanza. With snow blowing directly into his eyes, Igwebuike missed the kick, and the Bucs' best chance for scoring went by the boards.

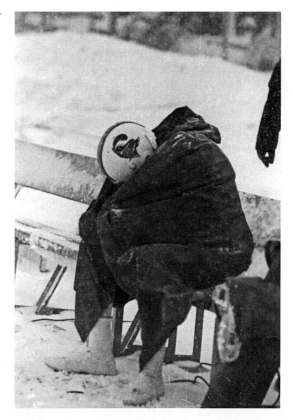

An anonymous Buccaneer is either attempting to stay warm or averting his gaze from the action on the field during the 1985 Snow Bowl. Arctic winds, frigid temperatures and 15 inches of snow conspired against the Bucs in the worst-weather game of the 1980s (*Tampa Tribune*, courtesy Tampa Bay Buccaneers).

The Packers scored one more time to make it 21–0 and for all intents and purposes the game was over, but the Bucs still had almost ten minutes of game play to endure. In that ten minute span the signature play of the game occurred with Steve Young being victimized.

Young dropped back to pass with a little over five minutes left in the game and was promptly sacked by Carreker for the fourth and final time. The momentum of Carreker's sack drove Young face first into a snow pile in the middle of the field. When Young got up, he was seen frantically pulling snow and mud out of his facemask before angrily ripping off his helmet. At first glance it appeared Young was just mad about once again landing in a wet pile of snow, but his teammates admit that Young was just trying to breathe.

"Young almost suffocated," Scot Brantley exclaimed. "It was just one of those frustrating, weird-ass games."[22]

"His whole face was one big snowball," said Sean Farrell.[23]

While Steve Young was able to extricate himself from the snow pile, the same could not be said for a great deal of Tampa Bay's equipment. Gloves, towels, scissors, cutters, pads and other assorted equipment were left buried in the snow. Once the snow thawed later in the week, the equipment was recovered and shipped back to Tampa.

The final statistics for the Snow Bowl were startling. The Packers gained 512 total yards, accumulated 31 first downs, and were buoyed by big days by their skill players. Lynn Dickey threw for 299 yards total with 106 yards going to James Lofton. The Packers also had two 100 yard rushers in the same game. Eddie Lee Ivery ran for 109 yards while Gerry Ellis contributed 101. By comparison the Bucs amassed only 65 total yards, 5 first downs and were led by Steve Young's 53 yards passing, James Wilder's 23 yards rushing and 33 yards receiving. If not for five Green Bay turnovers and a blocked field goal, the score could have been much worse.

As it was the Bucs' experience at Lambeau Field would actually be the easy part of their day. With the game over, the Bucs' thoughts turned to how they would get back home to Tampa Bay and the 81 degree weather that awaited them.

Once the final shower had been taken and the Bucs players had regained feeling in their extremities, they boarded the team bus for the ride to the airport. The snow had still not let up, and the Bucs looked out in amazement at the amount of snow that had blanketed the city of Green Bay.

Upon arrival at the airport many in the Buccaneers traveling party were feeling uneasy about the prospect of attempting to take off under the current weather conditions. That unease grew when they learned the airport was closed. What they didn't know was that Hugh Culverhouse was pulling strings with the airport authority to get his team out of Green Bay so they would not be trapped in Wisconsin for what could have been days.

"Apparently Culverhouse was working so hard with the airport authority to get the runways cleared and the plane de-iced," said Scot Brantley. "The storm was the front-end of a five or six day lockdown in Green Bay. Whatever they had done had convinced the captain of the plane."[24]

When some players learned their plane was going to take off during blizzard conditions, an intense discussion ensued. This discussion has grown into the stuff of legend over the past quarter-century.

For years it has been repeated that Scot Brantley refused to get on the plane until he spoke to the pilot. In the discussion, the pilot explained that he would never risk a dangerous take-off because he was a family man. At this Brantley was alleged to have demanded proof of the pilot's family, shouting "Show us pictures!"

When asked about this incident 25 years later, Brantley laughed and denied ever saying such a thing or even being one of the players that refused to get on the plane. In fact, Brantley stated he wanted to have a little something to drink, enjoy a meal and get the heck out of Green Bay.

"There was a group of players, but I wasn't one of them," Brantley contends. "I was the first one on the plane. I was ready to have something to eat. You would get two Budweisers when you got on the plane and a bag of ice. You drink a couple of beers and have a hamburger while getting ready for the flight home."[25]

Brantley states that it was actually offensive guard Sean Farrell who was the man that refused to get on the plane and demanded to see the pilot's family photographs. "There were about six or eight guys that refused to get on the plane," Brantley said. "They said, 'We'll get a hotel, pay for our own shit and come back out tomorrow.'"[26]

"That pilot had to get off the plane, go into that room, talk to those guys and convince them to get their ass on that plane and let's get out of here," Brantley continued. "Sean Farrell was one of those guys. A boy from Penn State who grew up in New York and been in snow his whole life."[27]

While Rick Odioso didn't state which players refused to get on the plane, he also recalled family photographs being offered into evidence by the pilot. "I was there when some of the players balked at getting on the plane and wondered whether it was safe or not," Odioso said. "I was there when the pilot pulled out the pictures of his kids and said, 'I wouldn't be taking off if I didn't think it was absolutely safe.'"[28]

When asked if he indeed demanded to see the pilot's family photographs, Sean Farrell laughed good-naturedly and stated his belief that his conversation with the pilot has been mythologized to point of becoming unrecognizable to him.

"I never asked for pictures of the family," Farrell said. "That's the way things get stretched to a level that is not true, but there is some fact to it. The airport was closed. It was snowing dramatically, nobody in and nobody out. I'm a pilot, and I wanted to make sure. I spent some time talking with the pilot about what the weather was and what we were facing, what the runways looked like. I just wanted to be abundantly clear that we were making a good decision. I wasn't too concerned about pictures of their family."[29]

Because of his experience as a pilot, Farrell inadvertently became the vocal leader of the six to eight players that were uncomfortable with flying, including quarterback Steve Young.

"Steve didn't know what he wanted to do," Farrell said. "He assumed that as long as I knew what I was doing, or thought I knew what I was doing, that if I was going to stay behind that he was going to stay behind. We ultimately had a good discussion. We all got on the plane and came home."[30]

Farrell's last sentence would imply that the take-off was relatively smooth and uneventful, but according to Brantley it was far from a routine procedure.

"When we took off you could feel the front end of the plane lift," Brantley said. "And when it lifted, it just stayed put. Then finally you could feel the wheels come off the runway and you think, 'OK, we're airborne.' Everybody starts clapping, but it stayed on a plane. Most times when you see a jet take off it just goes up at about a 45-degree angle. This thing kind of stayed at about a 10- to 15-degree angle forever it seemed like. Then all of a sudden we rise, rise, and boom, we pop out of the clouds, and we see blue sky and sunshine. It was a low front and boy everybody went crazy, clapping and high-fiving. We got back to Tampa, but it was a memorable moment in Buccaneer lore."[31]

Interestingly, the Bucs' participation in the game made big news but their safe return to Tampa was overlooked.

"We got back on time, but the next evening the *ABC Evening News* said we were snowed in," remembered Rick Odioso.[32]

Safely back in Tampa, the Bucs continued to play out the remainder of the 1985 season. The Bucs would lose their final three games, including a rematch with the Packers in the season finale at Tampa Stadium (with a balmy kick-off temperature of 55°F). The remaining games would be dedicated to providing Steve Young with as much playing experience as possible.

During those games, Young displayed the toughness that would become his trademark in the NFL, but he also showed a penchant for giving up on plays too early, recalled Leeman Bennett.

"Steve Young was not ready to play at that time," Bennett said. "When he was in Tampa he wasn't ready to play. He would much rather run than throw because the coverages were so much faster, and he thought his legs could carry him. That's not going to work over a long period of time in the NFL."[33]

In 1986 Young would alternate with Steve DeBerg as the Buccaneers' starting quarterback during a second consecutive dreadful 2–14 campaign. The only highlight for Young during that season was a fluky touchdown against the Chicago Bears. Trailing 42–0 in the 4th quarter, Young was intercepted by Chicago's Todd Bell. Bell attempted to make a big play by throwing a lateral to teammate Mike Richardson. Richardson then attempted a second lateral, only to have it intercepted by Bucs wide receiver Vince Heflin. The alert Heflin then raced 49 yards for a touchdown in an otherwise mundane 48–14 drubbing.

Due to the lack of any semblance of success, the Snow Bowl came to be the on-field face of Leeman Bennett's tenure in Tampa Bay. It also came to be defined as Steve Young's signature moment with the Bucs, enhanced by his face-first fall into a snow bank and his paltry statistics as Bucs quarterback.

Leeman Bennett's termination at the conclusion of the 1986 season would also spell the end of Young's time as the Tampa Bay quarterback. New coach Ray Perkins would elect to bring in his own group of players, including a Heisman Trophy-winner to build his team around. Perkins's decision made Young expendable.

It is only natural that Young's departure from Tampa Bay would be necessary to further an NFL dynasty and spark the most famous quarterback controversy in NFL history.

CHAPTER NINE

Building a Dominant Team
in the Other Bay Area

IN A PIECE BY *ST. PETERSBURG TIMES* columnist Tom Zucco, the very night Steve Young arrived in Tampa after extricating himself from his infamous 40-year, $40-million dollar contract with the USFL's Los Angeles Express, the young quarterback asked to be driven to the Bucs headquarters.

Around midnight, with all the lights turned off at One Buccaneer Place and just the faintest of noises from the nearby airport, Young looked around and said aloud, "Wow, the Bucs."[1]

And with that a brief but intense relationship between Steve Young and the Tampa Bay Buccaneers began.

How hard had Steve Young wanted to be a member of the Tampa Bay Buccaneers? He wanted it enough to pay over one million dollars for the privilege. In order to escape his Los Angeles Express contract, Young paid the USFL $1.5 million to get out of the deal.[2] Young then signed a $6 million dollar deal with Tampa Bay. After a legendary career at Brigham Young and a two-year period as one of the USFL's marquee names, Young presented Hugh Culverhouse with a legitimate name at quarterback and the pleasure of taking yet another shot at the league he had grown to despise.

Steve Young didn't join the Buccaneers until after the 1985 season had begun, joining the team in Week Two before a 31–16 loss to the Minnesota Vikings. Without having seen a second of training camp, Young had a lot of catching up to do and spent his first ten games on the sideline watching veteran Steve DeBerg run the offense. While Young didn't get to see much action on the field, he threw himself into each practice, exerting himself as

Quarterback Steve Young runs the offense through its paces during a 1986 practice. Young would go on to a Hall of Fame career, leading the San Francisco 49ers to a Super Bowl title. The Bucs' trade of Young garnered the team a pair of mid-level draft choices and an infusion of cash for owner Hugh Culverhouse (*Tampa Tribune*).

if it was the final moments of a Super Bowl and playing with the boundless energy of a high school athlete. Young's overwhelming love of the game was noted by his teammates.

"He is one of the only players I've ever seen who was really disappointed when practice was over," Buccaneers nose tackle Dave Logan told reporters in Tampa Bay.[3]

Former linebacker Scot Brantley took a liking to the young southpaw not only because of Young's infectious passion for football, but because of his unpretentious nature.

"I befriended Steve right when he first got here," Brantley recalled. "A normal California kid who never even tied his shoes, he had the pretty curly hair, a happy-go-lucky kid. A gym rat-looking guy who never dressed up but was a hell of a nice guy."[4]

Young's boyish enthusiasm wasn't limited to the field. The equipment staff would often work while Young lounged around the training room after practice watching cartoons.[5]

It was hard for teammates not to like a guy with the joy of life Steve

Young possessed. But aside from Young's bright personality there was little for Buccaneers players or fans to rally around in 1985. By the time the Detroit Lions came to Tampa Stadium for a Week Twelve encounter, the Bucs were 1–10 and going nowhere. Leeman Bennett elected to turn the reins over to Young to give him some experience.

In a tantalizing display of potential, Young rallied the Buccaneers to ten 4th quarter points to forge a 16–16 tie when regulation expired. Then, in overtime, Young drove the Bucs 56 yards for a game-winning field goal. The 19–16 victory in his first NFL start would be Young's high point in Tampa Bay. The Bucs would lose their final four games of the season, including the infamous Snow Bowl.

Heading into the 1986 pre-season Bennett left the starting quarterback job open to the winner of a competition between Young and Steve DeBerg. Young didn't enjoy a particularly stellar pre-season, turning the ball over four times in his first two games, including a three-turnover disaster against the St. Louis Cardinals in the pre-season opener. The Bucs' 26–10 loss to the Cardinals was played in sauna-like conditions at Tampa Stadium. With a game-time temperature of 86° F and 100 percent humidity, Young melted down on the sideline, venting to his buddy Scot Brantley that he couldn't handle Tampa Bay summers.

"I remember Steve coming up to me on the bench," Brantley said. "He had dropped the ball a couple of times in a pre-season game. He was frustrated. It was hot and humid and everything was soaking wet because everyone was sweating, and Steve Young could not hold onto the football. When he tried to grip it, it would just slip out.[6]

"He holds his hands up to me, because he is left-handed and I am left-handed," Brantley continued. "And he says, 'Scot, I've got small hands! I've got small hands! I cannot hold the football!'[7]

"It was just the heat and humidity," Brantley explained. "I mean he is from California and played in Utah where you don't have the humidity. That freaked him out to the point where he thought, 'I can't hold this football down here!'"[8]

Training camp 1986 was one of the few times that Young had to compete for a starting job. True to his word, Bennett made it an open competition and gave both Young and DeBerg equal opportunities. Young and DeBerg had a spirited competition, but the two men treated each other with respect. Unlike some competitions in NFL history that turned into full-blown controversies, the Buccaneers quarterback battle never divided the team.[9]

When the pre-season ended, Leeman Bennett named Steve DeBerg the starter. Interestingly, DeBerg had earned a reputation as being just good enough to mentor young talent, but not good enough to beat them out for long. In San Francisco DeBerg had started in 1979 and 1980 before relinquishing the job to Joe Montana. DeBerg was traded to the Denver Broncos and started in 1981 and 1982 before ultimately losing out to John Elway.

"Steve DeBerg was a tough competitor who tried to do what you wanted him to do," recalled Leeman Bennett when asked to describe DeBerg. "Not a great quarterback in all honesty but a guy who would fight for you."[10]

After two games in 1986 DeBerg played himself out of the starting job and, for the third time in his career, was replaced by a future Hall of Fame quarterback. Young started 14 games, completing just over half of his passes for 2,200 yards and 11 touchdowns. Young would also rush for over 400 yards, mostly to avoid being mauled by opposing defenses. Young would be sacked 47 times, hit on several more occasions, and hurried countless times. The incessant hits helped lead to 21 interceptions and more than one instance of Young being pulled to avoid serious injury.

Despite the rough season, Young had posted respectable statistics for a poor team and he felt confident that he had a bright future in the Tampa Bay area. With a new head coach on the job, however, his bright future was destined for a different Bay Area.

Ray Perkins was hired to succeed Leeman Bennett as the Buccaneers head coach on New Year's Eve in 1986. When Perkins looked over the roster he inherited from Bennett, the new coach experienced a case of déjà vu. The Buccaneers new head coach saw a squad that had won a total of four games over two years and was similar in talent and attitude to the team he had coached in his previous NFL stint.

In 1979 Perkins had been named head coach of a New York Giants team that had not made the playoffs in 16 years and was coming off six straight losing seasons. Perkins eventually fixed the Giants, leading the New Yorkers to the 1981 post-season and their first playoff victory since 1958. Perkins started his reclamation of the Giants by drafting a franchise quarterback in Phil Simms and building a solid defense through the draft. Perkins explained that his mindset going into 1987 with Tampa Bay was to follow the exact same plan.

"My basic philosophy is the philosophy of a lot of different people I'm sure," Perkins said recently. "I don't think you can go very far without a quarterback, and I don't think you can go too far without a defense. Those are the two places that I like to start when looking at a team overall to eventually take it to where you would like to take it."[11]

Eight years later, Perkins was looking for his next Phil Simms and believed that player was not on the Bucs' current roster. While Steve Young possessed talent, Perkins felt the Bucs would be better served by drafting Vinny Testaverde, the Heisman Trophy–winning quarterback out of the University of Miami. A six foot five, 215 pound quarterback with a strong right arm, Testaverde was universally proclaimed as the best quarterback prospect to come out of college since the famous 1983 draft class that produced John Elway and Dan Marino.

Perkins scouted Testaverde and immediately felt a level of comfort. The Heisman Trophy winner would be the coach's new Phil Simms. However there was some disagreement in the front office. Phil Krueger believed that Steve Young, fresh off a season of growing pains, would be the Bucs' best bet to turn around the sagging fortunes of the franchise.

"The only thing I was a little upset about was when Ray Perkins came in and I had Steve Young under contract and I really liked him," Krueger said. "I liked him as a player. I knew him from BYU, and he was a very good player and person. Perkins came in, and he had a feeling about Young. Young never really had a chance to prove himself with us. When Perkins came in he wanted his own guy like he had in New York. He had his eye on Vinny Testaverde."[12]

As had happened on numerous occasions in an organization without a strong voice on personnel, Hugh Culverhouse cast the deciding vote: the Bucs would take Vinny Testaverde. In April of 1987 the Bucs drafted Testaverde and Culverhouse signed him to a six-year, $8.2 million dollar contract. With Steve Young already earning $6 million over six years, it was pretty apparent to anyone with knowledge of Culverhouse's modus operandi that his salary budget wasn't big enough for the two signal callers.

"If you drafted Testaverde, there was no room for Young unless you wanted them to compete, which I wanted," lamented Phil Krueger.[13]

"It was a matter of us feeling strongly enough about Vinny Testaverde to pick him where we picked him," Ray Perkins explained. "If you are going to pick a quarterback where we picked Testaverde, you are pretty much saying he is going to be your quarterback. So that left Steve Young and Steve DeBerg as back-ups, so which one are you going to get the most for in a trade? You kind of put them out there and feel around. San Francisco wanted Steve Young so that is the route we went. This is where Phil Krueger, Mr. Culverhouse and myself were all involved in that particular trade. We talked about it."[14]

All three men may have talked about it, but Phil Krueger said it was Culverhouse who ended up doing the negotiating. When the 49ers first expressed interest in Young, Krueger tried to take a hard-line stance with San Francisco head coach and team president Bill Walsh. While Perkins and Culverhouse wanted Testaverde, Krueger knew that Young's yeomanlike performance in 1986 had caught Walsh's eye. With a reputation as a shrewd talent evaluator, Walsh's interest meant he viewed Young as an heir apparent. If Walsh viewed Young with such favor, Krueger wanted to make sure the Bucs were justly compensated. Krueger was demanding not only a straight-up trade for current 49ers in exchange for Young, but some of San Francisco's future draft picks as well.

"At that time the coach in San Francisco was Bill Walsh," Krueger remembered. "Steve Young was a valuable commodity, and I wanted some players and a pick"[15]

The reason Krueger was so demanding was so he could take advantage of what he perceived as leverage over the 49ers. With a limited market for viable starting quarterbacks, Walsh knew his best option was Steve Young. Despite the cool, calm façade that had earned Walsh the nickname "The Genius," the 49ers coach had major worries about the health of his starting quarterback, Joe Montana. Krueger was well aware of these concerns for the Buccaneers were the opponent during Montana's first comeback from injury.

The San Francisco 49ers burst onto the NFL's elite level in 1981 when, following a decade of futility, they won a Super Bowl championship. The face of that Super Bowl season was quarterback Joe Montana. A third-year player out of Notre Dame, Montana had captured the nation's attention when his miraculous last-minute touchdown pass to Dwight Clark defeated the Dallas Cowboys in the NFC Championship Game. The play, dubbed "The Catch," was replayed over and over again and helped to make Montana one of the most highly recognized athletes in the country.

In 1982 the 49ers came crashing back down to Earth, finishing the strike-shortened season with a record of 3–6. 49ers coach Bill Walsh was distraught over the season and felt let down by his players, particularly on offense. The rapid rise from perennial loser to Super Bowl champion and the resulting media attention caught the coach off guard. In Walsh's opinion, several of his players lost their focus and hunger while cashing in on their newfound celebrity.[16] Instead of mentally preparing for defending their championship, Walsh felt the team was preoccupied with filming commercials, writing books, and making personal appearances. This lack of focus led to ragged play on offense and increased pressure on Montana. The quarterback was sacked 20 times in just nine games and threw 11 interceptions. Fortunately for Walsh, Montana kept his health intact in 1982, but that streak didn't last much past the first 30 minutes of the next season.

In the 1983 season opener, Walsh was confronted immediately with an injury to Montana. The quarterback left the 22–17 loss to Philadelphia with a head injury in the second-half. 49ers back-up quarterback Guy Benjamin did throw a 73-yard touchdown in the game, but it was apparent the drop-off in talent was great. Walsh knew that he needed to find a quality back-up. Montana did return the next week and enjoyed a much better season, but, unfortunately, the quarterback couldn't prevent San Francisco from losing 4 of 5 games in the second half of the season. The nadir of the season was reached in Week 13 when the 49ers were held without a touchdown in a 13–3 loss to the Bears at Soldier Field. In the game, Montana looked largely ineffective, tossing two interceptions. Montana was also battered by the Bears, exacerbating nagging injuries he had suffered through the year including a painful charley horse. The late season floundering left the 49ers facing the very real prospect of finishing out of the playoffs for the second-straight year, but, fortunately, the Tampa Bay Buccaneers offered them a chance to redeem themselves.

The Buccaneers, at 2–11 and destined to finish with the worst record in the NFL, put up a strong fight and were trailing just 21–14 in the third quarter. Then Joe Montana went to work, coolly leading his team on two time-consuming drives (14 plays, 8:02 and 8 plays, 2:33 respectively), expertly mixing in passes and runs. The drives quickly put the 49ers comfortably ahead by three touchdowns in what ended up being a 35–21 victory. Montana's stat line, 21–31 for 227 yards and one rushing touchdown, was deceptively lethal. Whenever he needed a play, Montana executed. More importantly, Montana stayed upright the majority of the game, the only blemish being a sack by John Cannon.

It had taken almost four years since Walsh unveiled the West Coast offense in 1979 for his team to get comfortable with the system. On this Sunday, the 49ers were crisp and comfortable running every play in the game plan. In 1981, the 49ers offense had success in fits and spurts, but against Tampa Bay in 1983 the 49ers began an offensive hot streak that would last for almost two full years. Tampa Bay linebacker Scot Brantley believes the 49ers on that day unleashed the full effect of the West Coast offense, and he and his teammates were helpless to stop it.

"You look at San Francisco and they perfected that West Coast offense," Brantley said. "That means 1st and 10, throw a short pass. Second and 8, run the ball. Third and 2, throw another pass. Then its 1st and 10 again! I think one time I counted 15, 16 plays they were driving down the field and you get tired in that rhythm."[17]

For the first time in more than a month, the 49ers offense was in sync and they never lost momentum, winning their final three games to win the NFC West, defeating Detroit in the Divisional Round and succumbing to the defending champion Washington Redskins by only a field goal in the NFC Title Game.

The victory over the Buccaneers had knocked the 49ers out of the doldrums in 1983 and there was a supreme carry-over effect in 1984. The next year the 49ers won their second world championship, defeating the Miami Dolphins in Super Bowl XIX to cap an 18–1 season, at the time the most victories by one team in a single year. Fully focused and behind a stronger line, Montana was in total control of Walsh's West Coast offense and was named 1st Team All-Pro and Super Bowl MVP. Whatever worries Bill Walsh had about the health of his quarterback seemed to be satisfied. Unfortunately for Walsh, his team didn't handle success much better than they had in 1982.

The 49ers struggled to a .500 record after ten games, and only a superb effort over the final six weeks guaranteed a playoff spot. The 49ers lost to the New York Giants 17–3 in the Wild Card round, and Montana once again took a tremendous beating. The Giants defense sacked Montana four times and hit him on numerous occasions. Already suffering from a pulled chest muscle, Montana barely finished the game after another season of abuse. After watching his team's leader take shot after shot, Walsh headed into the 1986 season with renewed fears about the health of his quarterback.[18] In the season opener against Tampa Bay, the worst of those fears came true.

The 1986 season opener against San Francisco was the marquee event on an otherwise lackluster Buccaneers schedule. Having finished the previous season 2–14, the Buccaneers were presented with a less than stellar schedule as part of Pete Rozelle's continuing effort to bring parity to the league. Hosting Joe Montana and the San Francisco 49ers for the first time in franchise history, the Bucs PR staff pulled out all the stops.

"They hyped it all offseason," remembered linebacker Scot Brantley. "San Francisco and Joe Montana are coming to Tampa. It was supposed to be the introduction of Bo Jackson at running back. Usually early in the season they would make our home games start at 4 o'clock when it wasn't so hot. But they made this thing primetime, 1 o'clock first game of the day, first game of the year. It was 120 degrees on the field. It was the hottest day I ever remember at Tampa Stadium."[19]

Tampa Bay linebacker Scot Brantley was one of the most dependable and popular Buccaneers players in the 1980s. The former University of Florida standout saw it all during his eight seasons. Two players strikes, two playoff appearances, the Snow Bowl, Ray Perkins' initial training camp, a record-setting fourth quarter collapse and taking Bo Jackson bass fishing were just a few of the items on Brantley's résumé (*Tampa Tribune*).

Throughout the game Joe Montana was as hot as the temperature, finishing 32–46 for 356 yards and one touchdown. The only mistake Montana made was a second-quarter interception by Brantley when the 49ers were leading 14–0 and looking to put the game away early. Brantley returned the pass along the sideline and looked to score a touchdown before he finally ran out of gas after 57 yards. To this day Brantley is convinced he could have scored if not for a combination of the heat, humidity and San Francisco's style of offense.

"Joe threw a slant route and I picked it off," Brantley remembers. "If it had been the 2nd or 3rd play of the drive, I would have walked into the end zone. But they had had the ball so long, that's when that monkey jumped on my back. I got to the point where I said, 'Shit! Somebody catch me or I am going to have to stop!'[20]

"It was hot, and I was tired," Brantley continued. "Dwight Clark caught me from behind and as he tackled me he tried to knock the ball out of my hand. We both fell to the ground at the same time and landed facemask to facemask, and he was laughing! I go, 'Dwight, thank God you showed up because I was getting ready to have to stop!'"[21]

Sadly for Brantley and the Buccaneers, Montana's counterpart at quarterback that day was not having a good game. Steve DeBerg, winner of the pre-season competition with Steve Young, was facing his former team and, perhaps overanxious to prove himself to his former coach, pressed too hard. DeBerg threw a team record seven interceptions in Tampa Bay's 31–7 loss. The interceptions would lead to DeBerg losing his starting job to Steve Young the following week. One of those pick-offs came immediately after Brantley's big play.

"I'll be damned, we get the ball inside the 20-yard line and the crowd is going nuts and DeBerg comes in the game and throws an interception," Brantley said. "One play back on the sideline, and we are back on the field! It was just the way of the Buccaneers. If you put the franchise in a nutshell back then you could have put it all in that one series of plays."[22]

Late in the game Montana made an off-balance throw to running back Joe Cribbs. Montana was forced to twist his body oddly to make the throw and, shortly after releasing the pass, he was hit by Buccaneers linebacker Jackie Walker. At first nothing seemed amiss. Montana jogged off the field, grabbed a drink and began chatting with teammate Ronnie Lott. On the next series, Walsh inserted newly acquired back-up quarterback Jeff Kemp in the game. With a commanding 24–7 lead, Walsh was merely giving his new quarterback a chance to get some much needed repetitions with the first team. Kemp led the 49ers to their final touchdown of the game. When Montana jogged towards the locker room following the game, he gave no sign of discomfort or pain. Less than a week later everything for the 49ers, Montana and ultimately Steve Young would change.

On the flight home Montana complained of soreness and numbness in his legs and lower back. Late in the week Montana went to visit specialists to determine what was causing the pain and discomfort. The injury meant Walsh would be forced to start Kemp against the Rams in a key early season showdown. That Sunday the 49ers lost 16–13 on a last second field goal but when Walsh returned to the locker room he was presented with much more dire news. Montana's doctors at St. Mary's hospital diagnosed the quarterback with a ruptured disc at the base of his spine. The doctors explained to Walsh the only solution was spinal surgery which would put Montana out at least for the season and perhaps end his career. As Montana entered the operating room, Bill Walsh and fans across Northern California all held their collective breath.

When the surgery concluded, the operating team announced that Montana's injury was not as grave as first believed. Instead of fusing the disc, surgeons were able to remove the extended part of it making it possible for Montana to continue his career after a year of recovery.

One of San Francisco's team orthopedic specialists, Dr. Michael Dillingham, told the press that there was a good chance Montana would make a full recovery, but hedged the bet somewhat by stating a return to football was not guaranteed. "There is a chance he won't play again," Dr. Dillingham said before quickly continuing. "I think there is a general consensus that Joe will play again, but there is also the risk that even if the surgery is successful, it won't relieve the pain."[23]

While Bill Walsh was relieved that his star quarterback could one day return to lead the team, he was left with a quarterback quandary. Walsh had traded with the Rams to bring in Jeff Kemp as a backup. Like those in the position before him, Kemp proved to be no Montana. The 49ers muddled to a 5-3-1 record behind Kemp and Mike Moroski, who started two games when Kemp was injured. If not for the miraculous recovery of Montana, the 1986 season could have easily been lost.

In defiance of conventional wisdom, Montana returned to the field in Week Ten and led the 49ers to their fourth straight playoff appearance. Looking rusty from his time off, Montana nevertheless performed admirably down the stretch and culminated his unbelievable comeback with a 24–14 NFC West Division Championship–clinching victory over the Los Angeles Rams in the season finale.

Sadly for the 49ers there would be no continuation of the fairy tale in the playoffs. The 49ers were routed by the New York Giants 49–3 in the divisional round at Giants Stadium. Late in the second half, Montana was knocked unconscious by a Giants defender and spent the rest of game on the sideline in a concussion-induced haze. For the second year in a row, Bill Walsh's star quarterback had ended the season injured. Walsh decided the time had come to create a new back-up plan. Enter the Tampa Bay Buccaneers.

The Tampa Bay Buccaneers had provided Bill Walsh with a glimpse of what life without Joe Montana would look like, and he didn't care for that scenario one bit. In an example of irony that could have only befallen the "Necessary Team," the Buccaneers also provided Walsh with the ability to never have to worry about the impact of Joe Montana's health on his organization again.

Walsh was desperate for a back-up quarterback who could not just relieve Montana, but who also possessed a talent level akin to Montana's. In Steve Young, Bill Walsh felt he had found the man for the job. Walsh had reviewed countless tapes of Young in action in Tampa Bay and was immediately impressed with his arm strength, speed and leadership ability.[24] While surrounded with minimal talent in Tampa Bay, Young had managed to make impressive plays and had shown growth in the position. At 6' 2" and 200 pounds, Young was also a sturdier player than the fragile Montana.

Phil Krueger knew what he had in Young even if Perkins and Culverhouse didn't share his opinion. Krueger also knew of Walsh's desperation. Armed with that knowledge, he was holding out for a bevy of draft picks and players. Unfortunately for Krueger, Bill Walsh also was armed with information, information that would ultimately allow him to virtually steal Young in exchange for the football equivalent of magic beans.

Culverhouse's reputation for not spending a great deal on payroll and freely utilizing the cash flow from the Buccaneers to fund his real estate empire was known by many in NFL circles. Walsh's boss with the 49ers, Eddie DeBartolo, Jr., knew of Culverhouse's business operations and when Krueger took a hard line, the San Francisco owner advised Walsh to bypass Krueger altogether and deal directly with Culverhouse.

In Walsh's autobiography, *Building a Champion*, the coach wrote that DeBartolo, Jr. gave him permission to add a large amount of money to his efforts to acquire Young.

"Traveling through Florida, Eddie was calling from phone booths to discuss our strategy," Walsh wrote in his book. "He trusted our judgment implicitly, so after we agreed on the next step, he would hang up and call Culverhouse."[25]

David Harris' book *The Genius* theorizes the motivation behind Culverhouse's desire for cash instead of more lucrative draft picks was simple. Culverhouse wanted to recover some of the money he had paid to bring Young to Tampa Bay in the first place. He had paid Young $2 million in the previous two years and looked at the deep pockets of DeBartolo, Jr. as a chance to recoup some of his investment.[26]

In the end Culverhouse agreed to trade Steve Young to the San Francisco

49ers in exchange for the 49ers' second and fourth round draft choices in the 1987 NFL Draft and for monetary considerations. The deal shocked Phil Krueger, who was opposed because of the paltry draft picks. Krueger was also upset because those monetary considerations were large and went directly into Culverhouse's pockets.

"Culverhouse stepped in and talked to Walsh," Krueger recalled. "Steve Young went for money. He didn't go for a player. Culverhouse got a million something dollars. But that was one I didn't want to do. Culverhouse stepped in, and Walsh got a great deal. We were kind of conned on that one."[27]

Krueger may have felt conned, but Culverhouse got exactly what he desired. Coincidentally, in the same year Culverhouse received cash from the 49ers for Young, he parlayed his millions into a shockingly quick takeover of multiple Florida businesses.

First, he purchased the controlling stock of Florida Commercial Bank. (He ultimately sold the bank and cleared more than $23 million.[28]) Flush with those proceeds, he then went after controlling interest of Coast Federal Savings and Loan of Sarasota, a financial institution that owned half of Palmer Ranch. Culverhouse owned the other half of Palmer Ranch and went after the S&L with the intention of owning the entire land holding.[29] The purchase took two years and a lawsuit, but he ultimately prevailed, and Palmer Ranch was 100 percent his.

While the Buccaneers did not benefit from the Young trade as greatly as Culverhouse eventually did from the Palmer Ranch deal, in defense of the Bucs' scouting department, they made the most out of the draft picks obtained. While second and fourth round draft choices for a future Hall of Fame quarterback seemed unjust compensation, the fact is the Buccaneers selected two players who went on to solid NFL careers. The second round choice went for linebacker Winston Moss, who played five productive seasons for Tampa Bay before ending his 11-year career with Oakland and Seattle. The fourth round pick was wide receiver Bruce Hill, who went on to post a 1,000 yard season in 1988 and enjoyed five seasons as a highly regarded possession receiver.

While the picks the Buccaneers received in exchange for Young benefited the team, many in Tampa Bay were stunned to see the southpaw go for such a small return. Many of Young's teammates were also stunned to see him go because they felt Young had a bright future in the NFL.

"It's sad to see him go," tight end Jerry Bell told reporters. "I think he'll eventually replace Joe Montana and be a very successful quarterback."[30]

"The kid tried as hard as he could," lamented nose tackle David Logan.[31]

More than 20 years later, Scot Brantley can only shake his head at the memory of watching Young leave the Buccaneers.

"I knew he had what it took to be a great player," Brantley said of his friend. "The sad part is that they must have never seen that in Tampa. They didn't see it or they didn't think they could develop it."[32]

No one was more upset than Young himself, who had grown to love the Tampa Bay area and was determined to turn the Buccaneers around.

"I didn't want to get out," Young told the *St. Petersburg Times* from his off-season home in Utah. "I didn't want to be traded. I think things obviously could have been better there. That's why leaving feels so funny. There was something about coming from behind, no matter how bad it got, that I liked. It feels really funny. I thought I'd be there a long time, that I could turn it around.[33]

"My dream has always been to go into a filled up Tampa Stadium and see the Bucs play for a championship," Young continued. "Those fans—they want to be so proud of the Bucs. God, I can't wait until we're winning every week. I know I'll be watching how the Bucs do. You couldn't have gone through what I went through without feeling something. It's part of me.[34]

"I knew that it would be great one day," Young said in closing. "Now it'll be great somewhere else."[35]

Young would indeed be great somewhere else. In fact, he would be great much earlier than Bill Walsh or Joe Montana expected. Young's rapid rise led to one of the most famous quarterback competitions in NFL history. Unlike his competition with DeBerg, Young's battles with Montana would not be so pleasant. In their role as the "Necessary Team," the Tampa Bay Buccaneers would also play a large role in determining the winner.

Heading into the 1987 season, the question being asked around the NFL was, "Is Joe Montana healthy enough to be the 49ers' quarterback?" Coming off a season in which he underwent back surgery and suffered a concussion, it was a legitimate question, and no one was more uncertain of the answer than Bill Walsh.

Montana opened the season as starter and the 49ers split their first two games before the season was interrupted by a second players strike. When the regular players returned, Montana and the 49ers raced out to a 10–2 record and appeared to be the odds-on favorite to win the NFC. Unknown to many, however, the 49ers were not a harmonious group. During the course of the season Bill Walsh would periodically pull Montana from games and insert Young into the line-up. Walsh wrote in his autobiography that he did this out of concern for Montana's continued health.

"There were times I substituted Steve almost in desperation because we weren't protecting Joe well enough," Walsh wrote in *Building a Champion*. "I hoped Steve's running ability could take advantage of a situation."[36]

Montana was not pleased to be pulled from games for any reason and, in a late November contest at Tampa Stadium, he raised his game to such a level that Walsh couldn't possibly replace him. Facing almost no pass rush from the Buccaneers, Montana enjoyed one of his best days as a professional, completing 29 of 45 passes for 304 yards and three touchdowns, all to Jerry Rice, in a 24–10 victory. The only time Young saw the field in his old home stadium was during pre-game warm-ups.

The risk-free environment Montana enjoyed against Tampa Bay didn't continue for the rest of the season. Montana was forced to miss significant time late in the season after suffering a torn hamstring in a Week Thirteen Monday night contest against Chicago. Steve Young came in off the bench and was masterful, throwing four touchdown passes in a 41–0 victory. The next week Young started and threw for two more touchdowns in a 35–7 victory over the Atlanta Falcons. Young continued his hot streak, throwing for three more touchdowns in a 48–0 rout of the Los Angeles Rams in the season finale. Interestingly, Montana was inserted for mop-up duty in the final half. Being relegated to garbage time did not sit well with Montana. That indignity would be compounded two weeks later.

The San Francisco 49ers entered as the prohibitive favorite against the Minnesota Vikings in the playoffs. With a final record of 13–2 the 49ers looked to be a lock to return to the Super Bowl but after one half of play, they found themselves down 20–3 to the surprisingly strong Vikings. Montana had not looked sharp in the first half, throwing an interception and being sacked on numerous plays. In the third quarter, Walsh did the unthinkable: he pulled Montana from a playoff game and inserted Young. Young played well but couldn't overcome the deficit and the 49ers lost 36–24.

The benching left a sour taste in Montana's mouth and the relationship between him, Bill Walsh and Steve Young would never be the same. In the week leading up to the Vikings game, Montana had commented to the *San Francisco Chronicle* that he felt like Walsh was trying to ease him out of the starting line-up in favor of Young.

"I know there is a time when Bill's going to make a move," Montana told the paper. "All I can do is try to keep the clock moving backwards."[37]

The attempted move Montana spoke of almost occurred just months later. As the 1988 season approached, Walsh momentarily considered a lucrative trade package from the San Diego Chargers. San Diego offered two first round choices and a player to be named later in exchange for Montana. When Walsh broached the topic with his assistants, they unanimously voted no.[38] Rebuffed by his assistants, Walsh agreed to nix the deal and Montana stayed in San Francisco with the understanding that his hold on the starting job was tenuous at best. To keep the job, Montana needed to win big.

In 1988 Montana did just that, leading the 49ers to a Super Bowl victory in a rematch with the Cincinnati Bengals. The season was not a statistical masterpiece for Montana, but he did engineer several important victories including a 20–17 victory over the New York Giants in Week Two in which

Montana hit Jerry Rice with a 78-yard touchdown pass with just seconds to play. Despite his heroics, Montana had to share playing time with Young due to injuries and Walsh's desire to give his back-up experience. In 1988, Young had looked quite comfortable at the helm of the offense, subbing for an injured Montana in a key game on the road against the New Orleans Saints and starting in a rematch with the Vikings at Candlestick Park. Against the Vikings, Young scored on a stellar 49-yard scramble in which he broke six tackles to provide the winning points in a 24–21 victory.

In David Harris' biography of Walsh, the coach said he had brought Young in with the intention of replacing Montana in 1989 and but for a nixed deal with San Diego, Montana may have left a year sooner. However, the 1988 Super Bowl championship had provided Montana with a second chance to stay in the starting job. The dynamics of the Montana–Young competition altered dramatically after Super Bowl XXIII. Bill Walsh stepped down as 49ers coach following Super Bowl XXIII and was replaced by defensive coordinator George Seifert who was inclined to let Montana prove he should keep the starting job. Heading into the 1989 season Montana knew he had to make a good first impression on Seifert and naturally the Tampa Bay Buccaneers provided him a chance to cement his starting job.

In Week Two the 49ers trailed the unexpectedly stout Buccaneers 16–13 with less than two minutes to play. Montana took this opportunity to drive a dagger both through the heart of the Buccaneers' upset bid and Steve Young's chances of seeing much playing time in 1989. Calmly and methodically, Montana led the 49ers 70 yards down the field in 10 plays despite the Buccaneers' desperate efforts to stop him. Aided by two defensive holding penalties and a dropped interception by Buccaneers cornerback Ricky Reynolds, the 49ers faced second and goal from the four-yard line with 46 seconds to play. With vivid memories of "The Catch" of eight years ago in their minds, the Buccaneers secondary guarded the back of the end zone. This maneuver cost them as Montana sprinted left and raced untouched into the end zone for the winning score in a 20–16 thriller. The victory over Tampa Bay ignited Montana and the 49ers. San Francisco finished the season with a 14–2 record and a second consecutive Super Bowl victory.

Steve Young would not see much action in 1989 or 1990, starting only three games. Everything changed for good in the 1991 off-season. Montana suffered an elbow injury that cost him all of the 1991 season and most of 1992. During that time, Young thrived, leading the 49ers to the 1992 NFC Championship Game and being named NFL MVP. Young's play left the 49ers with a quandary. At 31 years old and at the peak of his career, Young was the logical choice to start over the 36 year old Montana. Montana made it known that he had no intention of returning to San Francisco as a back-up, so the 49ers traded him to the Kansas City Chiefs in 1993.

With something to prove, Montana threw himself into preparing for the 1993 season. On the opening weekend of that season, in his Kansas City debut, Montana enjoyed his best game in almost four years. The opponent was, logically, the Tampa Bay Buccaneers, the team that had sent the man who usurped Montana's position in San Francisco.

The opener was played on a blazingly hot day, reminiscent of the 1986 opener when Montana suffered the back injury which called his durability into question. On the very field where so much had changed seven years earlier, Montana played with the confidence and precision of his youth, completing 14 of 21 passes for 246 yards and three touchdowns. The final score was 27–3, but the contest was not that close and Montana left with most of the 4th quarter still to play. The game was just the beginning for Montana, as he led the Chiefs to an AFC Championship Game in his first year, and the Wild Card round in 1994. Montana retired after the 1994 season but not after gaining revenge against Young in a 1994 regular season contest.

In Week Two the San Francisco 49ers played the Kansas City Chiefs at Arrowhead Stadium in the only head-to-head match-up between Montana and Young. The Chiefs prevailed 24–17, with Montana out-dueling Young. Young ultimately had the last laugh in 1994, leading the 49ers to a Super Bowl championship. When Young yelled out, "Somebody take this monkey off my back," on the sidelines of Super Bowl XXIX, the former Buccaneer may have very well been talking about Montana.

The controversy between Montana and Young prodded them to raise their games to higher levels. Their heightened play catapulted the 49ers back into a dominant team that fell just short of the ever elusive Three-Peat. It is often forgotten that this entire era of San Francisco success was in no small part possible because the actions of the "Necessary Team." Ray Perkins' decision to start his reign with a new quarterback and Hugh Culverhouse's desire to recoup some of the money he had doled out to Young prompted the move which shifted the balance of power in the NFC back to San Francisco.

While Perkins may not have realized what he had in Young, it would be unfair to use Young's future success as an indictment of Perkins' ability to judge talent. With the exception of Bill Walsh and Phil Krueger, many in the NFL viewed Young as a stellar athlete too undisciplined to play quarterback at the professional level and were surprised by his career turnaround.[39]

An exception was linebacker Scot Brantley. The former Buccaneers defender said he saw bright potential for Young, but wasn't certain it would be fulfilled in Tampa. Brantley believes that had Young stayed in Tampa Bay he would have never reached the level of success that he did.

"It may have been the best thing to happen to him that he ended up going to San Francisco to resurrect his career," Brantley said. "Because it never really kicked off in Tampa Bay, and it is really a shame."[40]

The deal would be a rare win-win for all parties involved.

Ray Perkins would use the draft choices acquired from the Young trade to select linebacker Winston Moss and wide receiver Bruce Hill, both of whom would go onto solid careers in Tampa Bay. In addition to Hill, Perkins would select a second wide receiver in Mark Carrier and tight end Ron Hall. Teamed with Testaverde, these three receivers would provide the Bucs with an above-average passing attack during Perkins' tenure in Tampa Bay. Unfortunately for Perkins and the Bucs, they would never enjoy the same level of success as Montana, Young and the 49ers. If anything, the Bucs would be the anti-49ers. Where Montana's second act would be defined by dramatic come-from-behind victories, the Bucs of Ray Perkins would be haunted by a stunning series of come-from-ahead defeats. One of those late game collapses would be of such note that it would place the "Necessary Team" at the top of a most ignominious list.

CHAPTER TEN

What Is a Buc Worth?
Three Quarters!

WHEN RAY PERKINS TOOK OVER the Tampa Bay Buccaneers following the 1986 season the lack of talented depth on the roster was overwhelming. There were many solid professionals on the Bucs team at that time, men such as Scot Brantley, Steve DeBerg, Gerald Carter and Sean Farrell. In addition, defensive linemen David Logan, John Cannon and Ron Holmes, kicking specialists Frank Garcia and Donald Igwebuike, linebackers Jeff Davis and Ervin Randle, and offensive linemen Ron Heller, Rob Taylor and Randy Grimes all were solid if unspectacular contributors and popular players in the community. Unfortunately for these men, there was not enough depth on the team to supplement their contributions. Despairing losses piled on top of each other for four straight seasons as a result.

"Free agency didn't exist so what you had was what you had," Scot Brantley said of the state of the Bucs from 1983 to 1986.[1]

In addition to the toll the lack of depth took on the won-loss record, the physical punishment administered to the few dependable players on the roster was staggering. No one player personified the palpable effects of weekly beatings more than running back James Wilder.

Wilder had been a Pro Bowl player in 1984, accumulating over 2,200 total yards from scrimmage. In 1985, Wilder rushed for 1300 yards and scored ten touchdowns. In order to amass these numbers Wilder had been forced to carry the ball quite often. Wilder carried the ball a then NFL record 43 times in one game and touched the ball a record 492 times in 1984. In 1986, a season in which Bo Jackson could have spelled him in the backfield had the

Bucs organization had a better reputation, Wilder's production dropped off dramatically as he missed four starts, totaled just over 1,000 yards of total offense and ended the season on injured reserve.

Wilder never complained about the workload but by 1987, at just 28 years old, his best days were behind him. Former Buccaneers personnel executive Ken Herock explained that Wilder's plight personified the consequences of the Buccaneers' failure as an organization to utilize the annual draft to their best advantage. Over the course of the previous five years, the Buccaneers had squandered high draft choice after high draft choice beginning with a historic snafu in 1982.

"The one big hang-up we had was one year we had a guy named Booker Reese," said Herock of the start of the Bucs' annual draft misadventures. "That is one we should have done over. When we went to make the pick, we had two choices: Sean Farrell or Booker Reese. I told our equipment manager in New York, Pat Marcuccillo, 'We have two names: Sean Farrell and Booker Reese. We'll tell you who we want.' In those days there was a lot of noise and racket in New York. I said, 'Okay, we're going to pass on Farrell and we're going to take Reese.' Pat didn't hear that, he heard 'Sean Farrell' and turned that name in."[2]

The drafting of Farrell proved to be a boon for the Bucs as the guard from Penn State became a solid player, but he was not the player Tampa Bay had wanted with their top overall pick. Fearing that Reese, a mountain of a defensive lineman out of Bethune-Cookman, would be taken by another team, the Bucs front office overreacted and mortgaged their top pick in 1983 to acquire the man they considered the star of the 1982 draft.

"There was a bit of confusion," Herock continued. "The next thing that happens, someone says let's make a trade and get Booker Reese. It was a collective decision; it wasn't just one guy. Here is Reese still available; how do we get him? We don't have a second round pick, so what we did is trade our first pick next year for a second from Chicago."[3]

Reese ended up being a bust for the Buccaneers, never living up to the potential the team had envisioned. Instead Reese ended up out of football within three years. Ironically, had the Bucs not traded their 1983 top draft choice away to acquire Reese, Hugh Culverhouse's decision to low-ball Doug Williams in their negotiations may have never hurt the team. The Bucs' pick in 1983 would have been the 18th overall and a quarterback out of Pittsburgh named Dan Marino would have been waiting for them. Instead, as Herock explained, the Bucs' need for a quarterback instigated a trade of their top draft choice for the second year in a row. That trade brought in Jack Thompson.

"If they had said, 'We're not going to sign Doug Williams, Ken. Go get us a quarterback,' that would have been different," Herock admits. "But it was thrown in my face that we're going to take 'The Throwin' Samoan.'"[4]

In 1984 the Bucs would have had the number one overall choice in the NFL draft. That draft class included such stalwarts as linebackers Carl Banks and Wilber Marshall, and defensive linemen Alphonso Carreker and Keith Millard, all of whom could have helped the Bucs' rapidly aging defense. Instead, as Herock said, the Buccaneers lost out on prime talent and were left to patch their roster together as best they could with later round picks.

"I had been bringing in good players and now we're losing them," Herock recalled complaining to his boss before leaving. "You can't keep that up. After I left there was a big demise with that team. McKay hired a coach to place over personnel. That didn't work. Leeman Bennett comes in and that doesn't work."[5]

Factor in the Bucs' failure to sign Bo Jackson in 1986 and the Bucs' track record for number one draft choices was horrific. Their 1983 top pick went for a 1982 second round selection that resulted in a sub-par defensive lineman. Their 1984 top pick went for a journeyman back-up quarterback out of football within two years. Their 1986 top pick turned out to be a base-ball player. The only top pick the Bucs had in that span was the 1985 choice used on defensive end Ron Holmes of the University of Washington. Holmes had a solid NFL career, but not one commensurate of the value expected from a top ten selection.

In 1987 Ray Perkins came in determined to work with Culverhouse and Phil Krueger to stop the draft bleeding. Perkins attempted to make up for 5 straight sub-par drafts in one single year. In addition to trading Steve Young, the Buccaneers also traded offensive guard Sean Farrell to New England for a 2nd round draft pick. In conjunction with those deals, Perkins swapped other players and picks to maximize the number of selections at his disposal. By the end of the wheeling and dealing, the Buccaneers had 20 picks in the 1987 draft and Perkins made them count. Of those 20 players 14 would make the 1987 roster. In addition to the draft picks, Perkins invited dozens of undrafted free agents to a May mini-camp. A total of 121 players, including a staggering 69 rookies, reported for the mini-camp as Ray Perkins looked to wipe the slate clean and start out with a whole new foundation for Tampa Bay.

By the time summer arrived Perkins still had almost 100 players competing for positions. Before any of these would-be Bucs could dream of taking the field in the season opener however, they would have to endure a training regimen the likes of which the Bay Area had never seen before.

On July 20, 1987, the Buccaneers opened training camp at the University of Tampa's Pepin-Rood Stadium. A total of 97 players reported, geared to fight for 45 roster spots. In an attempt to maximize practice time, Perkins instituted a training schedule that had not been seen in years by the NFL: three-a-days.

"It was a concept that I had used in college at Alabama," Perkins said in an interview for this book. "What it is, your first practice is early in the morning at 8:30 A.M. and all you do is work on special teams. Then you go out with another practice before lunch and you work on certain aspects of your offense and defense. Then you go out at 3 o'clock in the afternoon and you work on other aspects of your offense and defense.[6]

"In other words," Perkins continued, "You have basically one special teams practice in the morning and two offensive and defensive practices before lunch and in the afternoon. But from a time standpoint, that is time spent running plays and plays run, you are really not spending any more time on the field. It's just a matter of how you are splitting it up and the fact you are going out three different times."[7]

In Perkins' mind, the three-a-day schedule accomplished two things: First it helped the Bucs cut down on lost practice time due to the torrential thunderstorms that are endemic to Tampa Bay in the summer and second, it would actually be easier on the players physically because it cut down the length of practice time.

"It helped us get in practices," Perkins said. "Like the practice before noon, to work on offense and defense because later in the afternoon in Tampa there are several times where you get rained out. That time of year there is almost always a rain shower in the afternoon.[8]

"It also takes care of players because they are out there for shorter periods of time," Perkins concluded. "Back then, it wasn't anything for a lot of teams to be on the field for two, two and a half hours, whereas we were always off the field in an hour and a half."[9]

The time on the field may have been shorter, but the practice sessions were intense, involving a good deal of sprinting and hitting under the unforgiving Florida sun. The schedule took many of the players by surprise, particularly the veterans who had grown accustomed to the common NFL structure of two-a-days, traditionally a two hour practice in the morning and a two to two and a half hour practice in the afternoon. Many participants in that 1987 camp admitted the schedule was a struggle.[10]

"Three-a-days in pads," exclaimed linebacker Scot Brantley. "We hardly went out in shorts. We wore shorts with helmets and shoulder pads. That was ridiculous. I was the old man. After that season, I was thinking to go through a camp like that at my age, this is not fun."[11]

To one veteran on the Bucs' roster, the training regimen looked all too familiar. Cornerback Jeremiah Castille had played at Alabama under Paul "Bear" Bryant and knew Perkins had mentored under the Crimson Tide legend. Castille was able to express what Bryant had meant to accomplish by driving players so hard in practice, and related to the press that Perkins was simply looking to do the same thing.

"He [Bryant] motivated by driving you to a point where you think you don't have anything left, but you find something," Castille told John Luttermoser of the *St. Petersburg Times*. "I think all men that played under Coach Bryant have some of it in them. You can't help but have some of the things that he taught you inside you."[12]

Mark Carrier, a rookie wide receiver out of tiny Nicholls State, remembered that while the camp was tough, Perkins did accomplish what he had set out to do, namely improve the talent level and toughen the mindset of the Buccaneers.

"I think Coach Perkins had a plan," Carrier said for this book. "His plan was to start everything fresh and see who really wanted to play and work through it and wean some people out. It was tough, really tough. It wasn't what I thought the NFL was, I can

Ray Perkins instructs his players during practice at his first training camp as head coach in 1987. Perkins instituted a three-a-day practice training regimen to fit in as much practice as possible between summer thunderstorms. The effect exhausted some players and saddled Perkins with an unfair reputation which culminated in *Inside Sports* magazine ranking him as the NFL's worst coach (*Tampa Tribune*).

tell you that. Growing up watching the NFL on television, growing up in Louisiana and watching the Saints, you didn't see that. It was culture shock for me. I didn't anticipate the work as it was. That was a rarity because not every NFL club did that. But I realized that once I made it through my rookie year training camp everything else was going to be a lot easier."[13]

During the 1987 pre-season it appeared that Perkins's methods were paying off. The Buccaneers were younger, faster and stronger than they had been in the previous four years. They also appeared to be more physically fit and mentally tougher than the opposition. The Bucs scored three touchdowns in the fourth quarter as Cincinnati wilted in the August heat; only a blocked extra point prevented overtime in the 31–30 loss to Cincinnati in the exhibition opener at Tampa Stadium. Tampa Bay scored two fourth quarter touchdowns in a 29–27 come-from-behind victory over the New York Jets in the next game and ten fourth quarter points in a 17–10 win over the Washington Redskins.

When the regular season opened in September, Perkins's Bucs were a radically different team from the one Leeman Bennett had left him. Gone were many veterans, including, ironically enough, Jeremiah Castille, who had welcomed the training camp methods of Perkins. The four-year starter at cornerback was replaced by Ricky Reynolds, a rookie out of Washington State.

The roster wasn't the only thing different about Tampa Bay; so was the way they played. In a 48–10 rout of the Atlanta Falcons at Tampa Stadium in the season opener, the Buccaneers' offense, defense and special teams excelled. Tampa Bay's offense amassed 460 total yards, 30 first downs and seven touchdowns. The defense held the Falcons to just 197 total yards, sacked Atlanta's quarterback four times and forced three turnovers. Despite kicking off eight times, the Bucs' special teams held the Falcons' return men in check the entire game. Only a missed extra point marred the Bucs' attempt at perfection. The following week the Bucs fell to the NFC Central Division bully Chicago Bears 20–3 at Soldier Field. The game was more hard-fought than the score indicated as the Bucs had four opportunities to score and misfired.

The NFL was hit with its second work stoppage in five years just two days after the Chicago game. NFL players walked out and stayed away for more than three weeks. When the players and owners agreed to a settlement, the first game for the Bucs was a rematch with the Bears at Tampa Stadium. Many viewed this game as a historic match-up between an up-and-coming young Buccaneers team and a vulnerable veteran club.

Instead what football fans saw was a preview of an unsettling trend by the Buccaneers that would foretell a historic collapse by the necessary team.

On Sunday, October 25, the Buccaneers met the Bears with a chance to tie Chicago for first place in the NFC Central Division. Throughout the majority of the first half it appeared the Buccaneers were ready for the top spot as they raced out to a 20–0 lead. The Bears rallied to close the gap to 23–14 but the Bucs' defense stiffened and held the Bears scoreless in the third quarter as Tampa Bay increased their lead to 26–14. With only a little over 5 minutes to play and a two touchdown lead the Bucs seemed assured of being in first place for the first time since John McKay had been head coach. Then everything fell apart.

The defense, which had stymied the Bears all day, got caught out of position on several occasions and gave up chunks of yardage. Chicago quarterback Jim McMahon led the Bears on touchdown drives of 85 yards and 71 yards, the last culminating in a six-yard scoring pass to Neal Armstrong with 1:28 to play in Chicago's 27–26 victory. The Bucs' offense didn't help matters by failing to convert key 3rd down opportunities which provided the Bears with the ball in a matter of seconds between scoring drives. If the opening win against Atlanta had been a team success, this loss was a team failure.

The next week in Wisconsin the Bucs shook off the disappointment of the previous week and once again raced out to a 20–0 lead against the Packers at County Stadium in Milwaukee. In the fourth quarter, the Bucs held a 23–3 lead with just over nine minutes to play when again the Bucs' defense surrendered back-to-back touchdown drives which narrowed the gap to 23–17 with just over three minutes left in the game. Unlike the previous week, the Bucs' offense was able to convert on third down to keep the ball away from the suddenly unstoppable Packers, and the Bucs held on for the victory. When asked after the game if he was nervous that the Bucs' defense had given up multiple scoring drives in similar fashion two weeks in a row, Perkins scoffed.

"I don't know about that déjà vu stuff," the head coach told the press in the locker room. "I'm not sure I know what that is."[14]

The next week in St. Louis Perkins was provided with a definition that would have made Webster's proud.

The St. Louis Cardinals were a moribund team going nowhere fast, at least as far as gridiron success was concerned. The 2–5 Cardinals were actually a franchise on the move. Shortly before the Bucs came to town, St. Louis owner Bill Bidwill had announced the team would be relocating following the 1987 season. While the final destination was not known at the time, their announced move was ending the Cardinals' quarter-century stay in St. Louis.

Needless to say Cardinals fans were not impressed with the decision, and they stayed away in droves. Only 22,000 attended the game against Tampa Bay. By the end of the afternoon, however, arguably enough people would claim they witnessed the contest firsthand that Busch Stadium's capacity of 54,000 would not have been enough to contain them.

Through the first three quarters the Bucs ran roughshod over their hosts in front of very dispirited fans. Quarterback Steve DeBerg continued a season in which he looked re-born, throwing three touchdown passes. The veteran, who had been replaced by Joe Montana in San Francisco and John Elway in Denver, entered the season with the understanding that he was once again considered a stopgap until another younger man was considered ready for the job. So far in 1987, however, DeBerg had played well enough to keep the Bucs in playoff contention at the halfway point, relegating Vinny Testaverde to being a spectator except for a handful of garbage time snaps against Chicago in Week Two.

Late in the third quarter Jeff Smith scored on a three-yard run to give the Bucs a seemingly insurmountable 28–3 lead. The few remaining Cardinals fans let loose with a sarcastic standing ovation as Vinny Testaverde put aside his clipboard and began warming up on the sideline. With the game apparently well in hand, Perkins was prepared to let Testaverde gain a quarter of playing experience before heading home with a 5–3 record that would put the Bucs at the top of the NFC Wild Card race. Before that could happen Tampa Bay began a late-game unraveling for the third consecutive week that would solidify a spot for the Buccaneers in the annals of NFL history.

For three quarters the Bucs' linebacker corps had displayed all of their athletic gifts and ability. A duo of young pros, Winston Moss and Ervin Randle, combined with seasoned veterans Scot Brantley, Chris Washington and Jeff Davis flew around the field harassing Neil Lomax and disrupting the Cardinals' passing game. Lomax was sacked four times, including two by Washington and one by Moss. As the fourth quarter began those same linebackers played as though their legs were encased in cement and they were unsure of their assignments. Neil Lomax easily took advantage.

"The great Neil Lomax brought them back," scoffed Scot Brantley many years later.[15]

The freefall began with a fourth and one from the Tampa Bay 43-yard line just as the final quarter began. Cardinals tailback Stump Mitchell ran a pattern out of the backfield and easily outraced Scot Brantley into the open field. Lomax rifled the ball to Mitchell, who raced to the four-yard line before being tackled by safety Rick Woods. One play later, St. Louis tight end Rob Awalt broke away from both Brantley and cornerback Rod Jones to catch a scoring pass in the back of the end zone. The extra point made the score 28–10 with 12:42 to play, and Testaverde quickly put away the football and picked his clipboard up once again.

Two plays later the Bucs' offense added to the defense's woes when James Wilder fumbled after being hit hard by a St. Louis linebacker. The ball bounced straight into the arms of Niko Noga, and the St. Louis defender raced untouched 24 yards for the Cardinals' second touchdown in just one minute. The extra point cut the score to 28–17 and a sickening sense of "here we go again" began to spread along the Buccaneers bench.

"You wonder why you get in those kinds of predicaments," Brantley said while looking back at the Cardinals game. "But with those kinds of teams, it happens."[16]

With just over eleven minutes left to play, Ray Perkins' mindset was to depend on his ground attack to run as much time off the clock as possible. On first down a carry by Jeff Smith gained three yards but the play was undone by a holding penalty on back-up center Dan Turk, who had entered the game for starter Randy Grimes. The holding penalty did three painful things to Tampa Bay. First, it pushed the ball back ten yards to the Tampa Bay 13. Second, it put Perkins in a position where he had to call pass plays in order to regain the lost yardage and sustain the drive. And third, it stopped the clock, which only benefited the Cardinals.

Two incomplete passes and a three-yard loss on an attempted draw play forced the Bucs to punt after taking only a little over a minute off the clock. Punting from his own goal line, Frank Garcia didn't get off a good kick, and the Cardinals started from the Tampa Bay 39 with ten minutes to play. In just two minutes the Cardinals were down by only one score. Neil Lomax continued to capitalize on the Bucs' linebackers' inability to cover the tight end, completing three straight passes to Rob Awalt to move St. Louis to the 11-yard line. With their linebackers struggling to keep up with the St. Louis tight end, Tampa Bay's safeties became pre-occupied with Awalt. This put the Buccaneers' young and inexperienced cornerback duo of Rod Jones and Ricky Reynolds alone on the outside. When St. Louis receiver J.T. Smith cut inside of the corners, safeties Rick Woods and Bobby Kemp were caught out of position. Smith was all alone in the back of the end zone and his touchdown reception cut the score to 28–24 with 8:18 to play.

Tampa Bay caught a break on their next drive as the Cardinals committed two defensive fouls which provided the Bucs with 30 free yards. The two penalties moved the ball from Tampa Bay's own 15 to the 45-yard line. Two safe plays by Jeff Smith and James Wilder moved the ball to midfield, and the Bucs faced a crucial third down. If the Bucs could gain five yards, they would be able to run three more offensive plays and force the Cardinals to burn their three remaining time-outs. In typical fashion this day, the Bucs came up just short.

Steve DeBerg threw a screen pass to Wilder at the St. Louis 46, one yard shy of first down yardage. Wilder turned and was hit immediately by Cardinals defenders before he could gain the needed yard. Garcia punted away with the ball landing in the end zone, giving St. Louis a first down at their 20-yard line with 5:41 to play. Lomax needed just 3:41 to score yet again.

After a 23-yard pass to Don Holmes moved the ball into Tampa Bay territory, Lomax again looked for his tight end and for the second time in the quarter the suddenly mercurial Awalt outraced Scot Brantley. The 27-yard pass over the middle moved the ball to the Tampa Bay 19. A two-yard run by Earl Ferrell was followed by a pass to Don Holmes in the end zone. The receiver ran the same route that J.T. Smith had used to score on the previous drive. This time, however, Tampa Bay cornerback Ricky Reynolds was able to cut inside at the same time Holmes made his move and tipped the pass away. That left the Cardinals facing third down from the Tampa Bay 17.

Realizing that he would have no help from the safeties because they would be preoccupied with Awalt and any other receivers that might cross the middle, second-year Bucs cornerback Rod Jones lined up against J.T.

Smith alone. At the snap Smith took off for the end zone with Jones in pursuit, but the cornerback just wasn't fast enough, and the Cardinals receiver hauled in the pass in the back of the end zone for a 17-yard touchdown. The extra point was good, and the Cardinals, who had trailed by 25 points just ten minutes ago, were now ahead 31–28 as the two-minute warning sounded.

The Buccaneers stood in stunned disbelief on the sideline. For the third time in three weeks, they had squandered a large lead.

"Oh man, we couldn't close the deal," a still embarrassed Scot Brantley said.[17]

Defensive back Paul Tripoli didn't see much action other than special teams that day, but could still vividly recall the absolute bewilderment he and his teammates experienced over their collective inability to handle success.

"I wasn't playing so it was more frustrating than anything, because I thought I could make a difference," Tripoli said recently. "It was falling apart for us, and we didn't know what was going on."[18]

With a first down at their own eight-yard line, the Buccaneers attempted to salvage the game behind Steve DeBerg. Throwing underneath the St. Louis coverage, DeBerg was able to methodically move the ball down the field. Unfortunately, DeBerg was forced to trade time and timeouts in exchange for the incremental progress and with only ten seconds to play the Bucs were at the St. Louis 41. The situation presented Ray Perkins with a dilemma. With no timeouts left Perkins could have Donald Igwebuike attempt a 58-yard field goal, which was slightly outside the kicker's range, or he could try to gain as many yards as he could with a quick sideline pass hoping his receiver would be able to get out of bounds to stop the clock before time expired. The odds were not in his favor with either move. Perkins elected for one last pass. DeBerg dropped back and saw no Cardinals run out wide with James Wilder along the far sideline. DeBerg threw a quick pass that Wilder caught. The tailback immediately ran out of bounds at the St. Louis 35. This made the length of a potential game-tying field goal 53 yards, which was within the range of Igwebuike, a strong-legged kicker who had booted a field goal of 53 yards against Minnesota the year before and who enjoyed an accuracy rate of almost 50 percent on attempts over 50 yards.

With just five seconds to play Igwebuike put all of his leg into the kick, and it set off straight down the middle. As the ball got closer, many Buccaneers players started to jump up and down in joy as it appeared to be a successful attempt. Steve DeBerg, who held on the attempt, jumped up and put his arms over his head to mimic an official's signal of a good field goal. But at the last instant the ball started to fall and it hit squarely off the top of the crossbar and bounced backward.

No good.

The game was over. St. Louis 31, Tampa Bay 28.

DeBerg, who had held his arms over his head, quickly clasped both hands to the side of his helmet, looking much like Willem Dafoe's character in the motion picture *Platoon*. His teammates likewise displayed differing paroxysms of rage and despair. Defensive lineman Kevin Kellin raced after the ball when it bounced off the crossbar and picked it up, looking at it as though it was a disappointing child. With the ball in hand, Kellin began walking toward midfield in a slightly disoriented way. Ray Perkins walked stoically over to St. Louis head coach Gene Stallings to offer a handshake of congratulations and headed to the locker room, followed by a roster of Buccaneers who almost looked zombie-like.

It wasn't until they reached the locker room that the impact of what they had done sunk in. The atmosphere was funereal.

"I still can't believe the ball came up short," a crestfallen Igwebuike told reporters.[19]

"We were supposed to win," Kevin Kellin said after the game. "That's not the way this is supposed to end."[20]

Kellin couldn't have been more wrong. It was only natural the necessary team would lose in such a fashion and lay claim to a most remarkable record in the process.

The 25 point lead they lost in just over ten minutes of play represented the largest fourth quarter collapse in the history of the National Football League. It is a record of infamy that still stands to this day. In 1980 the San Francisco 49ers had come from 28 points behind to defeat the New Orleans Saints but had done so in 30 minutes of play, not 15. In 1992 the Buffalo Bills would rally from a 32-point deficit to defeat Houston in a playoff game but once again would have 30 minutes in which to do so. The New York Jets scored 30 points in a fourth quarter comeback against the Miami Dolphins in 2000 on Monday Night Football, but had only trailed by 23 points heading into that final stanza.

Those comebacks have survived in memory because of the circumstances surrounding the games. The 49ers' game was seen as the first example of Joe Montana's amazing ability to pull out victories in seemingly impossible situations. The Bills' comeback was seen by a national television audience during the playoffs and the Jets' fourth quarter miracle was likewise broadcast nationally on Monday night. While better known, those games rank behind what the Tampa Bay Buccaneers did, or didn't do depending on one's perspective, on November 8, 1987. Almost a quarter-century later the Buccaneers' loss to St. Louis is the measuring stick by which all other late game collapses are measured.

The next day the jokes began. So did the questions.

"Bucs Only Worth 3 Quarters," blared the headline of the *St. Petersburg Times*.

"Bucs Crumble," countered the *Tampa Tribune*.

The *Times*' headline would provide grist for a joke that would be heard on Tampa Bay airwaves all week. "What is a Buc worth?" went the opening query. "Three quarters," was the standard reply.

"If any Buc accepts more than three-fourths of his paycheck this week, it's stealing," wrote longtime *Times* columnist Hubert Mizell in his day after review. "Three quarters is all they played. Perhaps team owner Hugh Culverhouse should consider a franchise transfer to the National Hockey League ... where playing three periods is enough."[21]

The Buccaneers would never recover from that loss, dropping their final seven games to finish 4–11. Steve DeBerg would ultimately be supplanted by Vinny Testaverde, and veteran players such as Scot Brantley, Gerald Carter and Frank Garcia would be released.

Shortly after the Cardinals game some in the Tampa Bay area wondered if the Bucs players wearing down in the fourth quarter was due to the strenuous training camp Perkins had run back in July and August during the dog days of summer.

The difference between the Bucs' performance in the first three quarters and the final quarter was striking. Tampa Bay outscored its first three opponents after the strike 74–20 in quarters 1, 2 and 3. In the fourth quarter of those contests however, the tables were dramatically turned with the Bucs being outscored 55–3.

Hubert Mizell alluded to as much when he took the team to task in his column following the Cardinals game. "Perkins had counted on his steamy, man-eating summer training camp physically toughening the Bucs so they would not be prone to fourth-quarter collapses," wrote Mizell. "Instead, they're wilting."[22]

Ray Perkins responded to questions of physical conditioning in the same column. "I think it's very simple," Perkins told the press when asked about those late game struggles. "In the fourth quarter, we're either not in as good a shape as I think we are, or we don't have enough guts to suck up what we need to suck up."[23]

When asked more than twenty years later if he thought his training camp schedule wore out his players and led to their late game struggles, Ray Perkins was polite, but blunt in stating that it did not.

"There wasn't a connection," he said.[24]

Many within the organization agree with him.

"I think that was speculation," said Perkins's longtime assistant coach Richard Williamson when asked if the Bucs had dead legs.[25]

"That's a bit deceiving because we weren't out there very long," continued Williamson. "We were out in the morning for an hour and worked individually or as a team. Then we'd go out about noon for an hour. Then late in the afternoon we'd go out for an hour and a half.[26]

"It wasn't the fact that you were on the field for a long time," Williamson stated. "It was just the way he [Perkins] had of trying to beat the heat. The biggest part was you'd have to take three or four showers a day. That was the hardest part. There was a lot of dressing and undressing and showering and drying off, but other than that you weren't beat up out there. Plus you weren't out in the sun nearly as much that way. You'd be out for three and a half hours, but it was spread over three times."[27]

While some players may not agree that they weren't beat up during training camp—Gerald Carter admitted he survived camp "by the grace of God"—events that transpired in the fall make it unlikely the effects of summer training had anything to do with the loss to the Cardinals. Former Buccaneers receiver Mark Carrier probably explained it best when he recalled his rookie season.

"You have to understand also that my rookie season we had the strike," Carrier said of the 24-day work stoppage. "It came right after training camp. Everybody was tired at the end of training camp, but we had the opportunity once the strike came to in essence regain ourselves and rest a little bit. But it did make for a long season because of the roller coaster of three-a-day practices and going through a strike."[28]

So what was the cause of the late-game collapse against St. Louis if not fatigue?

It can be argued that the Buccaneers were undone in that game by inexperienced and inexpensive players that were friendly to Culverhouse's bottom line. Many of the players on the defensive roster for that game were either in their first or second season and had yet to learn what it took to win in the NFL or were cast-off veterans with middling at best pedigrees. Young defensive backs Ricky Reynolds and Rod Jones gave up touchdowns against the Cardinals, but they were not helped much in the secondary by safeties Rick Woods and Bobby Kemp. Woods and Kemp were pre-season pick-ups in 1987 that never played a down of NFL football after being released following the season. In addition to Woods and Kemp, Mike Stensrud, Tyrone Keys and Don Anderson were other players who joined the Bucs' defense from other NFL rosters in 1987 that were out of football within a year.

"I think the biggest thing that caused us not to be successful as we could have been was when Coach Perkins came in he brought a lot of new guys and there was a lot of rebuilding," surmised Mark Carrier, one of Perkins' top draft finds. "Throughout his entire time there, there was a constant rebuilding. With a lot of young guys playing, that experience factor wasn't there. We just never as an overall team matured quick enough."[29]

The record-setting collapse in St. Louis portended what was to come during Perkins's regime. There would be many memorable collapses although none would reach the magnitude of the unprecedented contest in St. Louis. A theme would emerge during these collapses of young players or inexpensive veterans being victimized in key situations. In each case those games would erode Tampa Bay's confidence and lead to season-long tailspins.

In 1988, again against the Cardinals, the Bucs held a 24–23 lead late in the fourth quarter at Tampa Stadium. A week after a 13–10 win at Green Bay, the Bucs had a chance to move to 2–1 early in the season. For the second year in a row the Bucs couldn't cover Cardinals tight ends when it counted and Jay Novacek caught a 42-yard touchdown pass from Cliff Stoudt in the final moments as Tampa Bay lost 30–24. On the play the Cardinals caught the young Bucs defense in a shift. Only three Buccaneers defenders dropped into pass coverage against four Cardinals receivers. Novacek happened to be the one left all alone and by the time the Bucs' secondary realized it, he was catching the ball at the goal line. The loss spawned a streak that saw Tampa Bay lose eight out of ten contests to finish 5–11.

In 1989, second-year nickelback Donnie Elder was called for defensive holding just as it appeared the Bucs were about to defeat the San Francisco 49ers. The call came on a failed 3rd down pass attempt by Montana. Given new life, Montana scored on a roll-out moments later to provide the winning margin in a 20–16 contest. Just a month after losing to Montana on that quarterback keeper, the Bucs stood at 3–2 and were poised to tie Minnesota for first place in the NFC Central. Leading the winless Detroit Lions 16–10 the Buccaneers' defense surrendered a 76-yard drive in the final two minutes culminating in Lions quarterback Rodney Peete's 5-yard touchdown run on fourth and goal with 23 seconds to play. Peete's rollout looked eerily similar to the one Montana had run weeks before. On the play second-year left defensive end Rueben Davis rushed and got caught inside, leaving a wide swath of ground for Peete to use on the way to the end zone. The last-second loss was the start of a five game losing streak which led to a second consecutive 5–11 finish.

In 1990 the Buccaneers entered Week Seven with a 4–2 record and the opportunity to solidify their Wild Card positioning against the 2–4 Dallas Cowboys. The week before the game Rick Odioso had dinner with Perkins and both men agreed that it looked as though the Buccaneers were finally ready for a playoff push.

"We were 4–2, and we just came off a good win against Green Bay," Odioso recalled. "We were looking ahead and thinking playoffs. Everything was right in the world, as right as it had been in the Buccaneer world for a long time. Vinny Testaverde was finally getting it, the defense was playing pretty good, and it looked like we had gotten over the hump. Then the Cowboys beat us in diabolical fashion."[30]

The Buccaneers kicked a field goal with two minutes to play in the fourth quarter of a hard fought contest at Tampa Stadium. Trailing 13–10, Cowboys quarterback Troy Aikman engineered what became the first of many miraculous end-of-game heroics when he hit wide receiver Michael Irvin with a 28-yard touchdown pass with just 31 seconds to play in a 17–13 Dallas victory. On the play second-year cornerback Rodney Rice, a pick-up from New England in his first year with the Bucs, prematurely released coverage, thinking safety Mark Robinson was farther outside on Irvin. As Irvin celebrated his touchdown, Rice and Robinson were left to debate in the end zone which of them should have covered the Cowboys' receiver.

"I was in the end zone in front of Irvin when he caught the winning pass," Odioso said. "Then things fell apart and by Thanksgiving Perkins was fired."[31]

The loss to Dallas instigated a five game losing streak for Tampa Bay. By the time the Bucs righted the ship, defeating Atlanta 23–17 in Week Thirteen, it was too late for Perkins. Culverhouse terminated the man he had referred to as "my Vince Lombardi" just four years earlier.

To further put to rest any connection between Perkins' training camp and late-game fatigue, the previous collapses occurred during seasons in which the Buccaneers' training camp was much less strenuous than the 1987 version. Perkins never again did a three-a-day schedule, at least not as consistently as during his initial training camp.

"As the years went by, they may have been on the tough side of training camp, but not as brutal in subsequent years," admitted Odioso.[32]

In addition to the infamous collapses, inexperience played a large role in many of the Buccaneers' other 41 defeats under Ray Perkins. The young defense was the counterpoint to a young offense led by Vinny Testaverde, who threw a NFL record 35 interceptions in 1988. The growing pains of Testaverde led to many defeats in 1988 and 1989. One such game was a 1989 contest against the Cleveland Browns in which Testaverde had back-to-back passes intercepted and returned for touchdowns. Those 14 points proved the difference in a 42–31 loss. In addition to the growing pains of the passing attack, which featured four players (Testaverde, Carrier, Ron Hall and Bruce Hill) with less than four years experience, the Buccaneers' offensive backfield also shifted personnel often. In 1987 Jeff Smith and James Wilder were the primary ball carriers. In 1988 and 1989 it became Lars Tate and William Howard. In 1990, Reggie Cobb, Bruce Perkins and Gary Anderson joined the backfield. With almost every personnel move the Buccaneers' skill players got younger and younger. This led to a lack of continuity and offensive execution suffered.

What going with younger players took away from the playing field was more than made up for on the balance sheet. The problem for Ray Perkins, as it was the problem for John McKay and Leeman Bennett before him, was that the Buccaneers' payroll budget was restrictive in comparison to many other NFL franchises. In an era without a league-mandated salary cap, the Buccaneers operated under a Hugh Culverhouse-mandated cap. This was the result of Culverhouse's propensity to operate the Buccaneers with his priorities somewhat unequally divided between on-field success and the ledgers of his many business interests.

Culverhouse's love of deal-making continued to be insatiable. The Bucs owner would often wake up at 4:30 in the morning and work at his office until well past sunset. Any question whether the Bucs or his business empire came first was answered on the day of the Bucs' first pre-season game in 1976. The morning of the Bucs' game against the Rams at the Los Angeles Memorial Coliseum, Culverhouse rose early and attended a board meeting of Host International before conducting numerous business calls from his hotel suite. He did manage to squeeze in the Bucs' 26–3 loss to the Rams before flying back with the team.[33]

He was known to turn almost any casual conversation into a sales pitch. In the early 1980s Paul Stewart founded a British-based fan club of the Tampa Bay Buccaneers named Bucs UK. In 1988 Stewart made his first trip to Tampa Stadium and was made a guest on the sidelines by head coach Ray Perkins. During a brief encounter with Culverhouse, Stewart recalled being pumped for information by the Bucs owner.

"I only met Hugh Culverhouse one time during my first visit to Tampa in 1988," explained Stewart. "He appreciated the support for the franchise from across the Atlantic, but I always had the impression he was trying to work out if it could be financially successful to him. In those pre–Internet days, a group of at the time 20 to 30 fans in Great Britain were nothing more than a novelty so he moved on to more profitable conversations."[34]

The man who engaged in numerous profit-oriented conversations and oversaw Culverhouse's growing real estate empire was Stephen Story. Story, who eventually became his law partner, sometimes worked out of an office at One Buccaneer Place and was charged with making sure Culverhouse stayed liquid. One of the ways Story did this was by transferring funds from one entity to another. At the center of those entities was the cash cow Tampa Bay Buccaneers.

"I was more a money guy, even with no title, probably since the early 1980's," Story said. "I controlled all the cash flow for all the entities. In other words, I would give people budgets. In those years we were forced to use a lot of the operating income in our real estate ventures, probably one of the reasons we weren't real successful. You have profits in one entity and losses in another. You move the cash where you need it. That was done throughout the 1980's and 1990's. It was really cash flow needs, it wasn't necessarily losses. Cash flow as needed for various investments."[35]

The diverting of the Buccaneers' cash flow to other interests earned Culverhouse a reputation as a miser among some NFL owners.

"We couldn't conceive of anybody doing what Hugh would do and not put the best team on the field you could," said Steve Rosenbloom, son of Rams owner Carroll Rosenbloom. "The quest was to get the best players at any cost. Hugh's approach was kind of a novel approach. I would say most owners weren't squirreling it away. It appears his bottom line wasn't wins and losses but how much money could be put aside. The people in Tampa were cheated."[36]

In the interest of fairness, many NFL owners of that era were accused of running their franchises on the cheap including Art Modell in Cleveland, Georgia Frontiere in Los Angeles and Rankin Smith in Atlanta. Rick Odioso also argued that while Culverhouse was cheap in some areas, including personnel, he wasn't above paying above market if he felt the Buccaneers truly needed the acquisition.

"He wanted to win; he did sign some big contracts," Odioso argued. "When he signed Gary Anderson to a deal, that was a huge contract. The coaching contract he gave Ray Perkins was one of the biggest at the time, maybe the biggest. Testaverde's contract was huge. He would lay out good-sized money if he thought it had to do with winning, but he was always looking to cut costs around the edges.[37]

"I think if he was convinced it would help us win, he'd spend the money," Odioso continued. "I don't think he thought whether an employee made $27,000 or $31,000 had anything to do with us winning. I don't think there were that many lack of money issues that prevented us from having personnel that could win football games. We might have cut corners on the food players got in training camp or something might not have been as good."[38]

As head coach, Ray Perkins took the brunt of criticism for personnel decisions. Many years later he stated that the criticism didn't bother him, but it was unfounded because his was not the final say on how the organization was run or on how much of a personnel budget was allowed.

"I was the head coach, period. That was the job I took," Perkins said when explaining the organizational structure of the Bucs. "Krueger was the contract guy, bean counter if you will, for Mr. Culverhouse. I was involved in all the trades and drafts. I was very actively involved in all that.[39]

"If it was something kind of big it would go through Krueger to Mr. Culverhouse to get the final OK," Perkins continued. "If it was something of significance, I'd try to have enough respect for Mr. C as owner to run things by him.[40]

"You are talking about a guy who is a businessman whose expertise in football is very, very minute," said Perkins, who nevertheless admired his boss. "He was a great man. I really liked him a lot. He was a really fine businessman, but a football man he was not."[41]

To his credit, Ray Perkins refuses to lay any blame for the failures of the Buccaneers during his time as coach at the feet of Hugh Culverhouse. The Buccaneers had their share of bad draft choices. The 1987 draft class was excellent and the 1988 draft brought in stellar offensive lineman Paul Gruber and solid contributors Lars Tate, Robert Goff, John Bruhin, Shawn Lee and Reuben Davis. After 1988 however, the team misfired on draft day time after time. First round choices Broderick Thomas, Keith McCants and Charles McRae never panned out. A controversial decision to trade a number one draft choice to Indianapolis for quarterback Chris Chandler did little except to introduce a divisive quarterback controversy in 1990. Perkins admits the failure in these circumstances was his and not Culverhouse's.

"We got some good draft choices and then I would say I could have done a better job from a draft standpoint being involved as much as I was," Perkins said. "We missed on two or three guys that hurt us, in my opinion. Overall, the four years that I was there I just did not do a good enough job to get us where we needed to go, bottom line."[42]

The Buccaneers' payroll budget precluded bringing in veterans with a track record of success as situational back-ups. A comparison between the Buccaneers and the San Francisco 49ers and New York Giants may arguably be unfair, but it is telling. When the 49ers needed an additional linebacker in 1989, they signed Pro Bowl linebacker Matt Millen off the waiver wire. When the New York Giants needed running back depth in the mid–1980s, they traded for Pro Bowler Ottis Anderson. Both Millen and Anderson would play vital roles in winning Super Bowls for their respective teams. In comparison, the Buccaneers filled their need for linebacker and running back depth with the signings of Pete Najarian and Cliff Austin respectively. While Najarian and Austin did their best, the depth they provided paled in comparison to Millen and Anderson. When Najarian and Austin were ultimately released by Tampa Bay, they never set foot on an NFL field again.

In addition to not blaming budgetary constraints for his struggles, Ray Perkins also does not want to insinuate the contributions of players such as Rick Woods, Bobby Kemp, Cliff Austin, Pete Najarian or any other veteran pick-up were not appreciated by him. While these cost-conscious signings didn't lead to victories, Perkins is adamant that the players should be recognized for giving their all to the Tampa Bay Buccaneers and the head coach alone should be made responsible for the won-loss record.

"I don't want to chalk anything up to anything except I didn't get the job done," Perkins said. "I'm not blaming anybody. We had a lot of good

Ray Perkins shares a laugh with his team on the sidelines. Smiles were in short supply during Perkins' four seasons in Tampa Bay. Despite improving the talent level and competitiveness of the Buccaneers, Perkins was unable to post a winning record in Tampa Bay and was dismissed before the end of the 1990 season after posting a 19–41 record (*Tampa Tribune*, courtesy Tampa Bay Buccaneers).

players. Am I saying we had enough good players? Probably not. But we had a lot of good players that gave everything they had and were dedicated people. We had some really great coaches in my mind. I just didn't get the job done. Period."[43]

Ray Perkins' stay in Tampa Bay was tumultuous. A stern disciplinarian, Perkins was a hard man to read by those who played for him.

"He is very old school, very strict, kind of aloof," said Paul Tripoli, who played for Perkins at both the University of Alabama and Tampa Bay. "I knew him better than 95 percent of the kids on the Bucs, and I could never get real close to him. He was just very business-like and a hard worker."[44]

Perkins' passion for football boiled over at halftime of a 1987 game with the New Orleans Saints. During the intermission, offensive tackle Ron Heller and Perkins came to blows when the coach thought he heard the tackle tell his teammates to quit. The sight of their head coach in a physical confrontation with a teammate shook up the Bucs.

"I was going down on kickoff after halftime," recalled Tripoli. "I'm thinking, 'What did Perk do? Why did he do that?' It wasn't motivating to me at all."[45]

Perkins also didn't enjoy a particularly positive relationship with the Tampa Bay media. Press conferences at times could be testy and the general perception of Perkins as portrayed in the media made him a fan target. The nadir of Perkins's time in Tampa occurred when a fan boycott during a 1990 home game against Atlanta, complete with "Jerk the Perk" signs, presaged his termination the following day.

A final record of 19–41 overshadows the fact that Ray Perkins did vastly improve the talent level of the Buccaneers compared to the end of the McKay and Bennett regimes. While the losses were too much to overcome, Perkins did lead the Bucs to their first-ever season sweep of the Chicago Bears in 1989 and an upset of the burgeoning Buffalo Bills dynasty in 1988. Lost to history is also the fact that Perkins oversaw the best Buccaneers team of the 1980's in terms of winning percentage. Despite a tenure marked by turmoil and collapse, a team Perkins coached won 67 percent of its games, the best performance of any Tampa Bay team until Tony Dungy's 1999 Bucs won 68 percent of their contests.

As was the case with much of the NFL in the 1980s, Perkins' winning mark came as a direct result of Hugh Culverhouse's role as the most necessary man in the NFL.

CHAPTER ELEVEN

Strike Two: The B-Bucs

FOR THE SECOND TIME IN five years the National Football League Players Association staged a work stoppage following Week Two of the season. Less than 48 hours after their 20–3 setback at Soldier Field to the Chicago Bears, Buccaneers players were walking a picket line. The unresolved issues that prompted the walkout could be summed up in two words: free agency.

Free agency had been sought by NFL players for more than a decade. For a brief time in the late 1970s players had been awarded the right to offer their services on the open market by the courts. In the landmark Mackey vs. NFL decision of 1975, players had seen the Rozelle Rule deemed a violation of anti-trust laws, effectively ending the practice of the reserve clause. The NFL had appealed the decision, and while the appellate court had also found in favor of Mackey, it also stated that the reserve clause could be reinstated if it was agreed to in collective bargaining. Just two years after winning the right to move from team to team without requiring compensatory draft picks, the NFLPA bargained it away.

During the labor contract negotiations of 1977, NFLPA executive director Ed Garvey signed away the players' rights to free agency and agreed to the return of the Rozelle Rule in exchange for recognition of the NFLPA as the sole representative of the players and the right to collect dues from players who did not agree to NFLPA representation. Other cash considerations were granted to the NFLPA totaling more than $100 million over the five-year life of the labor agreement which expired in 1982.[1]

Bargaining away free agency in 1977 and being on the losing side of the 1982 strike had weakened Ed Garvey considerably and by 1987 he was out of the NFLPA altogether. Garvey was replaced as head of the NFLPA by Gene

Upshaw, a Hall of Fame offensive lineman for the Oakland Raiders from 1967 to 1981. Upshaw, while known as an intimidating, dominating presence on Oakland's championship teams, brought a more professional, player-oriented approach to the negotiations, recalled Jack Donlan.

"Gene was far more personable than Ed," Donlan said. "He knew the real player issues because he had been a player for so long. Gene had gone through those issues and knew how to respond. Gene was respected by his membership, and he was respected by the owners. The negotiations, I felt, were more professional."[2]

After the 1982 negotiations, Donlan had been retained in his role as chief negotiator by Hugh Culverhouse. Donlan remembered being approached directly by Culverhouse about staying on. "I had signed a three-year agreement in 1980," Donlan said. "So after the 1982 negotiations my contract was running out. He and I had a long conversation about whether or not I would renew my contract."[3]

Realizing that a second work stoppage in 1987 could be a distinct possibility, Culverhouse wanted to make sure he had Donlan's skill at hard negotiating at the table. This was especially important because, unlike 1982, the Tampa Bay owner would be much more of a public face during any possible strike.

During the 1982 strike, Culverhouse had played a key role in the owners' strategy by obtaining a line of credit for his fellow owners. That role was largely behind the scenes and didn't garner him much attention, but it made an impression on his fellow owners. One of the few times he became a public face for the league's point of view was towards the end of the 1982 battle. Culverhouse's financial summation before reporters undercut the NFLPA's remaining resolve right before the 57-day work stoppage ended. The performance made him a natural to succeed Billy Sullivan as the chair of the NFL Management Council.

"We had come out of the 1982 strike and all the money issues had been resolved because of his dealings," Donlan said of how Culverhouse worked to keep the league solid financially when that season's games were cancelled.[4] As a result of his work, Culverhouse was elected to chair the league's most powerful committee. "The six members are elected by the total group of 28 owners," Donlan explained of how the management council is staffed. "Then those six get together among themselves and decide who should be chairman."[5]

As chairman, Culverhouse had a powerful platform to fight against the imposition of free agency. Perhaps more so than just about any other owner, he was fearful of the impact free agency would have on the revenue source his Tampa Bay Buccaneers had become.

Free agency was growing in professional sports. Professional baseball and basketball players enjoyed some measure of free agency in 1987, but the National Football League continued to operate under the reserve clause. Jack Donlan's view was that the 28 NFL owners wanted to keep it that way when the contentious collective bargaining agreement from 1982 expired five years later.

"In 1987 I would say the sense of the owners was they did not want free agency," Donlan said. "They conveyed that to the management council, and that group conveyed it to me and my staff."[6]

During talks with the NFLPA negotiating committee, Donlan and his staff explored the possibility of adopting a similar form of free agency to one employed by the National Basketball Association. The NBA version of free agency involved committing rookie draft choices to their team for a set period of years before free agency began. More importantly, the NBA version maintained a competitive balance by imposing a salary cap on teams so that large market franchises couldn't corner the market on top talent at the expense of small market clubs. During those discussions, Donlan was informed that the owners didn't like the NBA plan because of two issues.

First, the NBA salary cap posed a problem for low revenue franchise owners. In addition to a cap, the NBA salary structure imposed a salary floor as well. Basketball owners were required to commit a minimum dollar amount annually towards payroll. Some NFL owners, particularly Culverhouse, didn't want a league mandated minimum, especially if it was more than Culverhouse normally paid.

The second issue was the NFLPA's demand that carried over from 1982 that 60 percent of the gross adjusted revenues of each team go towards salaries. That 60 percent would lead to a salary floor which would exceed what Culverhouse and many other owners wished to pay.

"We spent a lot of time looking at what I call the basketball system," Donlan said in summarizing the owners' point of contention. "Basketball had a system not unlike what football is today. A player can become a free agent after so many years, and there would be a salary cap. We kind of saw that more as a floor. When you talk about adjusted gross revenues, some things are negotiated out like loge boxes and things like that. Whatever the percentage is, when you take all the clubs' adjusted gross revenues, and you say 60 percent goes to the union, one of the issues is that every club has that responsibility.[7]

"That amount is 1/28th of the average," Donlan continued, laying out the math behind the disagreement. "So if you are a low revenue club, that 60 percent may represent 70 percent of your revenue. If you are a high revenue club, you may only be paying 50 percent of your revenue. So now you've got two football teams paying the identical amount of money with significantly different impacts on those teams based on what their revenues are."[8]

Throughout the majority of the 1980s, Hugh Culverhouse's Tampa Bay Buccaneers had been a high revenue club. If the NFL adopted the NBA form of free agency, Culverhouse's contribution to salary would have been less of a burden on his team's bottom line than on others according to Donlan's math. However, Culverhouse remained adamantly opposed to free agency for a very basic reason according to his son.

"He was against the salary cap because the floor was about $12 million above what he wanted to pay," said Hugh Jr.[9]

Culverhouse was not raised in affluence. The Alabama native grew up in modest surroundings and had attained his current level of wealth through hard work, calculated risk and iron will.

"People think we grew up wealthy," said Hugh Jr. "That's a canard and false. My dad went to Alabama on a boxing scholarship. If he hadn't, he wouldn't have gone to college. Dad put himself through law school by teaching accounting at the undergraduate level."[10]

Hugh Jr. recalled that following his military service and tenure in the Alabama attorney general's office, his father decided his future did not lie in politics. Instead, Culverhouse made the decision to enter into a whole new field of endeavor, the world of tax law. In order to learn more about taxes, he uprooted his family from their native land and took a much less lucrative position with the Internal Revenue Service. It was a major gamble. Culverhouse was giving up a prestigious job, high salary and family ties in exchange for mundane work, low pay and a long climb to attain a position comparable to what he was leaving behind.

"Dad decided the future for him was taxes," Hugh Jr. said. "He moved his family to Cincinnati. We lived in a mixed race government tenement. His salary was $3,900, down from $15,000 in Alabama."[11]

As the years went by Culverhouse's gamble paid off in abundance. By 1987 he was one of the nation's wealthiest men and the pre-eminent tax attorney of his time. The Tampa Bay owner had no intention of losing any percentage of his hard-earned wealth to the NFLPA's salary demands. Instead, he upped the stakes in his long-running war against the union.

"I can tell you what he did," recalled Hugh Jr. "He spent literally half the year in New York in the Regency Hotel. He was virtually full-time, and I would talk to him. I don't have a specific recollection, but there was no question he wanted to break the back of the union."[12]

When asked if his father had the ear of Jack Donlan during negotiations, Hugh Jr. answered quite strongly. "I would say it extended far beyond ear," he said. "Jack did what Dad said. There is no question about that."[13]

In 1982 Culverhouse had been instrumental in providing the financial resources his fellow owners had needed to win a 57-day war of attrition with the NFLPA. In 1987, as chair of the NFL Management Council, he finalized the use of a weapon that he and many others, including Dallas Cowboys president Tex Schramm, felt would crush the spirit of the union: scab players.

"If he didn't think of the scabs, the moment it was mentioned he thought it was brilliant," Hugh Jr. said.[14]

The thought of hiring replacement players, a much more palatable term than scab players, had first been broached during the 1982 strike only to be vetoed by Commissioner Pete Rozelle said Jack Donlan.

"When it became apparent that a strike was a good possibility, there were very many unresolved issues," said Donlan about 1982. "We had a talk about whether we should shut down or whether we would try to play. Pete Rozelle was very strong on the issue of not playing, and he argued very forcefully that if there was a strike, we should shut down. I really never got a sense one way or the other how strongly the management council felt. I think the results of what happened in 1982 led the management council to recommend in 1987 that we play through."[15]

As far back as April of that season, it began to leak out that should the NFLPA walk out on strike, the 28 NFL teams would field squads of replacement players to carry on the season so that no scheduled games would be missed. These teams would be stocked with players not under contract to any team whether they were cast-off veterans or inexperienced rookies that had failed to make a final roster. Ironically, these replacements would technically be free agents who could sign with any franchise should a walk-out occur. However, they were not the high-priced free agents the NFLPA desired or the owners feared. In addition to the replacements, the owners agreed to allow any current NFL player under contract who wished to cross the picket line a position on a replacement roster.

On September 22 the players walked, announcing their strike at the conclusion of a *Monday Night Football* game between the New England Patriots and New York Jets. Within hours coaches and general managers around the NFL began making phone calls to assemble rosters. The NFL Management Council, with Culverhouse as chair, elected to cancel the Week Three slate of games and resume play with replacement players during Week Four.

In addition to the irony of bringing in free agent replacement players, Culverhouse and the management council set a wage scale. Rookies would earn a minimum of $50,000 for the season while those with NFL experience could earn more.[16] No doubt this salary structure was more to Culverhouse's liking than the one being debated in New York by the two negotiating committees.

Shortly after the strike began Culverhouse met with reporters to offer the management perspective on the issues. As he had in 1982, he treated the press conference in a manner more befitting a trial. "Ladies and gentleman of the jury," Culverhouse quipped as he began his remarks, "I plead guilty by reason of insanity, but not my own."[17]

He made it clear during his remarks that the NFLPA was solely responsible for the work stoppage. Citing comments by NFLPA president and Tampa Bay Buccaneers offensive lineman Marvin Powell, Culverhouse claimed the NFLPA was guilty of a power-grab far beyond what any reasonable businessman should be expected to tolerate.

"Their president, Powell, said he wants control of the game," he said. "Well, we're not giving up control of the game and we're not giving up free agency."[18]

He also touched on the topic of replacement players, stating that the NFL season would continue with replacement players, all the way to the Super Bowl if need be. Unlike 1982, he promised, fans would not have to spend fall Sundays without NFL action.

According to the *St. Petersburg Times*, Culverhouse's message was clear: "Don't blame the owners, come watch the B teams and get ready for a 15-game season."[19]

Ray Perkins was one of those getting ready for the season.

At One Buccaneer Place, Ray Perkins arrived for work realizing that all the effort he had put in over the previous eight months re-shaping the Buccaneers roster was temporarily worthless. Now, with less than two weeks to prepare for a road game against division rival Detroit, Perkins was faced with teaching a new crop of players the pro game from the ground up.

"Not fun," said Perkins when asked what the atmosphere was like at the team headquarters.[20] Compounding Perkins's frustration over rebuilding a roster was the fact he disagreed with the strike in the first place.

"I'm not sure I can explain what it was like," Perkins said. "It wasn't a lot of fun I can tell you that. I resented it on the players' part because I look at the NFL, I look at college, and I look at the game of football as a great, great opportunity for any young man. I know that it is the livelihood of a lot of people when you get to the pros. I understand that and have an appreciation for that. But to go on strike? This happened to me in New York as well. I resented the players for actually going on strike because this is our game, this is the fans' game. I took it kind of personal."[21]

As chair of the NFL Management Council, it would benefit Culverhouse to field one of the stronger replacement teams. If the replacement team won games, the Tampa Bay fans would throw their support behind the fill-ins and severely undercut any support the strikers would have. When training camp began, it appeared the Bucs were attempting to get a head start on acquiring replacement talent for just such a reason. During training camp the Buccaneers had invited more than 100 players in an attempt to re-shape their roster. According to Perkins and Phil Krueger, this was not done with an eye on a possible strike, but with an eye on leaving no stone unturned in an attempt to increase the talent level. However, a side benefit was a large pool of players that would be trained in the offensive and defensive system of the Tampa Bay Buccaneers. When the players did walk out, the Buccaneers front office placed numerous calls to players that had been cut at the end of training camp when the final 45-man roster had been set.

One of the first calls went to a former player of Perkins' at the University of Alabama whom he had cut at the end of the 1987 training camp. Defensive back Paul Tripoli was across Tampa Bay in Pinellas County when he answered the call and remembers the conversation vividly.

"I was working for a friend of mine moving furniture in New Port Richey," said Tripoli. "My wife and my little baby and I lived with my dad in Largo. Coach Perkins called me up before the strike and said, 'Are you ready? We might need you for the Chicago Bear game coming up.' I said, 'Yeah, I'm ready.' But he didn't call me.[22]

"They went on strike the next week," Tripoli continued. "I had been in training camp to the final cut and could play all four secondary positions: corners, free safety and strong safety. Perkins called me up and told me about the replacement games, and I jumped at it."[23]

When asked if he had any qualms about crossing a picket line manned by men with whom he had gone through training camp, Tripoli stated he couldn't afford the luxury of a moral dilemma. "It wasn't difficult to make the decision to cross, not when you have to feed your wife and little girl," Tripoli said. "I just wanted the chance to show what I could do."[24]

In addition to Tripoli, other members of the replacement team roster who had spent time in Tampa Bay's 1987 training camp were linebacker Brian Gant, wide receiver Eric Streater and running back Dan Land. Training camp cut-down victims weren't the only avenue the Buccaneers explored; the Tampa Bay coaching staff also made use of their extensive network of contacts at the college level to turn up many players, including a prospective quarterback.

Prior to 1987 Mike Hold had pursued his football dream in a variety of leagues and capacities. When the Buccaneers found him he was back at his alma mater attempting to start a coaching career.

"I was a free agent with the Denver Broncos out of college," said Hold, a graduate of the University of South Carolina. "I went to part of training camp but never made it to the pre-season in 1986. I played a year of Arena Football in the summer of 1987 and went back to South Carolina as a graduate assistant. One of the USC assistants knew someone on the Bucs staff, and that is how my name came up. The next thing you knew, I was in Tampa."[25]

Much like Paul Tripoli, Hold had no reservations about crossing a picket line to play in the NFL because he wanted a chance to continue his dream of professional football.

"Some people wouldn't classify it as the NFL," Hold said. "There were a lot of people pissed off over this. The feeling that I had at that time was this is my dream. I understood the players' position but had I not played, I would have never had that shot. It was just one of those things where I said I'm going to do it and hope that it all goes well."[26]

Dreamers, romantics and idealists wouldn't be enough to win NFL games, even those of a replacement nature. Unlike the 1982 strike, the solidarity of the NFLPA was weak. Veteran players such as Gary Hogeboom of the Indianapolis Colts, Randy White and Ed "Too Tall" Jones of the Dallas Cowboys, Mark Gastineau of the New York Jets and several members of the St. Louis Cardinals all agreed to cross the line and play with the replacement teams. Tampa Bay, in contrast, was unified without any veterans crossing during the first week of the strike. In order to provide his replacement team with any semblance of veteran leadership, Culverhouse agreed to turn to a group of players whom he had once despised: members of the now defunct Tampa Bay Bandits.

The Bandits had gone belly-up two years earlier with the demise of the United States Football League. Some Bandits alumni had made it onto NFL rosters, most notably tailback Gary Anderson, who had become an effective weapon for the San Diego Chargers. For the most part, however, members of the Bandits had vanished from football and gone on with their lives.

That is until October of 1987 when the Tampa Bay Buccaneers called and offered them a chance to return to work at Tampa Stadium. All in all, a total of 17 Bandits joined the Buccaneers, headlined by former quarterback John Reaves. Reaves had been a number one draft choice of the Philadelphia Eagles and played 10 years in the NFL before joining the Bandits and becoming one of the most prolific passers in the USFL. In addition to Reaves, other Bandits joining the Buccaneers were running back Greg Boone, guard Rufus Brown, defensive tackle Fred Nordgren, center Chuck Pitcock, defensive back Jeff George and linebacker Sankar Montoute. Of the former Bandits, Montoute may have had the most compelling journey to the NFL.

"I think I am the only St. Leo player to make it to the NFL," Montoute said proudly.[27]

A native of Trinidad, Montoute had moved to the United States when he was eleven. A star basketball player in New York, Montoute was recruited to play for St. John's Military Academy in Wisconsin. While at St. John's, Montoute also picked up the game of football and played at a high enough level that he was offered a scholarship at the University of Wisconsin.

Montoute had difficulty making the adjustment to university coursework and transferred to St. Leo, a small college just north of Tampa in Pasco

County. With no football program, Montoute returned to basketball at St. Leo. After completing his time at St. Leo, Montoute tried his hand at football one more time, trying out for the Kansas City Chiefs. After failing to make the roster in Kansas City, Montoute returned to his adopted hometown of Tampa just in time to catch on with the Tampa Bay Bandits for their final season.

"My path was not typical," Montoute said of his route to the Bandits. "I wasn't well known so having proven myself to a coach like Steve Spurrier and him having faith in my ability was kind of my saving grace. I always knew because of my athletic ability I could do it. I was always very fast and had good range, I just needed experience."[28]

Montoute got that with the Bandits, playing the 1985 season at linebacker. His time with the Bandits convinced Montoute that he had the ability to play professionally, and he hoped that when Leeman Bennett was terminated by the Bucs in 1986 that the rumors about his former Bandits coach being hired by Culverhouse would prove true.

"Had he [Spurrier] gotten the Bucs' job I might have been retiring from the NFL after 14 or 15 years," Montoute said. "I truly believe that. You know if you've been around the game long enough there are a lot of players that can play the game and just need the right opportunity."[29]

Spurrier was not hired by the Bucs, so Montoute headed to the Canadian Football League. His time in Canada was not particularly memorable, but Montoute felt he benefited from his additional playing experience and the great timing of his release.

"After the USFL folded I went up to Edmonton and they traded me to Calgary," Montoute said. "I stayed in Calgary for maybe two or three games. I was released by them, but that was right when the NFL went on strike."[30]

Montoute also had no reservations about crossing the picket line. This was his best chance yet to make a living at football, and he intended to make the most of it. "I had no regular job," Montoute said. "I could make a couple of grand in a few weeks. When you have a family to take care of and bills to pay I didn't care that anybody else didn't respect what I was doing."[31]

The collection of rookies, cast-offs and veterans of the USFL that now constituted the Tampa Bay Buccaneers reported to One Buccaneer Place on Wednesday, September 23. Referred to by the local media as the B-Bucs, the replacement players were greeted with a smattering of snide comments and insults by the regular players walking the picket line nearby. The Buccaneers regulars didn't directly confront the B-Bucs and that set them apart from some notorious displays in other NFL cities.

An instance outside the Colts facility in Indianapolis was quickly making the rounds. A busload of replacement players was confronted by 100 members of the AFL-CIO and regular Colts players while in Denver eggs were thrown on cars in the parking lot by picketers.[32] In strong union cities such as Philadelphia, Detroit and Cleveland, striking players were supported by large labor unions. By comparison, the Bucs regulars were tame and that made life a little easier for the B-Bucs.

"I don't recall that we had to deal with picketers as much as other teams around the NFL," said Sankar Montoute. "I do recall having a bunch of players around but it was never confrontational to the extent it was with other teams."[33]

"There wasn't any violence," agreed quarterback Mike Hold. "We were staying at a hotel down the street and when we got back to the hotel, the regular players would be there to rib us. There were some guys who were truly pissed. That was a pretty young team they had that year, there wasn't a lot of guff from them. There wasn't really any bad blood like you heard from elsewhere."[34]

While they may not have been confrontational, the regular Bucs did not care for the concept of the B-Bucs.

"When they fielded that scab team; that was unbelievable," recalled Scot Brantley. "It was one of those things where you scratch your head and go, 'How in the hell?'"[35]

Wide receiver Mark Carrier, a rookie that season, sympathized with the replacements but was of a mind that the B-Bucs should not have been at One Buccaneer Place. "There were mixed emotions," Carrier said recently. "Some of those guys that came in were guys that were in training camp with you and were released a week or two into camp. I understood where they were coming from because they wanted the opportunity to play. But at the same time, this is my job and someone is taking my job."[36]

When the B-Bucs took to the practice field they were met by Ray Perkins and the rest of the coaching staff. Perkins made it clear that he was not going to treat the replacement players or their games any differently than he would if the regular Bucs were in front of him.

"I tried to," Perkins answered when asked if he treated the B-Bucs the way he treated the regular players. "What else could we do? We didn't have a choice. We had games on the schedule. So whatever players that we can get and gather up, put them on the field. Let's work at it and practice and prepare and try to win the games as we go. That's our job as coaches and as players."[37]

Mike Hold, for one, appreciated Perkins' approach. "I never felt like any of the coaches on that staff was against what we were doing," Hold said. "I'm sure they were torn because they understood the players, but the bottom line was they had a job to do and I felt they treated us with respect and never felt any animosity."[38]

Paul Tripoli admitted that in a locker room where players from across the country were thrown together on short notice, the respect of the coaches went a long way towards providing an environment conducive to learning. "We didn't know each others names," Tripoli said. "You spend all day together, you learn them pretty quickly. We had a good coaching staff, and they did a good job of gathering players together."[39]

That education would come in handy when things went wrong in a hurry during the opening stanza of the B-Bucs debut.

The Pontiac Silverdome had a seating capacity of close to 80,000 during its time as home of the Detroit Lions. When the B-Bucs lined up for the opening kick-off on October 4, 1987, only 4,919 fans were in attendance.

"Amazing that I can remember the attendance was 4,919," said Mike Hold about his recollection of his first NFL game.[40]

"I do remember there were a lot of empty seats," agreed Sankar Montoute. "Well, we didn't know what an NFL game would have felt like anyway. I didn't. I had never played in the NFL before that."[41]

The ride to the stadium from the team hotel had been relatively uneventful. As the center of the American automobile industry, Detroit is also the home of some of the largest unions in the country including the United Auto Workers. As a hotbed of union activity, Detroit was one of the focal points during the first week of replacement football. In other strong union cities, fear of confrontations had prompted the NFL to alter teams' normal schedules. In Philadelphia, the Chicago Bears and Eagles arrived for their 1:00 P.M. kick-off at 6:00 A.M. to avoid picketers. The move paid off as the Teamsters and other local unions joined regular players to walk the picket line. Picketers drove trucks around Veterans Stadium, pelted some fans with eggs, got into fisticuffs with others and even vandalized a car before the 35–3 Bears victory.[42]

The B-Bucs did not arrive at the site of their game as early as the Bears and Eagles, but they did take precautions, according to Mike Hold.

"We did experience some of the hostility because it is a union town," Hold said. "We had a police escort with a tractor-trailer in front of the bus to clear out any roadblocks on the way to the arena. There were people hooting and hollering at us as we pulled in. We kind of expected it, that there wouldn't be many people there, but it would be really loud."[43]

During the first quarter Tampa Bay gave the few Lions fans in attendance reason to be loud. Penalties, turnovers and missed assignments by the replacement Buccaneers helped Detroit race out to a 17–0 lead. Tampa Bay quarterback John Reaves, almost two years removed from his last football game, looked rusty. Ray Perkins had entered into the replacement game with a plan to alternate Reaves and Hold by quarters. When the second quarter began, Hold entered the game and Tampa Bay team rebounded.

Following a fumble recovery by Paul Tripoli inside Lions territory, Hold dropped back to pass and threw a flare to fullback Adrian Wright. Wright turned toward the end zone, ran over Detroit linebacker Alvin Hall at the five-yard line and scored the first B-Bucs touchdown, cutting the Lions lead to 17–7.

Hold was ecstatic over the throw but tempered in his enthusiasm by the fact it was a replacement game. "Realistically, it was great but it wasn't the same as what I imagined it would have been the year before or the year after," Hold said, comparing it to his time in NFL training camps. "I don't want to downplay it too much, but it was what it was. It was a replacement game. Was it truly the NFL everyone dreamed of? No, but I do have the stats!"[44]

Shortly after Hold's touchdown pass, safety Paul Tripoli snagged his second turnover of the game. Tripoli intercepted Detroit quarterback Todd Hons at the Lions' 15 and raced into the end zone with his first professional touchdown. The score cut the lead to 17–14. The first half thefts were just the beginning for Tripoli. In the second half, he would add a second interception, tip a pass that was ultimately intercepted by teammate Brian Gant and record tackles behind the line of scrimmage.

In addition to Tripoli's big game, Hold threw a second touchdown pass, 61 yards to wide receiver Eric Streater. The Bucs also added a touchdown run by Harold Ricks and five sacks by the defense in a wild 31–27 victory over the Lions. For the first time since 1980, the Tampa Bay Buccaneers had a winning record after three games.

While the B-Bucs were winning a road game over a divisional rival, the regular Bucs were also on the gridiron. South of Tampa Bay at Bradenton's Manatee High School the striking Buccaneers were playing a charity flag-football game against the police to raise money for a liver transplant for a local infant. On the sideline, Buccaneers players would gather around the portable television of safety Rick Woods to monitor the game in Michigan.

When asked what he thought of the replacement action, striking tight end Calvin Magee pointed to the flag football game and said, "This is probably more exciting than what is going on in Detroit."[45]

Unfortunately for Magee, the excitement was only just beginning.

On Monday, October 5, the striking NFLPA members woke up to a stunning reality: The game of football could go on without them. Television ratings and attendance were down, but the full slate of games in Week Four had gone on as scheduled. While the games were not of NFL caliber, many fans appreciated the effort of the replacement players. In Atlanta, fans at Fulton County Stadium taunted the striking players with chants of "We got jobs!" At Foxboro, Patriot fans answered the picketing players' chants of "Shame! Shame! Shame!" with the response "Game! Game! Game!" Following New Orleans' 37–10 defeat of the Rams, Saints fans exiting the Superdome yelled to the striking players, "Stay on strike!" Almost 40,000 attended a Broncos game in Denver. It was clear that the NFLPA was losing the public relations battle.[46]

In an attempt to lessen the impact of the replacement games, NFLPA head Gene Upshaw requested the recently played games be stricken from the NFL record book. The NFL refused, but rumors began to circulate that the owners would call off the replacement games in a display of good faith to kick negotiations into high gear. Hugh Culverhouse called a press conference to personally impress upon everyone those rumors were false. The Tampa Bay owner announced that not only would the recently played games count, the entire remaining schedule up to and including the playoffs and Super Bowl would be played by replacement players, if need be. "The striking players are operating under false impressions about management policy," Culverhouse said.[47]

The validation of the statistics and game results of the first week of replacement games was especially important for Paul Tripoli. Tripoli's stellar game against the Lions garnered the safety NFC Defensive Player of the Week honors. It is an award that Tripoli still cherishes, and he admits to still breaking out a recording of the game every once in awhile.

"It is one of the few games that I played professionally that I have on tape," Tripoli said. "My wife recorded it because it was in Detroit, and she went to Disney World and didn't see the game! The game was huge for me. I couldn't believe I was actually playing in an NFL game. I was so jacked up. I was even more excited because the morning of the game the kid that was supposed to start at strong safety came down with a stomach virus and couldn't play. I was moved to strong, and that was my natural position at Alabama. So I went out and just played under instinct. I had a nose for the ball and knew how to tackle."[48]

With the records and results of the games standing, the NFLPA had little choice but to continue their fight in the negotiating room. Buoyed by the success of the first week of replacement games, Culverhouse and the management council were in no rush to move off their stance against free agency.

No agreement was reached by the Tuesday deadline imposed by Culverhouse and the NFL for all players to be back on the field for Week Five. This decision led to many more defectors from the rank and file of the NFLPA, including Los Angeles Raiders defensive tackle Howie Long. The Buccaneers regulars held firm, however, and not a single one crossed the picket line meaning the upcoming home game against the San Diego Chargers would be a complete B-Bucs affair. When the players came out of the tunnel for the first time, they realized just what winning the Detroit game had meant to the fans of Tampa Bay.

More than 23,000 fans were in Tampa Stadium for the B-Bucs' home debut. While only at one-third of Tampa Stadium's capacity, the 23,000 fans represented about half the usual crowd for Buccaneers games during the Leeman Bennett era. It may have not been an overwhelming crowd, but enough fans came out to make the B-Bucs feel they had earned the respect of a good deal of Buccaneers fans. After all, the Buccaneers had only notched five wins over the previous two-plus seasons so any Tampa Bay victory was sure to be appreciated by a starving fan base.

"We won the week before so that probably had something to do with the turnout we did have," said Mike Hold, who saw more time at quarterback against the Chargers. "It was a cool feeling that at least half the fans respected us. So, it was a good feeling that they turned out and supported us."[49]

"They did support us," added safety Paul Tripoli. "I think Tampa Bay fans are knowledgeable. If they were in our shoes, they would have done the same thing."[50]

Sankar Montoute agreed, adding that the large number of ex–Bandits on the roster also probably helped attendance. "That was great playing at home," Montoute said. "I think because of the number of former Bandit players that were on that strike team had a lot to do with it."[51]

Unfortunately for the B-Bucs and their newfound fans, the new Tampa Bay team fell short in their quest for victory number two. In a hard fought and hard-hitting game, the Buccaneers fell to the Chargers 17–13. John Reaves started the game and looked less rusty the second week, leading the Bucs to a 10–0 lead after one quarter. The Chargers tied the score at 10 in the third quarter and took a 17–10 lead in the fourth behind future UCLA head coach Rick Neuheisel's passing. Mike Hold came in for a stretch per Perkins's alternating arrangement and used his mobility to good effect, racing 35 yards in the fourth quarter to lead to a field goal that cut the deficit to 17–13. Hold has no recollection of the play, the result of a hard hit by a Chargers defender earlier in the game.

"I got a concussion in that game, and to be honest I don't remember a whole lot," Hold said.[52]

Despite the loss, the B-Bucs played hard. The only thing they were upset about was the likelihood that it would be their last day as a team. Rumblings from New York pointed to a collapse of the NFLPA's united front and the resumption of regular games.

When the NFL announced that games would be played with replacement players, not many took them seriously. Even those that became replacements doubted the owners would follow through.

"I never really believed that we'd get in a game," Mike Hold admitted. "This is posturing to make the players do something. Then the next thing you know, we played a game!"[53]

The first week of games unnerved some veterans, who were missing paychecks and saw the NFL season continuing without them. The second week of games set off a flurry of defections, including some of the biggest stars in the NFL. Joe Montana returned to the San Francisco 49ers, Steve Largent returned to the Seattle Seahawks, and Tony Dorsett to the Dallas Cowboys. Even the Tampa Bay Buccaneers were not immune. Back-up center Dan Turk became the only regular Buc to cross the line when he returned to work at One Buccaneer Place. The series of defections weakened the NFLPA and, by Thursday of that week, the union agreed to end the strike and continue to bargain while regular games continued.

However, Culverhouse and the NFL announced that the players agreed to return too late in the week for them to get into proper game shape. For that reason, the NFL announced the replacements would play one final game.

The news irritated the regulars but was warmly received by the replacements, especially the B-Bucs. They would have the chance to go out as winners.

The third week of replacement games brought NFC Central Division rival Minnesota to town. The Vikings were a pre-season favorite to make the playoffs but their replacement team had lost both of their games. With a chance to not only finish the replacement games at 2–1, but improve Tampa Bay's overall standing to 3–2 and in the thick of the NFC Central title chase, the B-Bucs were highly motivated; so was Ray Perkins.

Realizing the importance of the game, Perkins elected to bring in a new quarterback. John Reaves had been inconsistent, and Mike Hold still had the lingering effects of a concussion, so the Bucs convinced former Seattle Seahawks and Green Bay Packers quarterback Jim Zorn to play the replacement finale. Hold was naturally depressed by the move but understood it. "Jim Zorn came in because Coach Perkins said, 'Hey, we really need to win this game,'" Hold said. "I respected it. It was a little disappointing, but that's the business."[54]

In an attempt to make the most of his final week as a Buc, Hold volunteered for dangerous duty in practice. "I played on special teams," Hold said. "I was on the punt return as one of the wings that covered the wide guys. I was also on kickoffs."[55]

Zorn would have little impact on the game, as he tossed two interceptions in a conservative game plan. The real story of this game would be the strong play of the B-Bucs defense. The defensive unit scored two touchdowns. The first was a recovery of a fumbled punt snap by Arthur Wells which put the B-Bucs up 10–3 in the third quarter. This was followed by a 30-yard interception return by Kevin Walker which sealed the 20–10 victory. Walker also snagged a second interception and would join Paul Tripoli in winning NFC Defensive Player of the Week honors. Tripoli would add yet another interception as would Sankar Montoute. In fact, Montoute's interception would be the final play of the B-Bucs defense.

"I didn't think that would be my last play," Montoute said. "I thought I would be playing in the NFL for a long time."[56]

Unfortunately for Montoute and the majority of the B-Bucs, the final game against Minnesota would be the end of a brief, but impressive, run of Buccaneers football.

A handful of B-Bucs were offered permanent positions on the Buccaneer roster following the return of the regulars. Based on his strong play, Paul Tripoli became a regular contributor to the secondary for the remainder of the 1987 season.

Tripoli remembered it being a bit of an awkward situation to go from replacement B-Buc to regular Buc.

"After three replacement games they asked me to stay on the team," Tripoli said. "When I got back we had Marvin Powell, who is president of the players union, on the offensive line. I kind of toed the line when walking by the offensive linemen. Once you get on the field and earn their respect, you just become their friends and brothers in battle."[57]

Tripoli saw significant playing time over the remainder of the 1987 season as an extra defensive back and special teams player. The highlight of his season was a start in the season finale against the Indianapolis Colts at the Hoosier Dome. That would be Tripoli's only start with the regular Bucs as he would be cut in the 1988 training camp and not play in the NFL again.

"The NFL was 'Not For Long' for me," Tripoli joked good-naturedly. "I had three interceptions in my first three games and, I am proud of the fact that when I did get to play, I played at a high level."[58] Today Paul Tripoli is a high school coach in Pensacola, Florida.

Tripoli was among the fortunate few. The majority of the rest of the B-Bucs went back to their former lives, never to play a down of NFL football again.

Mike Hold was offered a return to Buccaneers training camp in 1988, but for the time being he returned to his graduate assistant duties at the University of South Carolina. Hold admitted that he held out hope he would be retained in 1987.

"Deep down inside you hope they would keep you, but realistically I knew that they weren't," Hold said. "That's why I wanted to play special teams because I wanted to do something to hang around. The day I left I did sign a contract to return for training camp. I went through three pre-season games and played against Cleveland and Indianapolis."[59]

Hold was ultimately cut and returned to the Arena Football League, eventually becoming a head coach at that level. Today, Hold is the Athletic Club executive director at Newberry College in South Carolina.

Sankar Montoute was given a few weeks of practice time to try and make the Buccaneer roster, but he found that time frustrating.

"They kept me on the practice team after the replacement games," Montoute said. "They were going to give me a look because they liked what I had shown. The tough part was after the strike and the regular players came back, you can imagine what it was like being in the locker room. It was nasty, cold and disrespectful. It was horrible. I was released. The following year they said come back and start from scratch, but at that point I had been offered a position with the Hillsborough County Sheriff's Department."[60] Today Montoute is a lieutenant with the sheriff's office.

The 1982 strike had been a colossal failure for the NFLPA, failing to result in the increased salaries it was intended to produce. Likewise, the 1987 strike failed to garner the changes desired. The players returned without free agency and without a salary cap. The owners, behind Hugh Culverhouse's leadership, had won. The work stoppage lasted only 24 days compared to the 57 day ordeal of five years earlier. A key reason for the short duration was the use of replacement players to continue the season and prove that football could continue without NFLPA members.

Hugh Culverhouse won at both the league and franchise level, his replacement necessary team playing as vital a role as his regulars. As chair of the NFL Management Council, his stewardship had resulted in a crushing defeat of the union he despised because teams such as the B-Bucs maintained enough of an audience to make the endeavor worthwhile. The B-Bucs' success also meant the Tampa Bay owner was in possession of a team in the thick of a playoff chase. Many other NFC teams had failed to adequately prepare for the strike and now were looking up at the Buccaneers as a result of the B-Bucs 2–1 record in replacement games.

The Buccaneers' two victories came over NFC Central Division rivals, including the 20–10 victory over a Vikings team many picked to win the division crown. The victory gave Tampa Bay a key tie-breaker over the Vikings who went from 2–0 before the strike to 2–3 after the strike.

Other NFC teams that went winless included the Philadelphia Eagles and New York Giants. The Giants were defending Super Bowl champions and had virtually no shot at the playoffs after dropping three consecutive replacement games. In fact, except for the San Francisco 49ers and Washington Redskins, the Buccaneers arguably positioned themselves for a playoff run better than any other NFC team. The fact the 49ers had the services of Joe Montana during the replacement finale no doubt helped their cause, but the Redskins and Buccaneers both posted their winning marks without a single starter on their replacement rosters.

The playoff possibilities resulted in the Tampa Stadium turnstiles getting a workout as a sell-out crowd was expected for the first regular game against the Chicago Bears and ticket sales for the following home game against the 49ers topped 68,000. The return of capacity crowds would only help Culverhouse's revenue stream.

Ironically, although Culverhouse had championed the use of replacement players and his organization had fielded one of the more successful units, the Tampa Bay owner never personally thanked the B-Bucs, much less spoke to them.

"I do not remember Hugh Culverhouse addressing the team," said Mike Hold.[61]

"I never met Mr. Culverhouse," said Sankar Montoute.[62]

"No, as a matter of fact I can't even remember having a conversation with him," said Paul Tripoli.[63]

Despite the lack of recognition from their owner or any respect for their efforts from the regular Buccaneers who now benefited from a 3–2 record, the B-Bucs are proud of their time in Tampa Bay. To a man they feel they made the right choice to pursue their dreams and are excited that they left a winning record in Tampa Bay and put the Bucs in position to contend for the playoffs in 1987.

"We had a really good team," Paul Tripoli said. "We won two out of three ball games and should have won that third one. We were tied with the Bears for first place when the regulars came back! The replacement players were a good group of guys that really liked each other. When I look back at those games, they were some hard-hitting games."[64]

"I still have the team photo of the replacements and my jersey," said Mike Hold. "To some people it's more important than others. For me it was my opportunity to play in the NFL, and I'll always remember that. I also understand there is an asterisk by it. You have stats, and they can't take those away. I'd do it again because it got me a step closer to my ultimate goal and to training camp and I got a shot. I just wasn't good enough. I met great people. I played golf with Vinny Testaverde, Mike Shula and Ray Perkins. I've followed what they've done for the last 20 years. I don't care how anybody else remembers it. It is how I remember it and I've got great memories because of the friendships I've made."[65]

"Many times people will see my stats in the NFL records and say, 'Hey, you played in the NFL,'" said Sankar Montoute. "And I say, 'Yeah, I did. It was a strike team, but it was the NFL.'"[66]

The NFL Management Council's victory in the 1987 strike proved to be incomplete and temporary. The NFLPA was indeed weakened for years to come, earning the late Gene Upshaw a rebuke from HBO Sports broadcaster Bryant Gumbel, who infamously described the former Hall of Fame player as a dog on the leash of the NFL Management Council. Regardless of their influence, the NFLPA under Upshaw did live to see free agency in the NFL.

Despite the victory Culverhouse oversaw, free agency in professional football was merely postponed, not killed. In 1989 the NFL, in an attempt to control the introduction of free agency, unveiled a version of free agency known as Plan B. Under the Plan B system, a NFL franchise could only protect 37 players from being able to sign with other clubs leaving the remaining players free to negotiate. Naturally, the Plan B system left only the least desired players on the market. In the early 1990s the courts would determine that much like the Rozelle Rule, Plan B was a restraint on trade. Due to the court decision, the NFL was forced to join the NBA and Major League Baseball in allowing players to move freely once their contracts expired.

Free agency was a right the NFLPA fought for in a bitter battle. Although it was the courts and not the NFLPA that won free agency, veteran NFL players who lived through both strikes feel their effort to bring the right to negotiate on the open market should be much more greatly appreciated by today's players.[67]

Culverhouse's victories on the field proved to be as big a mirage as the death of free agency. With the end of the B-Bucs, it was up to the regular Bucs to make a playoff push. Alas, the regular Buccaneers could not carry on the momentum generated by the B-Bucs. The Bucs' regulars only won one more game the entire season and finished 4–11. The B-Bucs pulled hard for the regulars to make the playoffs for two reasons. The first is they had become fans of Tampa Bay, and the second was purely monetary.

"We were just hoping they made the playoffs in '87 so we'd get playoff money," said Mike Hold.[68]

If the Bucs had made the playoffs in 1987 it would have placed them on center stage and garnered them national television exposure for the first time in four years. As one of the least successful teams in the NFL, the Buccaneers were often relegated to the nether regions of the networks telecasts, and often blacked out in their own hometown. However, the Buccaneers made their television appearances count. As the NFL's necessary team, three Buccaneers games broadcast during the Culverhouse era would encompass the birth of a legendary broadcasting duo, the end of an iconic broadcasting career, and a seismic shift in who could be hired for the job of play-by-play.

CHAPTER TWELVE

Broadcast History Made at Tampa Stadium

ON NOVEMBER 25, 1979, the Buccaneers looked to make history. With a record of 9–3 the Buccaneers were just one victory away from clinching a spot in the playoffs and the NFC Central Division championship. Both accomplishments would be franchise firsts and leave the Bucs in contention to earn home field advantage throughout the playoffs. The Bucs fell short, losing 23–22 to the Minnesota Vikings when Neil O'Donoghue's extra point attempt was blocked with only 19 seconds remaining.

While the Bucs would need another three weeks to make their historic entrance to the NFL playoffs, viewers of the CBS telecast were bearing witness to a different type of history. A broadcast first took place high atop Tampa Stadium that day and fans of televised football would enjoy its reoccurrence for almost a quarter-century.

In 1979 the top broadcasting duo for CBS telecasts of National Football League games was Pat Summerall and Tom Brookshier. Summerall, a former kicker for the New York Giants, and Brookshier, a former defensive back for the Philadelphia Eagles, had been the A-Team at CBS for five years. Their pairing was a bold move by CBS. Both men were former players, and the industry standard for football telecasts was to have one professional broadcaster do play-by-play while a former player would be the color commentator. Summerall, who had been working as a television sports announcer for CBS for more than a decade, had earned his stripes as the professional broadcaster. Summerall had called the action in a variety of sports, including professional basketball and golf. Summerall's ability as a play-by-play announcer provided

CBS with a level of comfort to pair one ex-player with another in the booth. The move paid huge dividends for CBS.

Throughout the majority of the 1970s, the team of Summerall and Brookshier called multiple Super Bowls, numerous playoff games and over 50 regular season games. The easy, conversational manner of the Summerall-Brookshier partnership made them arguably the most popular broadcast team in football. The many Emmy Awards and nominations both men garnered during their illustrious careers act as a testament to the high regard in which their work was held.

However, on the day of the Tampa Bay–Minnesota game, Summerall knew he would be working with a raw rookie in the world of broadcasting. As Summerall explained in an interview for this book, holiday travel and family commitments prevented Brookshier from joining his partner at Tampa Stadium.

"That game was on the Sunday after Thanksgiving," Summerall said, stating that he and Brookshier had called the Detroit Lions–Chicago Bears game in Detroit on Thanksgiving Day. "Tom's daughter was in Philadelphia and had some kind of obligation, so he didn't work."[1]

"I worked with John Madden that Sunday afternoon," Summerall said of his partner in televising a game involving the necessary team.[2]

In hindsight, Summerall's initial broadcast with John Madden is akin to John Lennon and Paul McCartney beginning their collaboration with the Beatles. At the time however, Madden was simply filling in for a color commentator on family leave. In just his first season at CBS following a Hall of Fame caliber career as head coach of the Oakland Raiders, Madden had provided commentary on only a handful of CBS telecasts in 1979, including Tampa Bay's 21–3 victory over Green Bay at Tampa Stadium. A few weeks before subbing for Brookshier in Tampa, Madden had been interviewed as a guest on Summerall and Brookshier's call of an Oakland Raiders–Atlanta Falcons game at the Oakland Coliseum.

"I remember him being a guest," Summerall said of Madden's appearance in Oakland. "Brookshier was the analyst, and I was the play-by-play man. We interviewed John during the course of the game."[3]

The Bucs–Vikings game would be a huge step up for Madden as it would be his first time participating on CBS's A-Team telecast. Given the Bucs' chance to secure the first playoff appearance in franchise history, the game had national significance and was deemed worthy of the A-Team by CBS Sports executives. Pat Summerall explained what it meant to be on the A-Team.

"If we were the A-Team, they wanted us to be seen back in New York," Summerall said. "That is why an assignment is made, because the game was televised back to the New York market. The A-Team should be seen in New York at the network headquarters."[4]

Summerall had no doubts about the ability of his rookie partner, as he had come away impressed by Madden during their short time together conducting the in-game interview in Oakland.

"I knew that he was very articulate and very enthusiastic about the game," Summerall said.[5]

The Bucs–Vikings game was the type of contest Madden would become identified with. A fan of physical games played in inclement conditions, Madden's initial pairing with Summerall involved a tense, hard-hitting contest played in steady rain. To further add to the drama, the game came down to the final critical seconds. It may have been the type of game Madden loved, but the ex-coach wasn't quite ready to exhibit the energetic commentary he became famous for. A review of a tape of the game reveals that Madden was far from an arm-waving, overly-enthusiastic fan of the game. Absent his famous telestrator and such phrases as "Boom," "Whap," and "Doink," Madden was quite subdued and reserved in his commentary.

On the Buccaneers' last touchdown, a 13-yard run by quarterback Doug Williams, who somersaulted into the end zone after a hard hit, Madden calmly explained the touchdown was the result of a solid block by Ricky Bell and then allowed Pat Summerall plenty of room to call the action as the Bucs' extra-point attempt was blocked, preventing the game from going into overtime. Madden would need a couple of more seasons to grow into his role.

Following the Bucs–Vikings game, Summerall went back to regular weekly broadcasts with Tom Brookshier, but the top executives at CBS had seen something they liked in Tampa Bay. Madden continued to ply his trade at CBS, gaining experience working alongside Dick Stockton and Lindsay Nelson. By 1981 Madden had gained a reputation as an affable storyteller whose histrionics and booming voice were balanced by the nuanced understanding of football he had developed in his decade as a head coach. In 1981 CBS made the decision to switch Tom Brookshier to play-by-play duties and promoted Madden to the color commentator on the A-Team broadcasts with Pat Summerall.

From that point on Summerall and Madden were inseparable. Between 1981 and 2001 the two men called eight Super Bowls, dozens of playoff games and hundreds of regular season games. The partners won Emmys for their work. In a display of the respect they had earned, the Fox Network hired both men and immediately installed them as their A-Team when the fledgling network outbid CBS for the rights to NFL broadcasts in 1994.

One of the duos' more unique broadcasts occurred during the 1982 players strike. With a huge hole in their Sunday schedule, CBS elected to televise NCAA Division III football and dispatched Summerall and Madden to the campus of Baldwin-Wallace outside Cleveland for a game between the home-standing Yellow Jackets and the Wittenberg Tigers.

"That was a different experience going to a college campus and doing a game," Summerall said. "The coaches had us give a pep talk to the teams."[6]

A large measure of the popularity of the Summerall-Madden pairing was the apparent friendship the two men obviously shared. Their broadcasts were often viewed as two old friends, one outgoing and gregarious, the other dignified and erudite, discussing a game. In his autobiography, *Hey Wait a Minute (I Wrote a Book)*, Madden explained the balance Summerall provided him in the broadcast booth.

"Pat Summerall is as easy to work with as he is to be with," Madden wrote. "He's easy to hang out with, to tell stories with, and I think that comes across to the viewer. He's just a good guy. He has things I don't, but I don't think I have anything he doesn't. I like to bluster about a play, but Pat will sum it up in a few words."[7]

Madden wrote of an instance that summed up the perfect harmony in which the ex-coach's exuberance was perfectly counter-balanced by Summerall's brevity.

"One time I was raving about a great catch a wide receiver had made," Madden wrote. "About how he had juggled the ball like an acrobat before finally hanging onto it. 'That guy,' Summerall commented, 'should've been a waiter.' As simple as that. As quick as that. As good as that."[8]

According to Summerall, the respect was mutual. Despite his reputation for boisterousness, Madden was actually a consummate professional when it came to sharing air time with his play-by-play partner. From that first day in Tampa, Summerall knew that he and Madden could work well together.

"I think respect for each other, respect for the game and loyalty to each other," Summerall answered when asked what made the Summerall-Madden team work. "I think the fact the both of us listened to each other helped. I think people get into broadcasting and don't listen to what the other person is saying. We had chemistry from the beginning."[9]

Interestingly, as the A-Team for CBS and later Fox, Summerall and Madden would not call many Tampa Bay games. As the fortunes of the Buccaneers on the field sagged, their national prominence disappeared. As a result, Summerall and Madden called only five Buccaneers games in the 1980s.

Despite not covering the Buccaneers, Summerall still followed the exploits of Tampa Bay as an interested observer because of a long-standing friendship with none other than Hugh Culverhouse.

"Because of my friendship with Mr. C, I would keep up with what they were doing," Summerall said. "Mr. Culverhouse was one of my attorneys. I met him in Jacksonville long before he owned the Buccaneers."[10]

A native of Lake City in northern Florida, Summerall had been impressed with how Culverhouse had advised him during a challenging issue with the tax man.

"He represented me in tax situations," Summerall said. "I remember him telling me one time when there was a question if I owed the IRS, 'I'll take it as far as you want me to take it. I'll pursue it as hard as you want me to pursue it, but let me give you some advice. If it's not going to kill you, pay it. Don't let the IRS get after you because if they get after you once they'll stay after you.' He was a good friend as well as being an attorney and owner."[11]

In addition to being the site of the launch of the Summerall-Madden broadcast partnership, Tampa was also the site of the former coach's final airline flight. Madden became quite famous for his preferred modes of transportation to and from his CBS and Fox assignments. At first Madden traveled by train across the country, memorizing time tables and writing about his experiences in his best selling autobiography. Eventually the announcer moved on to the "Madden Cruiser," a customized bus that carried Madden to all of his assignments.

However, in 1979 Madden was still attempting to travel by jet as he had done as head coach in Oakland. There was only one problem: Madden quickly realized he could not handle the rigors of flying. A sense of nausea, claustrophobia and discomfort would envelop him on planes. This reaction to flying had been dormant while he was a coach. Madden was so preoccupied with game-planning for the upcoming opponent on the flight to a game and too wrapped up in pondering the execution of the game plan on the return flight that he never noticed anything unusual. Without the intense concentration on coaching to distract him, Madden was confronted by his aversion to flight and it came to a head on the first leg of his return flight to California following the Tampa Bay–Minnesota game in 1979.

In his autobiography, Madden wrote about the emotion that gripped him on the tarmac at Tampa International Airport.

"As soon as the flight attendant slammed that door shut, I got woozy," Madden wrote. "Worse than ever. That cold sweat and that weakness in my legs. I thought, 'Jump up and open that door and get the hell off this plane.' And then I thought, 'No, don't make an ass of yourself.' I was arguing with myself now, 'Get off. Stay on. Get off. Stay on.'[12]

"I stayed on," Madden continued. "That two-hour flight to Houston was the most miserable experience of my life. I tried to walk the aisle. I tried standing in the rest room. Nothing helped. In those two hours, I made up my mind that I was never going to fly again."[13]

Madden was true to his word and began taking the train to games the very next week.

In another example of how members of the Buccaneers had a knack for being involved in historic events during the Culverhouse era, it was a Tampa Bay public relations employee that drove Madden to the airport for that fateful flight.

"I am a historically familiar figure in that I drove John Madden to the airport to catch his final flight," said former Buccaneers director of public relations Rick Odioso.[14]

At the time Odioso was an assistant in the PR department and was assigned an errand following the loss to Minnesota.

"They said, 'John needs a ride to the airport, Rick. Can you run him over there?'" Odioso said. "I did. I drove him from the game, and I don't remember him being nervous or anything. I remember having a nice conversation with him. I am that historic person."[15]

Whatever conversation the two shared on the short trip to the airport must have been pleasant, because eventually the two would work closely together in television. When Odioso left the Buccaneers, he began working with the former coach on broadcasts, assisting Madden with keeping statistics during games.

"I was his booth statistician for five years after I left the Bucs," Odioso said.[16]

John Madden retired from broadcasting in 2009. His partnership with Summerall ended when Madden made the move to ABC's *Monday Night Football* in 2002. By the time Madden and Summerall left NFL broadcasting behind they had won numerous awards including the Pete Rozelle Radio/Television Award bestowed by the Pro Football Hall of Fame for broadcast excellence. And it all started with a game involving the necessary team in Tampa on a rainy Thanksgiving weekend Sunday.

Four years after hosting the beginning of one legendary broadcasting team, Tampa Stadium was the site of the end of another. A forgettable *Monday Night Football* game between the Tampa Bay Buccaneers and Green Bay Packers would be the last time Howard Cosell appeared on ABC's *Monday Night Football*.

Since its premiere in September of 1970, *Monday Night Football* had been a sensational boon for ABC, justifying the gamble the third-rated network had made when it agreed to give over a night of primetime programming for sports. Stuck behind CBS and NBC in the ratings, ABC paid the NFL $8.5 million for the rights to televise just one game a week in primetime.[17] In order to make the deal payoff, ABC needed to garner ratings that football fans by themselves couldn't generate. The network needed the game to be showbiz, generating enough buzz to attract the casual observer and steal viewers from the situation comedies and medical dramas offered by their competitors.

Enter Howard Cosell.

A lawyer by education, Cosell had come to broadcasting in his mid-thirties, beginning as a radio reporter and working into a role as the producer of sports specials. After climbing through the ranks of ABC, Cosell began announcing boxing matches on ABC's *Wide World of Sports* and became internationally known for taking up the cause of heavyweight champion Muhammad Ali. When Ali refused induction into the military during the Vietnam War, Cosell defended the boxer's rights and became known for his opinionated stance. Cosell parlayed that stance into a role of sports announcer and social critic, and he quickly became one of the first celebrity sports broadcasters in the nation. There was no more obvious choice to be the lightning rod in the broadcast booth on Mondays than Howard Cosell.

Over the course of the 1970s, *Monday Night Football* became appointment television largely because of the nation's fascination with Cosell. Cosell was egotistical, opinionated and never afraid to "tell it like it is." In addition to providing commentary, Cosell handled celebrity interviews during the course of the games, running the gamut from Ronald Reagan to John Lennon. At halftime, Cosell would narrate a package of NFL Films highlights from the previous day's games. Cosell's halftime highlights were viewed as the ultimate sign of respect by NFL players and coaches. If a team was not included in the highlights package, the assumption was they were simply not important.

The exposure Cosell received from his *Monday Night Football* duties catapulted him to the top of the ABC announcing hierarchy. Cosell quickly became the analyst on ABC's coverage of Major League Baseball, championship boxing matches for *Wide World of Sports*, Olympic events and the host of *Sports Beat*, a weekly sports magazine show. In addition to his sports duties, Cosell also dabbled in show business, making guest appearances on television shows such as *The Odd Couple*, a cameo in Woody Allen's film *Bananas* and even a stint as host of the eponymous variety show, *Saturday Night with Howard Cosell*.

But as the 1983 season approached Cosell gave signs that he was tired of the *Monday Night Football* assignment, hinting to Frank DeFord of *Sports Illustrated* that the upcoming season could be his last. Writing in his book *I Never Played the Game*, Cosell listed his reasons for wishing to walk away from football.[18] The 65-year-old realized that the grind of the schedule was becoming more than he could cope with, and he was looking to cut back and spend more time with his wife, Emmy. In addition to personal considerations, Cosell also stated he was tired of being the target of media hostility.

In his role as antagonist on *Monday Night Football*, Cosell had engaged in a running battle with the sports media, particularly newspaper reporters. The announcer labeled the vast majority of sportswriters as sycophantic mouthpieces beholden to the NFL, afraid to portray the league in anything but the best light. As a result, Cosell believed he was in the crosshairs of sportswriters eager to embarrass him. Thanks to a grave error he made in the 1983 season opener, Cosell had given them a large target.

The opening game of the *Monday Night Football* season was a thrilling 31–30 victory by the Dallas Cowboys over their arch-rival Washington Redskins at RFK Stadium. The Cowboys' dramatic comeback from a 23–3 halftime deficit was lost amid the furor created from the following comment Cosell made while analyzing the replay of a second-quarter reception by Redskins receiver Alvin Garrett, an African American player.

"Joe Gibbs wanted to get this kid and that little monkey gets loose, doesn't he?" Cosell said.[19]

Within moments, members of the press next door to the ABC broadcast booth started to write stories about the comment. Members of African American organizations began to fire off phone calls and telegrams to ABC's New York headquarters. The producers of the game let Cosell know that his comment was creating a furor, and the announcer was genuinely shocked, not believing that he had said any such thing. When the game resumed for the third quarter, Cosell addressed the growing furor outside the stadium, denying that he had called Garrett a monkey.

"According to the reporters, they were told I called Alvin Garrett a little monkey," Cosell said during a break in the action. "Nothing of the sort happened and you fellows know it. No man respects Alvin Garrett more than I do. I talked about the man's ability to be so elusive despite the smallness of his size."[20]

When the game was over and Cosell realized he had indeed uttered the phrase "little monkey" in describing Garrett, he apologized to the head of the Southern Christian Leadership Conference. Within days the furor passed, helped greatly by Alvin Garrett defusing the situation by stating that he was honored to have been singled out for recognition by Cosell. While Garrett wished Cosell had chosen a different phrase, he believed the announcer was not at all a racist man.

Although the tempest passed, Cosell was left with what he felt was the unfair task of having to earn back his reputation as a champion of civil rights all because of what he perceived as a vendetta against him by writers.

"Where were they when I fought for Muhammad Ali's rights?" Cosell asked rhetorically about the print media in an interview with the Associated Press. "Where were they when I created the Jackie Robinson Foundation? This is the cheapest kind of trash in the world. My record as far as race relations is supreme."[21]

If having his character impugned was not enough to drive Cosell to consider retirement, the weak schedule of games on the *Monday Night Football* line-up may have been the final straw.

Cosell had spent a good deal of the early 1980s railing about the business practices of the NFL. Cosell claimed he was growing disenchanted with the league and felt its on-field product had diminished.

"I no longer believed in the league, and I became increasingly disillusioned with what I felt was a deception of the American public," Cosell wrote in *I Never Played the Game.* "What was happening off the field began to sicken me. Greed and political chicanery became normal business practices. Their arrogance knew no bounds."[22]

Cosell believed the owners had focused so much attention on wringing money out of the networks, fans and players that the on-field product had suffered. Cosell argued the NFL could easily be surpassed by the rival USFL because of the upstart league's emphasis on family-friendly prices and the quality of talent being recruited. In contrast, Cosell said the NFL had become a bore.

"One week collided into another," Cosell wrote. "I got the distinct impression that I was watching a rerun of a game I had seen before. Teams lacked an identity, and they were populated by nameless, faceless players incapable of arousing the imagination."[23]

The Week 15 match-up between the 2–12 Buccaneers and the 7–7 Green Bay Packers was far from the marquee match-up generally associated with *Monday Night Football.* The Buccaneers had been a play-off team the previous two seasons, providing the NFL schedule makers with confidence they would be fighting for a third straight post-season. The Bucs collapsed without Doug Williams, however, and left Cosell and his broadcast partners with a dreadful game to sell to the nation.

The Bucs' contest with the Packers was filled with miscues and bad play. The two teams combined for seven turnovers, thirteen penalties and more excruciatingly dull play than a regulation 60 minutes could contain. Tampa Bay kicker Bill Capece missed a 35-yard field goal and an extra point in the fourth quarter, allowing Green Bay to send the game into overtime on Jan Stenerud's 23-yard field goal with under 30 seconds to play. The future Hall of Fame kicker then won the game in overtime on a second 23-yard kick. In yet another example of the Buccaneers being present for history, the 12–9 defeat to Green Bay saw Jan Stenerud set the NFL record for most career field goals in a game.

When the lights went off at Tampa Stadium following the game, Cosell set about preparing for his final assignment involving the NFL. There would not be a *Monday Night Football* contest in Week 16. Instead, the ABC crew would call a Friday night contest in Miami between the Dolphins and New York Jets.

When the season ended, Cosell took stock of his options and decided that he had had enough of the NFL. During the 1984 off-season Cosell announced he would no longer call *Monday Night Football* games for ABC. Instead Cosell dedicated himself to his sports program *Sports Beat.*

In explaining his reasons for leaving, Cosell had included the lack of a quality on-field product. As it turned out his final *Monday Night Football* appearance was the perfect illustration of his argument. Naturally, that illustration was provided by the Tampa Bay Buccaneers.

The most socially significant broadcast in Tampa Stadium history didn't make it onto live network television. Instead, a test broadcast from high atop the stadium attempted to blaze a trail for a group of broadcasters long shut out of football play-by-play. On Sunday, November 22, 1987, the Tampa Bay Buccaneers fell to the San Francisco 49ers 24–10 at Tampa Stadium. 49ers quarterback Joe Montana, trying to prove that he was fully recovered from back and arm injuries, tossed three touchdown passes against the Bucs. While Montana's comeback from injury was the big story of the day, there was an equally significant story in the Tampa Stadium press box.

Gayle Sierens, news anchor for Tampa's NBC affiliate WFLA, was calling the play-by-play of the contest, the first woman in NFL history to call a game. Sierens' broadcast was not visible to anyone other than the producers in a NBC control room. The game was actually a CBS production, but the network home of the NFC was allowing its rival network to piggyback off its coverage to provide Sierens and color commentator Dave Rowe the chance to get in practice for her upcoming debut. NBC planned to have Sierens call a game before the end of the season, and was using the Bucs-49ers game as her first live rehearsal. The story of how Sierens came to be in Tampa Stadium on that day included a few other historical firsts with the Bucs.

In 1979 Sierens was a sports reporter for WFLA when a female reporter for the *Ft. Myers News-Press*, Michele Himmelberg, was denied access to the Buccaneers locker room. The Ft. Myers newspaper threatened action against the Bucs for their denial of access to Himmelberg. The dispute led to the Buccaneers banning all reporters from the locker room, which adversely impacted the media's ability to get quotes for their shows and articles.[24] Eventually an interview room was set up, but it was a far-from-perfect solution. The Himmelberg dispute was an early skirmish in the battle for female reporters having access to players after games. In time women would be granted access to locker rooms, but it was many years before they were accepted.

Sierens recalls Himmelberg's plight and while sympathetic, she stated she never particularly wanted to go into the locker room out of respect for the players' privacy. In fact Sierens believes her principled stand helped her to become accepted by members of the Bucs.

"I never went in the locker room," Sierens said. "I stood my ground on that one, and the players appreciated it and came out the door to me. Many times I would get interviews before anybody else because they respected my opinion on that. I just wasn't comfortable doing it that way."[25]

In addition to covering the Bucs, Sierens also handled play-by-play duties for the Tampa Bay Rowdies of the North American Soccer League. The quality of Sierens' work was rewarded when she became the sports director of WFLA in 1983, the first woman with such a duty in a Top 20 market in television history.

Despite her success, Sierens was beginning to feel as though she would never be able to climb any further in sports because of her gender. While proud of her accomplishments and appreciative of WFLA's opinion of her work, Sierens couldn't help but notice the lack of professional female sports announcers at the network level.

"I had done sports for nine years at my station," Sierens said. "I had gotten tired of waiting for the networks to want to put women who really knew about sports in the sports division. At that point they were still using beauty queens. I was a little frustrated that I had knocked on a lot of doors."[26]

One mistake Sierens admits to making was not taking an offer from a fledgling cable channel seriously. "I had been given an opportunity at ESPN to do some work," Sierens recalled with a laugh. "But that was in their infancy and I was thinking, 'I'm not moving to Bristol, Connecticut, to go to a network that no one has heard of!' I mean, come on, tractor pulls? But now look at them."[27]

Sierens believed the reason for the lack of upward mobility from the affiliate level to the network level was a paucity of recognition by network executives in regards to the abilities of females to cover sports. Too many executives believed the world of professional sports was an inherently male domain.

"What was interesting about that time was there was so few of us [women] doing sports that everyone had a raised eyebrow when they saw you coming," Sierens said. "In a classic way, you had to be better. There was no showing up for an interview or an event unprepared, because someone was waiting for you to be exposed for what you really were: 'Some girl that wanted to get in the locker room.' That is what a lot of people thought. They couldn't wrap their arms around the idea that you might actually be interested in sports and cover it like any guy would. If you made a mistake it would be amplified like crazy, but if a guy would do it, it would be, 'Ah, he's just having a bad game.'"[28]

So in the mid–1980s Sierens left sports behind and joined Bob Hite as the co-anchor of WFLA's nightly newscasts at 6:00 and 11:00. The move proved beneficial to Sierens as she and Hite formed a respected duo. After time in the news anchor chair, Sierens was a little surprised when she received a call from NBC Sports executive producer Michael Weisman.

Weisman felt the time had come for a woman to be more than window dressing on a broadcast. In Sierens Weisman believed he had the best candidate to break the gender barrier. Weisman had first noticed Sierens's ability when he watched tapes of her WFLA coverage of Super Bowl XVIII. The Super Bowl between the Los Angeles Raiders and Washington Redskins had been played at Tampa Stadium giving Sierens plenty of exposure.

"We believe this is long overdue," Weisman told the press. "There are outstanding women announcers on the local level that deserve a shot and we're confident it will lead to other women getting a chance."[29]

"I was thinking my sports day were behind me," Sierens said. "I had left sports behind and moved to the news department when I got the phone call."[30]

Her bosses agreed to allow Sierens to moonlight as NBC's play-by-play announcer on two conditions, she recalled. One was the side job must not interfere with her anchor duties and secondly her games could not be broadcast in the Tampa Bay area.

"That was something my bosses requested," Sierens said. "My bosses were extremely reluctant to let me do the games because they had just been spending all this money, time and energy to try and get people to forget that I was the sports girl and respect me as the news anchor. They allowed me to do it with conditions. They didn't want people thinking of me as the sports girl again."[31]

During her free time, Sierens worked extensively with NBC's Marty Glickman. Glickman had made a name for himself as a mentor of broadcasters. Those that benefited from Glickman's tutelage were Marv Albert of NBC and Johnny Most, the legendary radio voice of the Boston Celtics.

"Marty was very special, a very wonderful man," Sierens said of her broadcasting coach. "He just wasn't going to let me fail. He was going to have me as prepared as he could have me."[32]

Part of that preparation was an audio test during the Tampa Bay–San Francisco game in November. Sierens and Rowe performed a similar test at Cincinnati's Riverfront Stadium two weeks later during a Bengals game against the Kansas City Chiefs. The following week Sierens and Rowe did a full-scale dress rehearsal at Tampa Stadium when the Bucs hosted the Detroit Lions. The Lions game was also a CBS broadcast but unlike the 49ers game, the rival network was not as gracious a host to Sierens and NBC the second time around.

"I did two practice games at Tampa Stadium," Sierens said. "One there was a little controversy. CBS was doing the Buccaneers game at the time, and NBC asked if we could use the live feed from their truck so I could practice with a monitor and CBS said sure.[33]

"Unbeknownst to us, they were running tape of my audio during the practice game," Sierens continued. "CBS released a statement to the national papers saying, 'She's not ready. She's not going to be ready.'"[34]

Weisman and the rest of NBC Sports were outraged at the move, arguing that it was poor form by CBS to publicly critique the performance of a NBC employee in such a manner.[35] The backlash prompted the president of CBS Sports, Neal Pilson, to personally apologize to Sierens for his network's actions.

Sierens admitted to the local media that she had made some mistakes during the rehearsal but nothing worthy of condemnation. She viewed the CBS slight as another example of a double-standard for women broadcasters.

"The incident was pretty ugly and unnecessary," Sierens told the *St. Petersburg Times*. "I don't have to be good. I have to be terrific, better than the rest if that's possible. Yes, just because I'm a woman."[36]

When asked how she thought she would do in her live debut, Sierens was candid.

"It won't be the best game I ever do. It'll probably be the worst," she said. "It'll be a typical broadcaster's first broadcast—man, woman, whatever. Look, if I go out there and fail miserably—which I have no intention of doing—but if I do, the worst anyone can say is, 'Gayle Sierens couldn't do play-by-play.'"[37]

The next week Sierens made her national television debut, calling the play-by-play of the Seattle Seahawks–Kansas City Chiefs game at Arrowhead Stadium. The game took place the Sunday after Christmas and although it was the season finale for two average teams seen by only 10 percent of the nation, NBC promoted the contest heavily. Shortly before kickoff Sierens was interviewed by Bob Costas during the NBC pre-game show *NFL Live*. Sierens was totally unfazed by the attention.

"I had known Bob for years from when I did sports," Sierens said of the nationally televised interview. "He would always be down in the Bay Area for Spring Training because he is a huge baseball fan. Bob was a familiar person and a friend to me. What was kind of funny is we taped ahead of time and we had to redo it because he went on and on."[38]

After the interview Sierens called the action of Kansas City's 41–20 victory and for the most part received positive reviews. She had made a mistake on the opening play, mistaking the Chiefs' kick returner for another player on the roster, but quickly recovered and enjoyed the rest of the game. Sierens joked that in addition to being the first female to call a NFL game, she may go down as the only pregnant woman to call a NFL game.

"I was two months pregnant when I did the game," Sierens said. "The good news is I had no morning sickness and that was my worst fear, that I was going to wake up and have morning sickness, or be hoarse or that I was going to feel terrible."[39]

Instead Sierens went to the booth healthy and at ease. The reviews of her performance were positive for the most part. Sierens recalls the local media was a little rougher on her than the national press, but not inordinately so.

"Truthfully, I didn't see too many reviews that weren't positive," Sierens said. "People would say, 'She's going to be good.' I think people were pretty generous. I don't have any complaints about it. I personally thought the local papers were tougher on me because I think they felt they had to be."[40]

NBC felt Sierens did well enough to invite her back during the 1988 season in a more prominent role. Sierens was named temporary host of *NFL Live* while the majority of the network was in Seoul, South Korea, for the 1988 Summer Olympics.

"I filled in for about six weekends," Sierens said.[41]

Once the regular cast returned, Sierens was asked to do more play-by-play, including Tampa Bay games versus the Miami Dolphins and Buffalo Bills at Tampa Stadium. In deference to her primary employers and her burgeoning family, Sierens turned down the offers.

"They offered me six more games," Sierens said. "At that point the Bucs weren't selling out so they wouldn't have been shown in Tampa anyway. My station was pretty resistant to doing that. I was in a really new phase of life and not ready to roll the dice on some chancy thing when I had a really good thing at home. I just couldn't get on airplanes every weekend. I couldn't quit my job because it was paying bills. If had been single and younger I would have said, 'What the heck, I'm going to give it a shot!' Life is all about timing.[42]

"I was completely okay with that. In 1989 I was pregnant with my second child. I got out of the football business and turned into a baby-making machine for three years," Sierens said with a big laugh.[43]

Sierens' turn as the first female play-by-play announcer in NFL history did not have the impact she and Michael Weisman hoped. In the close to quarter-century since Sierens' turn behind the microphone, no other female announcer has called a NFL game. The closest women have gotten is as sideline reporters. When asked to assess her impact on women in football, Sierens is not entirely sure what to make of it.

"I don't think I can answer it," Sierens said. "I think it was an important first but it wasn't enough to blow open the doors to other women. When I did it, it was an experiment. It wasn't a gimmick, I don't believe for one minute that it was a gimmick because they asked me back the following year, and I opted out."[44]

What started out as a test run from the press box in Tampa Stadium may not have resulted in a stream of female broadcasters on NFL telecasts, but it did change the opinions of enough executives that women calling men's sports has become accepted. Pam Ward, Lesley Visser, Robin Roberts and Andrea Kremer have all either called game action or reported on men's games for years. Ward in particular has become known for her play-by-play duties on ESPN's coverage of college football and men's college basketball. According to Sierens, Ward is the most logical woman to follow her into a NFL booth.

"Why isn't Pam Ward doing NFL games right now?" Sierens asks. "I don't know because I think she is immensely talented. I think she does a fabulous job."[45]

While she may have blazed a play-by-play trail for Ward and others to follow, Sierens prefers to look at her practice games at Tampa Stadium and her time with NBC Sports as professional fulfillment.

"I'm delighted with the fact that I did it. It was a dream of mine," Sierens said.[46]

With NFL games being called on all three networks and two cable networks, it is probably just a matter of time before Pam Ward or another female broadcaster follows Sierens to the microphone. Sierens is confident that person will be seen as less of an experiment than she was.

"The bottom line is just that someone has to step up at the network level and find some women to do play-by-play that are very good and let them do it," Sierens said. "I think the world is ready for it. I don't think it will be some huge experiment."[47]

Despite the broadcast history that occurred at Tampa Stadium, the Buccaneers appeared on national television only a handful of times during the 1980s. As loss after loss mounted, the nation continued to largely ignore Hugh Culverhouse's football team. For years he had attempted to run his franchise in as financially efficient a manner as possible. The philosophy paid off monetarily, but now in his mid-seventies, Culverhouse desired to return his franchise to on-field prominence. He offered Bill Parcells a king's ransom and complete control over the Buccaneers in late 1991, a 180-degree turn from his previous belief.

When Parcells backed out of the deal at the last moment, Culverhouse looked defeated. What people didn't realize at the time was just how much desperation played a role in his pursuit.

CHAPTER THIRTEEN

Left at the Altar in the End

By DECEMBER OF 1991 Hugh Culverhouse may have been arguably the least popular man in Tampa Bay. A billboard along local roadways showed a picture of a metal screw next to a picture of the Buccaneers owner. The symbolism was clear: "Screw Hugh."

"Tampa Bay has endured a miserable NFL generation of awaiting real answers from a stingy, stubborn, inefficient Bucs owner who should be ashamed over what long has been the game's most inept, poorly managed, poorly coached franchise," fumed longtime *St. Petersburg Times* columnist Hubert Mizell in a 1991 opinion piece on the state of the Bucs.[1] Mizell's column was cordial compared to the letters to the editors.

"Is Culverhouse ignorant or blind?" asked one fan in a letter to the *Times*.[2]

"He [Culverhouse] knows one thing about football: How not to succeed," wrote another.[3]

Those same fans were beginning to stay away from Buccaneers games, disenchanted by a decade of losing while reading about Culverhouse's astronomical profits. A final straw came in the late 1980s when Culverhouse announced an across the board ticket price increase following a fifth straight season of ten or more losses. Compounding the problem was his stated intention to investigate the possibility of playing two or three home games a year at Orlando's Citrus Bowl Stadium. The deal with Orlando never materialized, but Culverhouse's intentions alienated even the staunchest Bucs fan.

What the fan base of the Buccaneers didn't realize was that Culverhouse was undergoing a transformation. Contrary to popular opinion, the owner of the Tampa Bay Buccaneers was desperate for a winning franchise, but now those desires were being driven by a most pressing motivational force.

Culverhouse was in seriously declining health. Diagnosed with prostate cancer, he was not promised many more years. While keeping his medical condition private, he gave hints of an increasing level of commitment to his franchise when he stepped down from the NFL Management Council and NFL Finance Committee in March of 1989. When he made the announcement he stated it was so he could devote more time to his football team and other business interests.

A hint of Culverhouse's increased attention appeared when he fired Ray Perkins late in the 1990 season. Unlike his previous short coaching searches, he took his time in hiring a replacement. According to his son, Culverhouse's action in the January 1990 search was more deliberate than his previous emotional hires of Leeman Bennett and Ray Perkins.

"He tried to marry every head coach," Hugh Jr. said.[4]

In addition to a new head coach, he was also willing to turn over control of the football team to a general manager. It was a stunning concession for a man who had viewed a football czar as a needless level of bureaucracy between him and his football team.

In January of 1991 the first man Culverhouse pursued was recently retired San Francisco head coach Bill Walsh. Walsh had retired from the 49ers following the 1988 season but had been sending out signals he was interested in returning to the NFL if the right opportunity came along. For close to a month, Culverhouse pursued Walsh, trying to persuade the former coach to take on the role of head coach and head of football operations. Ironically, Walsh wanted the football operations job, but walked away when Culverhouse demanded he also be head coach.

"I took my time and thought about it," Walsh told the Tampa Bay media after turning down the job. "It was a hard decision but I think it's better to leave coaching to the young turks."[5]

Much like the speculation about Parcells's rejection a year later, it was opined that Walsh had grave doubts about working for Culverhouse's organization. Walsh went out of his way to deny that was a consideration, politely recognizing the community, the owner and the franchise as a solid employment opportunity for a younger coach more interested in a cross-country move.

"Tampa Bay is a wonderful place to live," Walsh said. "They have a solid, young team and I feel it can be turned around quickly. Hugh Culverhouse is a very admirable man. It's not only his grace and charm I appreciated, but he is very knowledgeable. But at this stage of our life, we're very happy here [in California]."[6]

In hindsight Hugh Culverhouse, Jr., feels his father wasted a little too much time going after Walsh, believing from the start that the former 49ers coach had no interest in a cross-country relocation.

"That was total bullshit. Not even close," Hugh Jr. said.[7]

When Walsh said no to the job, Culverhouse decided to promote his chief contract negotiator. In February of 1991 Phil Krueger assumed the general manager duties and began to assist in a search for a new coach.

Sadly, the dalliance with Walsh may have cost Culverhouse the chance to hire a future Hall of Fame coach. One of the more intriguing names to interview for the position was a New York Giants defensive coach named Bill Belichick. The young Bill Parcells protégé was definitely the favorite of Phil Krueger.

"The guy I interviewed was Belichick," said Krueger. "He was young, and I was impressed. That was my recommendation. I recommended Belichick. He had a nice interview, and we all hit it off so well."[8]

Unfortunately for Krueger, Belichick also hit it off well with Cleveland Browns owner Art Modell, who hired Belichick before the Buccaneers could call him back.

With his dream candidate not interested and a young, highly-respected assistant now unavailable, Culverhouse offered the head coach position to Richard Williamson. To label Williamson the choice of last resort would be unfair and demeaning to his contributions to the Bucs. Williamson had been named interim coach following Perkins's dismissal and had done a solid job of keeping the young team together, winning his debut against the Minnesota Vikings 26–13 before dropping the final two contests. The former receivers coach had also interviewed well and had the added benefit of being the players' choice.

Williamson was ecstatic for his first NFL head coaching job, but the long interview process had placed him behind the eight-ball in assembling a staff and putting together an off-season regimen.

"I interviewed for it early," Williamson said in an interview for this book. "I felt my interview was good, and I was just hoping that I would have a shot to be coach the next year. We had to wait around because of the procedures they set up to interview all of those different people so we had to just wait and see. Mr. C called me in and told me I was going to be the head coach. It was late, I remember that. I had to scramble to get assistant coaches because a lot of teams that had changed coaches had already hired them. We had to scramble a little bit. That's the way it is and you can't control it. You just do what you can do the best you can."[9]

Williamson's season as Bucs coach would be a disappointing 3–13 campaign marked by excruciatingly close losses in the beginning of the year and lopsided defeats towards the end. As the end of the season closed in, speculation began to swirl that Williamson was going to be dismissed at the end of the year. Rumors abounded about Williamson's possible successors. An early candidate was former Philadelphia Eagles head coach Buddy Ryan.

Ryan had been one of the candidates interviewed following the 1990 season. A defensive specialist, Ryan had rebuilt the Eagles into a playoff team but had lost each of his playoff games, a fact that may have worked against him. Some speculation surrounded current Tampa Bay defensive coordinator Floyd Peters. Following a successful stint as the defensive coordinator of the Minnesota Vikings, Peters, nicknamed "Sgt. Rock" due to his intimidating appearance, had done a decent job of cobbling together a top five pass defense in Tampa Bay.

Given Ryan's lack of playoff success and Peters' lack of head coaching experience, it was no surprise that neither name gained much traction over the second half of the 1991 season. It became suspected that Culverhouse wanted a candidate with head coaching experience and a track record of playoff success. Shortly after the calendar turned to December, the name Bill Parcells began to surface in connection with the Tampa Bay job. At first, few took the Parcells stories seriously for several reasons. First, the two-time Super Bowl champion Parcells was in the first year of a high-profile studio analyst job for NBC Sports. Second, midway through December Parcells underwent an angioplasty to clear a blocked artery.[10] The procedure led many to believe that Parcells was not physically fit for a return to coaching. Third, having gone out on top following New York's victory in Super Bowl XXV, many wondered why Parcells would risk tarnishing his legacy by working for the toxic Buccaneers franchise.

However, weeks after the angioplasty, Parcells was reported to have engaged in serious discussions about the Buccaneers job with Culverhouse. The discussions took place through intermediaries and appeared to be positive. So positive that it was announced in the local papers that Richard Williamson was all but through as head coach of the Bucs.[11]

Despite the rumors about Parcells, Williamson persisted in getting his team ready for games. In the season finale, Williamson led the Bucs to a 17–3 victory over the Indianapolis Colts. While the 1–15 Colts were a truly dreadful team, it said a good deal for Williamson's character that he still had his players giving effort in the final week of an abysmal season. Unfortunately for Williamson, the final victory was not enough to save him. The coach was let go in what was believed to be a deck-clearing for Bill Parcells's introduction. Williamson had an inkling he would be let go from reports he was reading in the paper leading up to the finale.

"I was not informed they were going to interview anybody," Williamson said. "But of course they had no reason to inform us. Phil Krueger and I talked about it some and I knew the situation was shaky and things could be happening. I felt things were happening because I read it in the news."[12]

Many years later Williamson is left to ponder what might have been if one or two breaks had gone the Bucs' way during their first four games, a streak of four losses by a combined 13 points, including a heartbreaking 17–10 loss to the defending AFC Champion Buffalo Bills that ended with the Bucs at the Buffalo eight-yard line when time expired.

"I always wondered what would have happened if we had won two or three of those early games and given us some confidence for the rest of the year because we had some players that could do some things," Williamson said.[13]

Daily reports in the local papers continued to detail the ongoing negotiations with Parcells. The day after the season ended, Culverhouse reportedly flew to Newark, New Jersey for further conversations with Parcells. According to news accounts, Parcells had a long list of demands and expectations. Some accounts listed a total of 38 considerations including total control of the football operations. Later stories indicated that Culverhouse had agreed to every single request. One of the considerations was reportedly the naming of Jerry Vainisi as the next Buccaneers general manager. Vanisi was a highly regarded executive who had been the general manager of the 1985 Chicago Bears when they won Super Bowl XX.[14]

When Phil Krueger voluntarily stepped down as general manager after less than a year on the job credence was given to the Vainisi hiring. When Krueger mentioned Parcells by name in his resignation announcement, it became accepted that Parcells was indeed the next Buccaneers head coach.[15]

On the morning of Sun-

New York Giants head coach Bill Parcells addresses the media during the week leading up to Super Bowl XXV in Tampa. Parcells led the Giants to a 20–19 victory over Buffalo to win his second Super Bowl ring. Less than a year later, Buccaneers owner Hugh Culverhouse would stand behind a similar podium to announce that Parcells had "jilted him at the altar" (*Tampa Tribune*).

day, December 29, stories appeared in the Tampa Bay papers that Bill Parcells had agreed to terms to become the next head coach of the Tampa Bay Buccaneers. The former Giants coach would be paid $7 million over five years and would have complete control over the entire Tampa Bay organization. Jerry Vainisi would accept the job as Parcells' hand-picked general manager and both men would go about reshaping the Buccaneers organization from the playing roster on down to the type of letterhead to be used by the administrative assistants.[16]

Culverhouse then announced that Bill Parcells had left him at the altar. Thinking he had landed the man to redefine his legacy as owner, he was now targeted with further hostility from the Tampa Bay area.

Culverhouse's public humiliation was complete and while he looked devastated that morning he did not find an overwhelmingly sympathetic community of support. A decade and a half of poor public relations and team performance had soured the Tampa Bay area on his leadership. The sad irony was that despite going all in for the biggest name in coaching, Culverhouse was being blamed for Parcells's decision to back out of the agreement.

This scapegoat effect had been enhanced by the unsubstantiated claims by some newspapers that Parcells backed out of the deal when he learned what kind of man Culverhouse was. It was speculated in a Hubert Mizell column in the *St. Petersburg Times* that Parcells had talked to some of his friends who had worked for Culverhouse and gotten a less-than-rosy picture of being a Tampa Bay employee. Names such as Ron Wolf, Ray Perkins and Ken Herock were hinted at as suspected sources of unkind references.[17] When asked about any advice they may have given Parcells, the aforementioned parties admitted to differing levels of conversation but denied advising Parcells against working for Culverhouse.

Ken Herock, who had worked diligently to restock the Buccaneers roster with talent under Culverhouse's tight budget, admitted that once he patched up his differences with the owner in the mid-1980s he would have been happy to return to Tampa Bay. "I would have always considered working for him again," Herock said.[18] Those aren't exactly the words of a man that would have steered Parcells away.

The man who may have had a great deal of sway with Parcells was former head coach Ray Perkins. Parcells had been one of Perkins' best hires in New York, and the two had become good friends.

"I met Bill Parcells when he was coaching at Texas Tech about 1976 or 1977," Perkins said when asked about his relationship with the former Giants coach. "When I first went to the New York Giants I called Steve Sloan, who was coaching Ole Miss and was a good friend of mine from Bama. I asked Steve, 'Who is the best linebacker coach in college football? I want to try to hire a college coach to linebackers in New York.' Sloan said Bill Parcells is the best. I said, 'Where is he?' He was at the Air Force and that's where I hired him from.[19]

"We brought him in and he coached our linebackers," Perkins continued. "But he had some personal things he had to do and he quit during training camp. This is a story a lot of people don't know. He was out for a year, he had to leave and go home to Colorado. We went out to play St. Louis, and he called me to have dinner the night before the game. He asked me to help him get back in the league. Ron Erhardt at New England had lost his linebackers coach and I hooked them up and Ron hired him to coach linebackers the next year. The next year I hired him to be my defensive coordinator, and I have nothing but a great deal of respect for him and he is a great friend today."[20]

As the man who was responsible for giving Parcells his first shot at the NFL, Perkins's advice could have carried a great deal of weight. However, when asked if he spoke to Parcells about the Buccaneers job, Perkins responded that he could not recall specifics of the conversation. Perkins did state that if he did offer advice, it probably would have been in the realm of demanding total football authority.

"I remember him calling me," Perkins said. "I don't remember whether it was for advice or just asking me a question. The only way I would recommend any coach to any team is if the coach could get full control of the situation. If you can't get total control, leave it alone. I think having full control of the program increases your chances of winning by 40 percent."[21]

In light of the fact that Culverhouse was on record as being willing to cede total control to Parcells, it would appear that Perkins' condition for his former assistant to accept the job was met.

It is possible the impact of the references made by former Buccaneers employees on Parcells has been greatly overstated. As for Bill Parcells himself, the former coach said nothing about the Buccaneers organization or Culverhouse leading him to back out of the job. Parcells claimed he knew both Culverhouses and the Bucs' reputation going in and didn't feel either was worthy of walking away from a return to the NFL.

"That didn't make any difference," Parcells said. "In all these jobs that you wind up going to in the NFL, if things were going well they wouldn't need you. There is always a reason these jobs become available. Most of the time, the problems are the same. It's not that complicated. They just can't get the combination of talent acquisition, player development and coaching on the same wavelength. A lot of organizations can't get that structure in place at the same time. They may have decent player acquisition, but no one there who can develop them. Or, the coaching may not be up to par. Or, the coaching is pretty good and maybe there is a development plan, but the scouting and management isn't up to par. If one of those is missing, it's a disaster and you can't function. You've got to be able to acquire players, have a philosophy on personnel and have someone to implement it."[22]

If the story had simply ended with Bill Parcells leaving Culverhouse at the altar, it would have just been an interesting footnote in the history of both men. Less than two weeks later however, both men would meet again with the Buccaneers job on the line and their actions would cement certain elements of their legacies forever.

Lost in the controversies surrounding Doug Williams, two NFL strikes, low payroll budgets and using the revenue of the Buccaneers to aid cash flow for other endeavors is one often overlooked fact: Culverhouse wanted the Tampa Bay Buccaneers to win. Unfortunately, his lack of public relations savvy and desire to run an organization in as fiscally efficient a manner as possible prevented his desire to bring a championship to Tampa Bay from receiving any recognition from the media or fans.

"'I want to win, Ken,'" Ken Herock recalled hearing from the owner on more than one occasion. 'I want to be in the Super Bowl.'[23]

"I watched every Tampa Bay home game with Mr. C," Herock continued. "No question in my mind that he wanted to win. He thought whenever he hired a coach that he had hired a winner. When I sat up in the booth with him he lived and died with that team during a game. Maybe he didn't know what it takes to win, or what it was to win. He was a successful businessman and when you're successful in one end you think you'll be successful in another."[24]

"He wanted to win," agreed former general manager Phil Krueger, adding that Culverhouse simply didn't believe in reckless spending on players the way Eddie DeBartolo of the 49ers and Jerry Jones of the Dallas Cowboys had done. "But I don't think he was going to buy a team the way some owners did.[25]

"The team was quite profitable," Krueger added.[26]

Culverhouse's ability to make money off the Tampa Bay Buccaneers set him apart from many NFL owners. However, his ability to win on the ledger went unrecognized and unappreciated because no one who followed the Bucs wanted to watch the books. Fans and media wanted to see the team beat the 49ers and Cowboys on the field, not the bank account. This realization may have finally begun dawning on Culverhouse in the late 1980s and early 1990s. He may have been a better businessman than either DeBartolo or Jones, but he wasn't viewed as the better owner. Former linebacker Richard "Batman" Wood succinctly summed up why Culverhouse's business acumen met with little appreciation when compared to his team's losses.

"The bottom line in sport is what?" Wood asked rhetorically. "The championship. The bottom line is put a product on the field to win football games. The bottom line is to win football games, win and be a champion. That is what everyone remembers."[27]

Culverhouse's decision to go after Bill Parcells with everything he had was borne out of more than just a desire to win football games. It was also his chance to shape his own legacy as an NFL owner. The Tampa Bay boss knew in 1991 that he didn't have much time left to live. According to his son, the owner's decision to scrap the way he had conducted Buccaneers business for almost twenty years wasn't an easy decision, but he felt it was his best chance to go out on top.

"He struggled with it," Hugh Jr. said of his father's internal turmoil over assigning complete control of the franchise to Bill Parcells. "There is no question about it. At that time my father had already undergone treatment for prostate cancer that people didn't know about. Dad underwent radiation treatment and didn't want people to know. So when we are dealing with Bill Parcells there is a cognizant influence of, 'I don't have long to live so I had better try this one last time because what the fuck does it matter?' That is the influence that was happening. If I had to guess, I'd say Bill Parcells was going to be his final Hail Mary."[28]

When Parcells said no, the result on Culverhouse's psyche was devastating, his son recalled. "He was totally crushed," Hugh Jr. said.[29]

"It was embarrassing for him," added Stephen Story, Culverhouse's law partner who also advised him on business matters with the Buccaneers. "Hugh was just a man of his word. I can't think of the number of transactions that involved billions of dollars that I saw him make merely on a hand-shake."[30]

Culverhouse was left to pick up the pieces. In the days following Parcells's rejection, he interviewed three men for the Bucs job. For the second year in row, Buddy Ryan interviewed and appeared a solid candidate. Following Ryan to the interview room was former Cincinnati Bengals coach Sam Wyche, who had led the Bengals to the brink of a Super Bowl championship in 1988. While Culverhouse clearly favored former head coaches, he did interview a well-regarded assistant coach who had made an impression on every team he spoke to. Mike Holmgren, offensive assistant on the San Francisco 49ers, met with the owner for nearly three hours and, from all accounts, interviewed well.[31] However, Holmgren's interview coincided with an astonishing bit of news. Bill Parcells was calling Culverhouse to tell him he was having a change of heart and wanted to be considered for the Tampa Bay job again.[32]

Parcell's apparent desire to reconsider the Tampa Bay job put Culverhouse in an interesting dilemma. He had been humiliated on national television by Parcells's rejection. Culverhouse had proven over the past 20 years that when embarrassed or challenged, he could both hold a grudge and engage in grueling battles. His ownership of the Buccaneers had been prompted by his one-man lawsuit against the entire NFL over his failed attempt to buy the Los Angeles Rams. His stature as vice commissioner was helped by his ability to out-duel Ed Garvey and the NFLPA in 1982 and scuttle the USFL. His Buccaneers remained one of the most profitable teams in the NFL because he was unwilling to concede on free agency and was willing to take a hard line stance when necessary.

Unfortunately, not all of these victories were without cost. Doug Williams, John McKay and Ken Herock had all left in differing levels of frustration with Culverhouse's penury. The absence of a strong voice in control of football had led to a streak of futility for the Buccaneers. Now a man Culverhouse had truly believed could end that streak was willing to admit a mistake and join the team. The question was: could he forgive and forget? Or would he tell Parcells thanks, but no thanks, and go forward with one of his back-up candidates?

Culverhouse agreed only to meet with Parcells and his representatives. A meeting was set up in a private home in Maryland, just outside of Washington, D.C. On January 8, Culverhouse boarded a plane and flew to Maryland to meet with Parcells. Joining him on the trip was Stephen Story, acting in his capacity as financial advisor, and Rich McKay, the Buccaneers general counsel.

"He so much wanted to win," said Story. "I think that is the only thing that took him to Maryland to begin with."[33]

For two and a half hours the two sides discussed the situation. After the conversation, Culverhouse asked to be excused so he, Story and McKay could adjourn to a side room and discuss their options in private. What happened in that room became the final, defining moment of the era.

When Culverhouse returned from the room he told Parcells that he was no longer a candidate for the job.

"He came back and he said, 'Hey, we can't do anything,'" Parcells recalls of the decision.[34]

Then Culverhouse, Story and McKay flew back to Tampa Bay. According to Story, it was he who was assigned the duty of informing the Tampa Bay community that Culverhouse turned down Parcells. The way he was volunteered for the assignment still causes Story to chuckle to this day.

"When we flew back from that meeting, Culverhouse and McKay got out of the jet way on the tarmac, and I was left to do the interviews," Story said. "I call that drawing the short straw."[35]

The contents of the sidebar conversation between Culverhouse, Story and McKay depend on the recollection of the individual.

Hugh Jr. claims his father told him that he had looked to McKay and Story for advice on what the owner should do.

"My father, Stephen Story and Rich McKay all met with Parcells," he said. "My father excused himself and confabbed with Story and McKay.

McKay said, 'Hire him. Swallow your pride. You wanted to hire him, hire him.' Story said, 'Fuck him.' Dad went with Story."[36]

Stephen Story did not recall using language quite as blunt or explicit as this, but he does admit to advising Culverhouse against hiring Parcells. "We had some concerns about health issues and whether the same thing was going to happen again," Story said, stating that Parcells' initial rejection had to do with health problems that all involved were not convinced were resolved.[37]

Story also recalled that in addition to concerns over Parcells' health, Culverhouse was still hurt by the public embarrassment of being rejected in public. "I don't think he ever got out of the back of his mind Bill walking away the first time," Story said. "That is human nature. This was not a meeting to set up to embarrass Bill Parcells. That never entered the conversation."[38]

As for the man who reportedly was for hiring Parcells, Rich McKay would prefer to not divulge his recollections of the conversation. As general counsel for the Buccaneers at the time, McKay believes it would be inappropriate to share the contents of the conversation. "I think that is one of those situations that I would not feel comfortable speaking about," McKay said, adding that Bill Parcells is probably the best source for information about the Maryland meeting. "I think coach Parcells represents the story well."[39]

Parcells was never privy to the conversation that occurred between Culverhouse, Story and McKay, but he was perfectly understanding of the decision reached by the Tampa Bay owner. "I don't know what happened, but it was okay with me," Parcells said. "I didn't really have high expectations going in there. I was prepared for the result, I really was."[40]

One of the reasons Parcells was prepared was that he understood what his rejection of Culverhouse's initial offer had done to him. Parcells knew Culverhouse was humiliated. He felt horrible about the gamut of abuse Culverhouse ran through because he felt the man didn't deserve it.

"If I was Hugh Culverhouse I would have been pissed off at Bill Parcells too," Parcells admits. "And I think he was. I'm not denying that or making any excuses for it. Nobody knows that because nobody cares to know that. He was a good man.[41]

"I wanted to work for the Bucs, I really did," Parcells continued. "I felt so bad about the situation. I was hoping that I could rectify it somehow, and it turned out we couldn't. And I don't blame him for not wanting to rectify it because he had every right to be upset."[42]

Hugh Jr. certainly understood his father's emotions regarding Bill Parcells. However, the younger Culverhouse wishes his father could have overcome his anger and embarrassment to bring in the man who would go on to rebuild four franchises in his Hall of Fame career.

"He was totally crushed, but here is the flip side," Hugh Jr. argued. "What is it that you want? How do you turn lemons into lemonade? You host another press conference and have Bill Parcells right beside you. Bill Parcells says, 'I'm sorry.' And you have Bill put his arms around Dad and say, 'This guy is a hell of a guy. He gave me a second chance nobody else would have given me.' Then Parcells says to Dad, 'Now, get the hell out of here. I'm going to run your team and win a Super Bowl!' Is your ego strong enough to do that?"[43]

In light of the aftermath of the negotiations, it would become apparent that the ego that voided any reconciliation was short-lived. Any anger Culverhouse may have had was quickly dissipated as proven by his actions over the following months when Parcells' health continued to get worse.

"My physical condition kind of continued to deteriorate as the year went on," Parcells said. "Eventually I had to wind up getting an operation on my heart. The day that happened, a little time after, I got a long letter from Mr. Culverhouse telling me he was sorry to hear about my heart surgery and that he hadn't realized the extent of what my problems were. So I wrote him back thanking him for the letter and he sent me back a book and we started to communicate.[44]

"The important thing to me is as we went forward down the road about a year later we ended up having quite an interesting relationship, and I am pretty sure hardly anybody knows that," Parcells said.[45]

While ego played a role, the decision to not hire Parcells was also motivated by Culverhouse's inability to overcome another personality trait: frugality.

Stephen Story recalled advising Culverhouse of the financial impact the Giants coach would have on cash flow. Both men realized the amount of money Parcells was going to burn through in order to put together a new organization.

"Bill wanted certain control features that Hugh was prepared to turn over," Story said. "With Bill you always had to worry about an unlimited budget because he has a reputation for spending money on large staffs and that was going to be a total opposite for Hugh. We had always had from a cash flow standpoint one of the leanest operations.[46]

"I was emphasizing cash flow and my concerns in that area," Story continued in describing his argument against hiring Parcells. "When you had the real estate empire he had, and highly leveraged, you had to take those thoughts into consideration. I was certainly very vocal about my concerns in that area because I am responsible for running all his businesses. It may have worked out fine, but it may have been a disaster. It's hard to say."[47]

In the end Culverhouse agreed with Story's assessment. Instead of Parcells, Culverhouse ended up hiring Sam Wyche as the team's head coach.

Wyche was a bargain at $550,000 a year compared to the more than $1 million annual salary Parcells was offered.[48] In addition to hiring Wyche, the Bucs also later promoted Rich McKay from general counsel to general manager, a stunning promotion for a 33-year-old with no previous NFL experience.

The positive financial impact on the bottom line in the hiring of Wyche and promotion of McKay were readily apparent. Despite suffering two more dismal seasons in 1992 and 1993, Culverhouse's Buccaneers continued to enjoy profitable seasons.

"His average profit was $11 million which is not bad when you paid $16 million in 1974," Hugh Jr. said.[49]

But unfortunately Culverhouse could not take it with him. He was growing sicker and sicker. Due to his bout with prostate cancer, he had been slowly handing over the reins of the franchise to others. His daughter, Gay Culverhouse, was named team president in 1992. Hugh Jr. took his father's place at league meetings and Stephen Story, Fred Cone and Jack Donlan became trustees. As the 1994 season approached, it was apparent that Culverhouse was not going to be around for the season opener against Chicago.

"His cancer had spread throughout his body to the point where it was almost beyond hope," Hugh Jr. said. "He underwent treatment at Moffit Cancer Center in Tampa, St. Joseph's Hospital in Tampa and then an experimental treatment in New Orleans where they give you a nuclear injection to eradicate the cancer cells."[50]

The treatments failed to curb the cancer and on August 25, 1994, Hugh Culverhouse, once the most powerful owner in the NFL, died quietly in seclusion at Louisiana Regional Medical Center in New Orleans. He was 75 years old.

Before he passed away, Culverhouse continued to maintain correspondence with Bill Parcells. The man he had once hoped would become the savior of his franchise was now a source of comfort while he struggled with his own illness.

"We exchanged letters three or four times between that time [the initial letter by Culverhouse] and the time Mr. Culverhouse died," Parcells said. "We exchanged books on a couple of different subjects, and I started to communicate with him on a different scale. I don't think the term 'good friends' is appropriate. Certainly we had a relationship that became mutually important. It was important to me because he had reached back to me and said, 'Hey, man, I didn't know exactly what you were talking to me about, but I got it now.' And in light of him getting sick, I was kind of communicating my best wishes to him."[51]

While these conversations were going on Bill Parcells was making his return to the NFL. In 1993 Parcells was named head coach of the New England Patriots. Within two seasons, Parcells had the Patriots back in the playoff and in a Super Bowl within three. Following his stint in New England, Parcells rebuilt the New York Jets and rehabilitated the Dallas Cowboys. As head of football operations of the Miami Dolphins, Parcells enjoyed the distinction of turning a team that finished 1–15 in 2007 into a division champion in 2008.

An unanswerable question is, how would the 1990s have turned out for Bill Parcells had Culverhouse made a different decision in January 1992? What if the Tampa Bay owner had truly thrown financial caution to the wind and turned over his organization to Parcells?

What impact would Parcells' medical condition have had on the franchise and coach? If a medically unsound Parcells had flopped in Tampa Bay, would he have been granted the opportunities he enjoyed in New England, New York, Dallas and Miami? Would Culverhouse have been pilloried for overpaying?

Conversely, had Parcells been able to regain his health while guiding the Bucs to a Super Bowl appearance, how would the histories of the Patriots, Jets, Cowboys and Dolphins be altered? Would Hugh Culverhouse be remembered today with the respect afforded to other Super Bowl winning owners?

Such is the nature of the NFL's necessary team. Even on the eve of his own demise, far removed from the corridors of power of the NFL, Culverhouse's final major act as the head of the Tampa Bay Buccaneers reverberated for years to come.

Epilogue

IT IS DIFFICULT TO GAIN a complete picture of Hugh Culverhouse.

Immediately following his death, it was learned that had prostate cancer not taken his life, he may have had to part ways with his football team. After years of transferring the revenue from the Buccaneers to his other business ventures, the new NFL economy was going to stop the flow of cash.

In 1994 a salary cap of $34.6 million was introduced. Lost in the focus on the cap was the $12 million dollar salary floor. In order to comply with the new salary structure the Buccaneers would have to pay no less than $12 million in payroll for the season. According to Hugh Jr. that floor would have been more than his father was willing to pay. The son finds the timing of the cap and his father's death eerily appropriate.

"I always thought he did it on purpose," he said of his father dying shortly in advance of the salary cap and floor. "He died right before the salary cap came in. There was an average in the salary cap. You had the ceiling with the Eddie DeBartolos in San Francisco, but you had a floor with the Cincinnatis and Tampa Bays. The average would have required higher payroll. I think the last year we made $11 million. The floor was $12 million, so consequently we would have lost $1 million unless we found a way to increase revenue. So there's a reason economics were in the back of Dad's mind because he was paying banks, interest and trying to keep afloat businesses by trying to go cheap on talent."[1]

In the early 1990s, Culverhouse needed every penny of Buccaneers revenue he could get his hands on. An almost compulsive deal-maker, he was in danger of losing money because he was over-leveraged. In the 1970s and 1980s, he had saved many owners from themselves by setting a debt limit on

Hugh Culverhouse addresses the media at One Buccaneer Place. While an unpopular owner, Culverhouse should be remembered as the man responsible for professional football in Tampa Bay. He should further be remembered as the owner most accountable for the astounding profitability of the National Football League (*Tampa Tribune*).

teams. This prevented owners from over-leveraging their teams with debt in order to stay in the NFL. In a 180 degree turn, Culverhouse had overleveraged his outside businesses and was over-dependent on the Bucs to bail him out. When the NFL instituted free agency and a salary floor, Culverhouse would have not been able to generate the revenue he needed to support his other businesses.

"If I had known his overall finances, I'd have probably strangled him," Hugh Jr. said. "When he died, he owed millions of dollars."[2]

It also came out in the years following his death that Culverhouse had engaged in an extra-marital affair with Susan Brinkley, wife of ABC news-caster David Brinkley.[3] This was one of multiple affairs and the revelations were personally embarrassing for his widow, Joy, and his two adult children. The handling of his estate would also lead to controversy as Hugh Jr. would file suit against the trustees of his father's estate, including Stephen Story and Jack Donlan, stating he and his sister were denied entry to a condo-minium his father owned.[4] Later, Culverhouse's widow sued the trust, chal-lenging a settlement.[5]

The revelations of infidelity, the contentious disposition of his estate and lingering bitterness by the fans of the Tampa Bay Buccaneers over his frugal methods did little to provide a positive legacy for Hugh Culverhouse.

And yet to remember only those controversies would be to sell the man short. While unpopular in many regards, Culverhouse was also a generous benefactor to many worthwhile causes. Unwilling to part with his money when it came to the Buccaneers, he gave away countless sums to charitable endeavors throughout Tampa Bay and to his beloved alma mater.

"When he died, he donated millions of dollars to the University of Alabama," said Hugh Jr. "Now the entire school of commerce and business is named after Dad. The school of accountancy is named after Dad."[6]

Culverhouse was also generous with his time and understanding of others. Bill Parcells's story about the relationship he and Culverhouse formed shortly before the owner's death is unknown to many. Parcells stated that he was willing to share such a personal story because of his belief that Culverhouse deserves to be remembered for more than just losing football.

"I want to be able to tell someone about what eventually happened with myself and Mr. Culverhouse, because I think people would find that a little unusual. He was a good man," Parcells said.[7]

Such is the paradox of Hugh Culverhouse: A generous philanthropist on one hand and a philanderer on the other. The owner was a rock-ribbed, fiscal conservative who wouldn't dare overpay and crushed numerous attempts to place players in a free market. Yet, he was a risk-taker in real estate and other acquisitions, often placing himself at the brink of insolvency to pull off a deal. His son is left to speculate on his father's mindset, one that could house such disparate personal and business traits.

"A lot of times people are afraid of success," said Hugh Jr. "You see that in every aspect of life. So a lot of times it is easier for people to lose. I think in certain aspects of his life he was afraid of success, period."[8]

Many players and individuals who had run-ins with Culverhouse, such as Doug Williams, Dave DeForest-Stalls and Steve Rosenbloom, don't have a particularly fond recollection of the man. The reasons Williams, DeForest-Stalls and Rosenbloom have for their feelings are understandable and well-chronicled both in this book and in others. However, despite his well documented confrontations, Culverhouse is also remembered fondly by many other men who worked for him. Additionally, some men who were not fond of his handling of the organization have an appreciation for the fact that without his patience with John McKay, they may have not had NFL careers at all.

"The man gave me a job, and I really appreciate it," said Richard "Batman" Wood, who was not pleased with how his time in Tampa ended but nonetheless has pleasant memories of his Buccaneers career. "I tried to be positive about the whole situation. I'm not bitter. There are a lot of memories that are good but a lot that baffle me."[9]

Fellow linebacker Scot Brantley recalled that Culverhouse was approachable. "Mr. Culverhouse was always nice to me," Brantley said. "He always had a big smile and would shake your hand. I could call Mr. C at any time and say, 'I need to get in touch with so-and-so,' and he'd help me. That meant a lot to me."[10]

Tom Bass, one of the first hires of the Culverhouse era, recalled an owner who in the beginning wanted to win. After Bass left however, he wonders if Culverhouse became sidetracked. "I saw Mr. Culverhouse a great deal," Bass said. "He was a good owner. He was always positive and always tried to give you what you needed. He had coaching changes, personnel changes. There were a lot of things going on that I didn't really know anything about and couldn't understand at the time."[11]

According to former public relations director Rick Odioso, Culverhouse's frugality was overblown. During his time in Tampa Bay Odioso found the owner to be a reasonable man who just wanted expenses to be justified.

"I'll say this about Mr. C, he wasn't a bad guy to be around as long as you weren't talking about money," Odioso said. "If you were just shooting the breeze or watching practice, I think he cared about his employees and their families. He wasn't a bad guy. I always found that if you took a deep breath and laid out your reasoning for doing something, he would listen to you respectfully."[12]

Perhaps the fairest legacy Culverhouse could have is that he is the man who made the Buccaneers of today possible. It is easy to forget that when the Tom McCloskey ownership group fell apart, there was speculation the Tampa Bay franchise would be relocated before it was even given a team name. It was Culverhouse's financial commitment of $16 million that gave the team that would become the Tampa Bay Buccaneers its true start. The only reason the NFL turned to him was because of his lawsuit over the Rams controversy. According to his son, that should be enough for Tampa Bay fans to give his father's memory more respect.

"I would say the fans of Tampa should appreciate one thing," Hugh Jr. said. "Had it not been for my father, they would not have a football team. So whenever they get good and pissed off, they should think back to the origins. The only reason they got it was the federal lawsuit by my father. Is a shitty 19 years heading up to a better ownership group enough of a penalty to pay to at least have something called big-time NFL football? My answer is of course!"[13]

That better ownership group turned out to be the Glazer family. In 1995 Malcolm Glazer purchased the Buccaneers for a then-record $192 million.

At the time the trustees that ran the Bucs following Culverhouse's death were believed to be holding out for the highest bidder with no regard for keeping the franchise in Tampa Bay.[14] Rich McKay argued nothing could be further from the truth, and the fact that the Buccaneers ended up staying in Tampa Bay had everything to do with the demands of Hugh Culverhouse.

"The good part of Mr. C's legacy will be that he was the original owner of the franchise and established a franchise in the NFL that will be in Tampa forever," McKay said. "I think that is a credit to him because in his estate plan, the instructions he gave to us charged with selling the team were very clear on how he wanted the team to stay in Tampa. His estate worked in a way to encourage that. The wishes of Mr. C were we structure the deal in a way that the new owner would be encouraged financially to keep the team in town. His legacy is the permanency of the franchise."[15]

Culverhouse's legacy is also felt in the way the NFL operates today. The financial and tax expertise he provided to the NFL was invaluable. His role as chair of both the NFL Management Council and Finance Committee saw the NFL safely through two work stoppages, a multi-million lawsuit against a rival league and the deft handling of two potentially embarrassing franchise ownership transitions in Los Angeles and Philadelphia. Even in the throes of illness, when Culverhouse dispatched his son to league meetings, he could still shape the structure of the NFL.

In 1989 Pete Rozelle announced his retirement as commissioner, effective immediately after a successor was named. New Orleans Saints general manager Jim Finks emerged as the favorite early in process. The possible ascension of Finks did not sit well with Culverhouse. Although he had officially stepped out of the NFL power center, he quietly enlisted his son to derail the Finks candidacy and guide a choice more palatable to the Bucs owner's tastes.

"My dad called me and said, 'You always wanted to work with the team. I've got a job for you to do,'" Hugh Jr. remembered.[16]

"I said, 'Great, what do you want me to do?'" he continued, stating that he thought his father was about to complement him on his skills as a litigator by asking for expert advice.[17]

"I want you to do what you do best: fuck things up," Culverhouse told his son.[18]

"'The league wants to appoint Jim Finks and you don't need to really know my relationship, but I don't like Finks and I don't want him to be commissioner,'" Culverhouse said. "'I got along with Rozelle, I couldn't get along with Finks.'"[19]

"What do you want me to do?" Hugh Jr. asked.[20]

His father left the course of action up to him but offered the following warning.

"If anybody asks me about what you're doing, I'm going to disown you," the father said. "I'm going to tell them you are an unguided missile."[21]

Knowing that he was on his own, Hugh Jr., did what he knew best. He scoured the operating rules of the league to find a method with which he could derail the Finks candidacy. "I did shareholder litigation," Hugh Jr. explained. "My first instinct was show me the rule book."[22]

He learned the NFL bylaws spelled out a procedural hurdle that could be implemented to prevent the needed two-thirds majority required to name a new commissioner. He realized that by not electing to cast a vote, and convincing others not to cast a vote, the two-thirds majority needed would be unattainable.

"I got out there and got Norman Braman, Eddie DeBartolo, Billy Bidwill and Bud Adams, all the guys that were the outs," Hugh Jr. said. "Because there is a little clause that the owners hadn't looked at when they were going to appoint Finks that says to vote on the issue of commissioner, it takes two-thirds vote approval. So, it was pretty easy. Just take a position of not voting. Not vote no, but just not vote and sign an agreement. We signed an agreement to vote as a bloc, and I think we went through three months of hearings before the other side gave up. Then we all agreed Paul Tagliabue seemed like a hell of a guy."[23]

While he was working to derail Finks's candidacy, his father was watching from afar. True to his word, the elder Culverhouse feigned ignorance of what his son was doing, telling those who asked that Hugh Jr. was acting independently.

In truth, father and son worked closely together, but the elder Culverhouse kept his involvement low-key. According to his son, there was a method to the delegation of duties. "I went out to the league meetings because he had quote-unquote removed himself from being active," Hugh Jr. said. "He was telling people he didn't know what I was doing because I was off the reservation. He had plausible deniability."[24]

In November of 1989 after months of acrimony, the NFL owners voted to elect Paul Tagliabue commissioner of the league. The move paid great dividends for Hugh Jr. "One of the first things he did was appointed me to the finance committee," he said.[25]

In his role on the finance committee, Hugh Jr. helped prevent Art Modell and other owners from losing their teams when the economy sputtered in the early 1990s.

"One of the first things I did was to bring in a league-wide credit facility," he said. "The Resolution Trust Company was taking over everybody's bank. Art Modell was going to lose his team because his two banks were taken over by the federal government. The government took over banks that had bad real estate loans and a lot of the owners had loans from banks now owned by the government and the government was calling in the loans.[26]

"We needed to get in a bunch of big banks," Hugh Jr. explained, stating that it would be necessary to change how the loans were collateralized to get the best rate possible.[27]

"Your biggest asset is not the 45-man roster," he said. "Your biggest asset is your television revenue. When you think about it that is the biggest asset any team has today. If you securitize the television revenue, you will get the lowest, cheapest loan rate humanly possible."[28]

The results were dramatic. By securitizing the television revenue many banks clamored to loan the NFL owners millions at a rate barely above the London Interbank Offered Rate (LIBOR) banks charge each other.

"Where else were you going to get a loan at LIBOR plus 5/8ths of a point with no personal guarantee?" Hugh Jr. asked rhetorically. "Most of these guys were paying prime plus three to five points and personally guaranteeing the loan! The difference in interest was 10 to 15 percent."[29]

The plan worked, saving each owner untold millions.

Like father, like son.

The derailment of the Finks candidacy was one of the last major projects father and son would work on, and one that meant a great deal to Hugh Jr.

"He and I never had more fun than getting Paul Tagliabue in," he said. "We were on the phone six to seven times a day. We had a ball. My dad and I had passionate ups and passionate downs. I adored the man."[30]

While these feats may have not been appreciated by Tampa Bay fans, they went a long way towards providing the Buccaneers and the other 27 teams in the league a secure financial structure.

"He certainly held the league together during some very tough times," recalls Jack Donlan, the man Culverhouse hired as chief negotiator during the 1982 and 1987 players strikes, both overwhelmingly crushing defeats for the NFLPA. "We went though some difficult periods. Teams had different problems and different issues. I saw him as a problem solver. He was a man that was not a shrinking violet. He always kept his eye on what he was trying to accomplish."[31]

As for Culverhouse's inability to field a winning franchise despite his business skills, Donlan chalks it up to the vagaries of the game.

"It's funny how you can have great success in one area and not in another," he said. "There have been owners who couldn't get out of their own way but could field championship teams."[32]

Rich McKay, who would one day go on to become president of the Atlanta Falcons and co-chairman of the NFL Competition Committee, also believes the NFL today would not be nearly as successful if not for the intervention of Culverhouse in the league's finances.

"I have great memories of Mr. C," McKay said. "He never gets enough credit for how brilliant a man he was from a business standpoint and what he did for the NFL from a business standpoint when he was chairman of the finance committee. The effects are still felt today with the debt ceiling and deferred compensation and other things that really continue to give our league a much more solid footing than other sports leagues. I really feel he deserves a lot of credit for that."[33]

The name Culverhouse still reverberates through the NFL today. Twenty years after becoming one of the highest-ranking women in NFL history, Gay Culverhouse is spearheading a crusade to provide retired players with the medical and psychological help they need.

The Gay Culverhouse Players' Outreach Program was founded in response to the 2008 death of Tom McHale, a Buccaneers offensive lineman from 1987 to 1992. The 45-year-old McHale died of a drug overdose, but later tests showed the former player's brain had characteristics of early onset dementia. That condition is becoming more prevalent among retired players and Gay Culverhouse is convinced the NFL should do more to treat retired players.

She has put her own money behind the cause. With little support from charitable contributions, she has footed the bill for flying in players from around the country to undergo medical and psychological evaluations. As far as she is concerned, it is simply the right thing to do. Necessary, also.

"It is only fair that we find a way to give back to all retired players who now have needs," Culverhouse told John Barr of ESPN in an April 2010 interview.[34]

When asked if she was taking up the cause of retired player health to atone for the miserly ways of her father, Gay Culverhouse said no. "My father has to answer on his own merit," she told ESPN. "No one can make up for someone else's mistakes."[35]

What should be the ultimate legacy of Hugh Culverhouse's Tampa Bay Buccaneers, the necessary team? From 1976 to 1993 the Buccaneers' on-field record was an abysmal 81-194-1, a winning percentage of roughly 42 percent. Aside from three playoff seasons and a handful of All-Pros and Pro Bowlers, the Tampa Bay Buccaneers of that era are a largely forgettable team, especially in light of the World Championship and multiple playoff appearances the team would enjoy in the 2000s.

But to ignore the contributions of those players would be to disregard the role they played in the history of the NFL and professional football in Tampa Bay. The Bucs under Culverhouse may not have enjoyed much on-field success, but they became cult heroes. The Buccaneers rarely sold out in the 1980s, but the fact Tampa Stadium averaged 48,000 fans per game from 1985 to 1990 during the height of the futility is testament to the admiration the fans had for the players, if not the owner.

"I give the fans so much credit, because the stands were packed even when we were 0–26," recalled Richard "Batman" Wood.[36]

Fan support during even trying times is what made Louisiana native Mark Carrier decide to make Tampa his permanent home when his playing days ended. "When I was drafted I actually fell in love with the city," Carrier said.[37]

Even Ray Perkins, the man who many fans wanted run out of town on a rail, admitted that despite the way his tenure ended, he always enjoyed the city and appreciated the fans' passion.

"I appreciated the great opportunity that Hugh Culverhouse gave me with the Tampa Bay Buccaneers," Perkins said. "I have nothing but fond memories of the city of Tampa and living there. My only regret is that I didn't do a better job than what I did."[38]

Perhaps Scot Brantley summed up best what it meant to be a Buccaneer during that time and the impact he and his teammates had on the future of the franchise. "I love the Buccaneers," the ex-linebacker said. "They've gone through some changes, but they're still the Buccaneers, and we were the building blocks. We are still the foundation of what they are today."[39]

At the time of the interview with Brantley, the Buccaneers had announced they would wear the Bucco Bruce uniforms of the 1976 to 1996 era. The orange and white uniforms had been replaced in 1997 by a radically different pewter and red color scheme. The Bucco Bruce helmet logos were jettisoned in favor of a crimson battle flag replete with skull and crossbones. For years the Glazer family refused to entertain the thought of a throwback game in which the Bucco Bruce uniforms would be worn. The argument was that the Culverhouse era was so unpopular the Glazers wanted nothing to do with recognizing that period of Buccaneers history. Ultimately, the Glazers agreed to a throwback game in 2009. While the retro uniforms worn on November 8, 2009, in a 38–28 victory over the Green Bay Packers were meant as a nod to the 1979 NFC Central Division champions, they were also a way for Buccaneers fans to recognize the contributions of those who toiled during the Culverhouse era. Scot Brantley, for one, was pleased by the recognition.

"It's about time they recognize it because you can't change the past," Brantley said. "You think the Philadelphia Eagles always had great and storied teams, or the New York Giants? Hell no! They sucked for years. All teams have. I have no regrets. I was so fortunate to have never left the state of Florida, from high school to college and the pros. I would not live anyplace else in the world. I'm fortunate to have raised my family here. I couldn't imagine living anywhere else. All because the Tampa Bay Buccaneers drafted me!"[40]

The Tampa Bay Buccaneers of the Hugh Culverhouse era are memorable not just because of the games they lost, but because of the role they played in NFL history. The owner and the team were both blessed and cursed with an uncanny ability to be at the focal point of modern NFL history.

This book is meant as a further recognition of the men who played and worked for the Tampa Bay Buccaneers from 1976 to 1993. They were many things. They were entertaining yet baffling, endearing and infuriating, sincere but unsuccessful.

They were also something more important.

They were necessary.

Chapter Notes

Introduction

1. Rick Stroud, "Krueger Leaves Bucs," *St. Petersburg Times*, 29 December 1991, 1C.
2. Ibid., "Parcells Turns Down Bucs Job," *St. Petersburg Times*, 30 December 1991, 1A.
3. Ibid.
4. Ibid.
5. Ibid.
6. Ibid.
7. Ibid.
8. Ibid.
9. Ibid.
10. Hubert Mizell, "Hugh, Bucs Left Crying at the Altar," *St. Petersburg Times*, 30 December 1991, 1C.
11. Ibid.
12. Bill Parcells, telephone interview, 29 May 2009.
13. Ibid.
14. Ibid.
15. Ibid.
16. Ibid.
17. Ibid.
18. Ibid.
19. David Harris, *The League: The Rise and Decline of the NFL* (New York: Bantam Books, 1986), 304.

Chapter One

1. Michael MacCambridge, *America's Game: The Epic Story of How Pro Football Captured a Nation* (New York: Anchor Books, 2004), 15–17.
2. Ibid.
3. David Harris, *The League: The Rise and Decline of the NFL* (New York: Bantam Books, 1986), 193–195.
4. Ron Martz, "He Didn't Pay $16 Million for a Toy," *St. Petersburg Times*, 15 August 1976, 17H.
5. Rick Stroud, "Bucs Owner Loses Fight Against Cancer," *St. Petersburg Times*, 26 August 1994, 7A.
6. Ibid.
7. Ibid.
8. Harris, 193–195.
9. Ibid.
10. Hugh Culverhouse, telephone interview, 14 May 2009.
11. Ibid.
12. Ibid.
13. Ibid.
14. Ibid.
15. Ibid.
16. Steve Rosenbloom, telephone interview, 28 April 2009.
17. Harris, 193–195.
18. Culverhouse, telephone interview.
19. Martz, 17H.
20. Culverhouse, telephone interview.
21. Ibid.
22. Harris, 193–195.

23. "Suit Filed by Attorney," *Spokane Daily Chronicle*, 21 December 1972, 22.
24. Culverhouse, telephone interview.
25. Ibid.
26. Rosenbloom, telephone interview.
27. Ibid.
28. Ibid.
29. "Baltimore's Owner Eyes Rams' Purchase," *The Free-Lance Star* (Fredericksburg, VA), 23 June 1972, 6.
30. Rosenbloom, telephone interview.
31. John A. Fortunato, *Commissioner: The Legacy of Pete Rozelle* (New York: Taylor Trade, 2006), 29.
32. Rosenbloom, telephone interview.
33. Ibid.
34. Ibid.
35. Culverhouse, telephone interview.
36. Ibid.
37. Harris, 193–195.
38. Rosenbloom, telephone interview.
39. Ibid.
40. Culverhouse, telephone interview.
41. Ibid.
42. "NFL Franchise Awarded to Tampa," *Canton Repository*, 31 October 1974, 49.

43. Hubert Mizell, "Jacksonville Attorney Tampa NFL Owner," *St. Petersburg Times*, 6 December 1974, 1C.

44. Tom McEwen, "The McCloskey Progress Report," *Tampa Tribune*, 22 November 1974, 1C.

45. Ibid., "New Millionaire in Town," *Tampa Tribune*, 7 November 1974, 1C.

46. Harris, 193–195.

47. Mizell, 6 December 1974, 1C.

48. Culverhouse, telephone interview.

49. Ibid.

50. Ibid.

51. Mizell, 6 December 1974, 1C.

52. Culverhouse, telephone interview.

53. Martz, 15 August 1976, 17H.

54. Ibid.

Chapter Two

1. Sports Media National, *Bucs Reflections* (Tampa: Sports Media National, 1979), 12.

2. Hubert Mizell, "Jacksonville Attorney Tampa NFL Owner," *St. Petersburg Times*, 6 December 1974, 1C.

3. Ron Martz, "He Didn't Pay $16 Million for a Toy," *St. Petersburg Times*, 15 August 1976, 17H.

4. Tom Bass, telephone interview. 2 April 2009.

5. Ibid.

6. Jack Harris, telephone interview, 19 January 2006.

7. John McKay, and Jim Perry, *McKay: A Coach's Story* (New York: Atheneum, 1974), 332.

8. John Underwood, "A Three Hour Time Difference," *Sports Illustrated*, 23 August 1976, 17.

9. Ron Martz, "Witty McKay Leaves 'em Laughing," *St. Petersburg Times*, 5 December 1975, 1C.

10. Hubert Mizell, "McKay's Decision: Put Cards on Table," *St. Petersburg Times*, 1 November 1975, 1C.

11. Ibid.

12. Ron Martz, "McKay: I'm Tickled You Picked Me," *St. Petersburg Times*, 1 November 1975, 1C.

13. Underwood, 16–17.

14. Jim Murray, "McKay: Outside Looking In," *Los Angeles Times*, reprinted in *The Bulletin* (Bend Deschutes County, OR), 11 November 1977, 12.

15. Underwood, 16.

16. Roger Kahn, "Aboard the Lusitania in Tampa Bay," *The Fireside Book of Pro Football*. Ed. Richard Whittingham. (New York: Simon & Shuster, 1989), 116.

17. "McKay Unleashes his Wrath," *Palm Beach Post*, 10 November 1976, D2.

18. *Lost Treasures of NFL Films: Birth of the Bucs*. Dir. Steve Sabol (NFL Films, 2001).

19. Jack Gurney, "Bucs' Fame Grows With Every Defeat," *Sarasota Herald-Tribune*, 10 December 1977, 1C.

20. Bruce Lowitt, "Is Tampa Bay Really Worst Team, or is it McKay's Incapable Coaching?" *Ocala Star Banner*, 15 November 1977, 1C.

21. Dave Klein, "You're Wrong McKay," *Pro Football Weekly*, 24 October 1977, 6.

22. Ibid.

23. Ibid.

24. Ibid.

25. Bass, telephone interview.

26. Ibid.

27. Lee Roy Selmon, personal interview, 1 November 2004.

28. "John McKay," *Pro: The Official Magazine of the National Football League (Buccaneers Edition)*, 16 August 1980: 23.

29. Mike Tierney, "McKay's Preference? How About LA?" *St. Petersburg Times* 19 December 1979: 1C.

30. *Lost Treasures of NFL Films: Birth of the Bucs*. Dir. Steve Sabol (NFL Films, 2001).

31. Hubert Mizell, "State of Bay Bucs: Wading in Black Ink," *St. Petersburg Times*, 7 December 1978, 1C.

Chapter Three

1. Michael MacCambridge, *America's Game: The Epic Story of How Pro Football Captured a Nation* (New York: Anchor Books, 2004), 53.

2. MacCambridge, 49.

3. John A. Fortunato, *Commissioner: The Legacy of Pete Rozelle* (New York: Taylor Trade, 2006), 10.

4. MacCambridge, 73.

5. Steve Rosenbloom, telephone interview, 28 April 2009.

6. Ibid.

7. Fortunato, 30.

8. MacCambridge, 183–185.

9. Ibid., 167.

10. Hugh Jr. telephone interview, 14 May 2009.

11. Rosenbloom, telephone interview.

12. Ibid.

13. David Harris, *The League: The Rise and Decline of the NFL* (New York: Bantam Books, 1986), 589.

14. Ibid., 207–209, 217–219.

15. Ibid., 196–197, 476–477.

16. Culverhouse, telephone interview.

17. Harris, 589.

18. Ibid., 304.

19. "Rams' Owner Drowns," *Ocala Star-Banner*, 3 April 1979, 3B.

20. Rosenbloom, telephone interview.

21. Ibid.

22. Harris, 373, 416.

23. Ibid., 374.

24. Rosenbloom, telephone interview.

25. Ibid.

26. Ibid.

27. Ibid.

28. Ibid.

29. Ibid.

30. Ibid.

31. Ibid.

32. Ibid.

33. Harris, 465.

34. Rosenbloom, telephone interview.

35. Rick Odioso, telephone interview, 7 March 2005.

36. "Feds Say Frontiere Scalped Super Bowl Tickets," *United Press International*, 2 December 1986.

37. Rosenbloom, telephone interview.

38. Ibid.

39. Ibid.

40. Ibid.

41. Harris, 466.

42. Ibid.
43. Ibid.
44. Ibid.
45. Rosenbloom, telephone interview.
46. Ibid.
47. "Avocations by the Millions," *Mohave Daily Miner* (Kingman, AZ) , 2 April 1985, A9.
48. Stephen Story, telephone interview, 22 July 2009.
49. Harris, 556.
50. Story, telephone interview.
51. Harris, 556.
52. Ibid.
53. Story, telephone interview.
54. Ibid.

Chapter Four

1. John A. Fortunato, *Commissioner: The Legacy of Pete Rozelle* (New York: Taylor Trade, 2006), 151–152.
2. Ibid., 154.
3. David Harris, *The League: The Rise and Decline of the NFL* (New York: Bantam Books, 1986), 544.
4. Marc Gunther, and Bill Carter, *Monday Night Mayhem: The Inside Story of ABC's Monday Night Football* (New York: Quill, 1988), 269.
5. Harris, 543.
6. Dave DeForest-Stalls, telephone interview, 5 August 2009.
7. Ibid.
8. Mike Tierney, "Bucs Tabbed as a Rich, Low-Paying Club," *St. Petersburg Times*, 27 February 1982, 1C.
9. Ibid.
10. DeForest-Stalls, telephone interview.
11. Ibid.
12. Tierney, op. cit.
13. Robert H. Boyle, "The 55% Solution," *Sports Illustrated*, 1 February 1982, 30.
14. Hugh Jr. telephone interview, 15 May 2009.
15. Fortunato, 158.
16. Mike Tierney, "One Owner's View: We'll Never Cancel," *St. Petersburg Times*, 30 October 1982, 4C.
17. Boyle, 31.
18. Ibid.

19. Jack Donlan, telephone interview, 14 August 2009.
20. Ibid.
21. Ibid.
22. Ibid.
23. Patrick Zier, "Bucs Select Selmon New Player Representative," *Lakeland Ledger*, 23 May 1982, 3D.
24. DeForest-Stalls, telephone interview.
25. Ibid.
26. Ibid.
27. Ibid.
28. Ibid.
29. Donlan, telephone interview.
30. Ibid.
31. DeForest-Stalls, telephone interview.
32. "Donlan, Garvey to Resume Talks," *St. Petersburg Times*, 25 September 1982, 1C.
33. David Harris, *The Genius: How Bill Walsh Reinvented Football and Created an NFL Dynasty* (New York: Random House, 2009), 173.
34. Tim McDonald, "Potential Football Strike is on Their Minds," *The Evening Independent* (St. Petersburg, FL), 7 July 1982, 1C.
35. Scot Brantley, telephone interview, 20 September 2009.
36. DeForest-Stalls, telephone interview.
37. Ibid.
38. Ibid.
39. Patrick Zier, "Bucs Vote to Show Support," *Lakeland Ledger*, 14 August 1982, 5D.
40. DeForest-Stalls, telephone interview.
41. Ibid.
42. Ibid.
43. Ibid.
44. Ibid.
45. Patrick Zier, "Owners Set to Play if Players Aren't?" *Lakeland Ledger*, 26 September 1982, 1D.
46. Harris, *The League*, 544.
47. Donlan, telephone interview.
48. Ibid.
49. Gerald Carter, telephone interview, 2 September 2009.
50. DeForest-Stalls, telephone interview.
51. Donlan, telephone interview.

52. Ibid.
53. DeForest-Stalls, telephone interview.
54. "Culverhouse Says Wage Scale Not a Bad Idea," *Ocala Star Banner*, 6 October 1982, 3C.
55. Mike Tierney, "Bucs Boss, Stalls Discuss Options," *St. Petersburg Times*, 4 October 1982, 3C.
56. DeForest-Stalls, telephone interview.
57. Ibid.
58. Ibid.
59. Harris, *The League,* 546.
60. Donlan, telephone interview.
61. "Colzie Joins Williams in Opposing the Strike," *The Evening Independent* (St. Petersburg, FL), 9 November 1982, 3C.
62. Tim McDonald, "Culverhouse Makes Point; Where Was Counterpoint?" *The Evening Independent* (St. Petersburg, FL), 9 November 1982, 3C.
63. Ibid.
64. Harris, *The League,* 542.
65. McDonald, op. cit.
66. Ibid.
67. DeForest-Stalls, telephone interview.
68. Ibid.
69. Donlan, telephone interview.
70. Harris, *The League,* 548.
71. Phil Krueger, telephone interview, 18 May 2009.
72. Donlan, telephone interview.
73. Brantley, telephone interview.
74. Culverhouse, telephone interview.
75. DeForest-Stalls, telephone interview.
76. Patrick Zier, "Bucs Contacting Their Players on the Sly," *Lakeland Ledger*, 10 October 1982, 7D.
77. Culverhouse, telephone interview.
78. DeForest-Stalls, telephone interview.

Chapter Five

1. Doug Williams, telephone interview, 25 July 2005.
2. *Breaking the Huddle:*

The Integration of College Football. Dir. Mike Tollin (HBO, 2008).

3. Ken Herock, telephone interview, 2 June 2009.

4. Ibid.

5. Ibid.

6. Ibid.

7. Ibid.

8. Williams, telephone interview.

9. Tim McDonald, "Performance Chart Says He Did it Again!" *The Evening Independent* (St. Petersburg, FL), 4 January 1983, 16C.

10. Paul Zimmerman, "Pro Football '82 Scouting Report," *Sports Illustrated*, 1 September 1982, 202.

11. Stephen Story, telephone interview, 22 July 2009.

12. Ibid.

13. Ibid.

14. Herock, telephone interview.

15. Ibid.

16. Ibid.

17. Ibid.

18. John Underwood, "Gone With the Wins," *Sports Illustrated*, 24 October 1983, 44.

19. Ibid., 41.

20. Hugh Jr. telephone interview, 14 May 2009.

21. John Smith, "Bucs Owners: Million-Dollar Men With Lots of Sense," *The Evening Independent* (St. Petersburg, FL), 2 March 1976, 1C.

22. Story, telephone interview.

23. Phil Krueger, telephone interview, 18 May 2009.

24. Ibid.

25. Doug Williams, and Bruce Hunter, *Quarterback: Shattering the NFL Myth* (Chicago: Bonus Books, 1990), 106.

26. Williams and Hunter, 107.

27. Krueger, telephone interview.

28. Ibid.

29. Rick Odioso, telephone interview, 4 May 2009.

30. Ibid.

31. Mike Tierney, "Agent Says Odds Good Williams to Join USFL," *St. Petersburg Times*, 19 July 1983, 1C.

32. Scot Brantley, telephone interview, 20 September 2009.

33. Herock, telephone interview.

34. Culverhouse, telephone interview.

35. Williams and Hunter, 110.

36. Krueger, telephone interview.

37. Ibid.

38. Herock, telephone interview.

39. Krueger, telephone interview.

40. Williams and Hunter, 112.

41. Krueger, telephone interview.

42. Williams and Hunter, 127.

43. Krueger, telephone interview.

44. Ibid.

45. Ibid.

46. Frank Litsky, "Redskins Settle on Williams to Start," *New York Times*, 31 December 1988, B8.

47. Tom Zucco, "Super Bowl MVP? It's a Fairy Tale Come to Life," *St. Petersburg Times*, 1 February 1988, 4C.

48. Dave Steele, "Past Haunts Doug Williams," *St. Petersburg Times*, 8 January 1988, 1C.

49. Ibid.

50. Ibid.

51. Thomas George, "20 Years Later, Williams' Super Bowl Performance Remains Fresh," *NFL.com*, 25 January 2008.

52. Richard Wood, telephone interview, 20 April 2009.

53. Bruce Lowitt, "Ex-Bucs Wonder What Might Have Been," *St. Petersburg Times*, 2 February 1988, 4C.

54. Odioso, telephone interview.

55. Wood, telephone interview.

56. Ibid.

57. Ibid.

58. Brantley, telephone interview.

59. Odioso, telephone interview.

60. Wood, telephone interview.

61. Culverhouse, telephone interview.

62. Krueger, telephone interview.

63. Ibid.

64. Ibid.

65. Paul Stewart, telephone interview, 3 August 2010.

66. Culverhouse, telephone interview.

67. Ibid.

68. Ibid.

69. Williams, telephone interview.

Chapter Six

1. Barry McDermott, "Here's Carling, Her Daddy's Darling," *Sports Illustrated*, 27 June 1983, 90.

2. David Harris, *The League: The Rise and Decline of the NFL* (New York: Bantam Books, 1986), 229.

3. McDermott, 88.

4. Ibid., 91.

5. Mark Johnson, "Dog-gone, Burt, They're the Tampa Bay Bandits," *St. Petersburg Times*, 5 August 1982, 1C, 3C.

6. Ibid.

7. Ibid.

8. Ibid.

9. Mark Johnson, "Bandit-Ball: The Thing in Spring," *St. Petersburg Times*, 14 September 1982, 6C.

10. "Spurrier to Coach Bandits," *Ocala Star-Banner*, 23 November 1982, 4C.

11. Ibid.

12. Jim McVay, telephone interview, 11 June 2009.

13. "Bandits Already Ahead," *St. Petersburg Times*, 2 October 1982, 5C.

14. Ron Martz, "The Community Owns Nothing," *St. Petersburg Times*, 15 August 1979, 7C.

15. "Robbie Calls Truce in Battle of Florida," *Ocala Star-Banner*, 11 August 1979, 1C.

16. Hugh Jr. telephone interview, 14 May 2009.

17. Dave Reeves, "Bandits Want to be Attractive," *Lakeland Ledger*, 14 January 1983, 1D, 8D.

18. Ibid.

19. Ibid.

20. McVay, telephone interview.

21. Mike Flanagan, Mike. "It Was Different Kind of Football," *The Evening Independent* (St. Petersburg, FL), 1 March 1983, 1B.

22. Ibid.
23. Ken Herock, telephone interview, 2 June 2009.
24. Patrick Zier, "Bucs Don't Care for the New Kid in Town," *Lakeland Ledger*, 28 March 1983, 1D.
25. Ibid.
26. Richard Wood, telephone interview, 20 April 2009.
27. Sankar Montoute, telephone interview, 19 September 2009.
28. Herock, telephone interview.
29. Ibid.
30. Phil Krueger, telephone interview. 18 May 2009.
31. Herock, telephone interview.
32. McVay, telephone interview.
33. Montoute, telephone interview.
34. *Small Potatoes: Who Killed the USFL?* Dir. Mike Tollin (ESPN 30 for 30, 2009).
35. McVay, telephone interview.
36. Ibid.
37. Ibid.
38. Culverhouse, telephone interview.
39. Ibid.
40. Dave DeForest-Stalls, telephone interview, 5 August 2009.
41. Ibid.
42. Patrick Zier, "Bucs' Selmon May Consider USFL Team," *Lakeland Ledger*, 28 October 1982, 1D.
43. Paul Zimmerman, "The Choice is Leftovers," *Sports Illustrated*, 30 April 1984, 32.
44. *Small Potatoes.*
45. William Nack, "Give the First Round to the USFL," *Sports Illustrated*, 7 July 1986, 27.
46. Dave Reeves, "Bandits Finally Had to Reach for Checkbook," *Lakeland Ledger*, 11 May 1983, 1C.
47. *Small Potatoes.*
48. Ibid.
49. McVay, telephone interview.
50. *Small Potatoes.*
51. Ibid.
52. Ibid.
53. Ibid.
54. Ibid.
55. John Luttermoser, "Bandits Will Refuse to Play Fall Schedule," *St. Petersburg Times*, 27 March 1985, 1C.
56. McVay, telephone interview.
57. Jerry Greene, "Culverhouse Reacts to Tales of USFL-NFL Merger: 'Hogwash.'" *Orlando Sentinel*, 24 December 1985, 4C.
58. "Cosell's Testimony Entertains," *Reading Eagle*, 26 June 1986, 48.
59. Jack Donlan, telephone interview, 14 August 2009.
60. Ibid.
61. Nack, op. cit., 22.
62. Culverhouse, telephone interview.
63. Ibid.
64. Rich McKay, telephone interview, 10 June 2009.
65. "Many Believe the Victory May be Fatal to USFL," *Los Angeles Times*, 30 July 1986, 1.
66. McVay, telephone interview.
67. DeForest-Stalls, telephone interview.
68. Wood, telephone interview.
69. Montoute, telephone interview.
70. Ibid.
71. McVay, telephone interview.
72. Culverhouse, telephone interview.

Chapter Seven

1. Hugh Jr. telephone interview, 14 May 2009.
2. Stephen Story, telephone interview, 22 July 2009.
3. Leeman Bennett, telephone interview, 26 May 2006.
4. Paul Tripoli, telephone interview, 26 September 2009.
5. Phil Krueger, telephone interview, 18 May 2009.
6. Bo Jackson, and Dick Schaap, *Bo Knows Bo* (New York: Jove Books, 1990), 55–56.
7. Culverhouse, telephone interview.
8. Ibid.
9. Dave Scheiber, "Buc Boo-Boo Costs Bo his Baseball Eligibility," *St. Petersburg Times*, 29 March 1986, 1C, 8C.
10. Ibid.
11. Jackson and Schaap, 113.
12. Rick Odioso, telephone interview, 4 May 2009.
13. Scot Brantley, telephone interview, 20 September 2009.
14. Odioso, telephone interview.
15. Brantley, telephone interview.
16. Jackson and Schaap, 117.
17. Bennett, telephone interview.
18. Ibid.
19. Ibid.
20. Krueger, telephone interview.
21. Odioso, telephone interview.
22. Jackson and Schaap, 116.
23. Odioso, telephone interview.
24. Ibid.
25. Ibid.
26. Krueger, telephone interview.
27. Ibid.
28. Culverhouse, telephone interview.
29. Ibid.
30. Odioso, telephone interview.
31. Jackson and Schaap, 147.
32. Ibid., 148.
33. Brantley, telephone interview.
34. Ibid.
35. Odioso, telephone interview.
36. Bennett, telephone interview.

Chapter Eight

1. Leeman Bennett, telephone interview, 26 May 2006.
2. Ibid.
3. Scot Brantley, telephone interview, 20 September 2009.
4. Ibid.
5. Ibid.
6. Ibid.
7. Ibid.
8. Bud Lea, "Bucs Can't Weather Packers," *Milwaukee Sentinel*, 2 December 1985, 1.
9. Mike Flanagan, "Brrrr!" *The Evening Independent* (St. Petersburg, FL), 2 December 1985, 1C.
10. Brantley, telephone interview.
11. Ibid.

12. Gerald Carter, telephone interview, 2 September 2009.
13. Sean Farrell, telephone interview, 11 January 2010.
14. Ibid.
15. Brantley, telephone interview.
16. Bennett, telephone interview.
17. Carter, telephone interview.
18. Farrell, telephone interview.
19. Ibid.
20. Ibid.
21. Rick Odioso, telephone interview, 12 May 2009.
22. Brantley, telephone interview.
23. Farrell, telephone interview.
24. Brantley, telephone interview.
25. Ibid.
26. Ibid.
27. Ibid.
28. Odioso, telephone interview.
29. Farrell, telephone interview.
30. Ibid.
31. Brantley, telephone interview.
32. Odioso, telephone interview.
33. Bennett, telephone interview.

Chapter Nine

1. Tom Zucco, "Uneven Exchange: 49ers Stole Best Bucs Had to Offer," St. Petersburg Times, 25 April 1987, 3C.
2. Ibid., "Young, Bucs on the Brink of Finalizing Agreement," St. Petersburg Times, 10 September 1985, 1C.
3. Zucco, "Uneven Exchange," 1C.
4. Scot Brantley, telephone interview, 20 September 2009.
5. Frank Pupello, telephone interview, 3 August 2009.
6. Brantley, telephone interview.
7. Ibid.
8. Ibid.
9. Gerald Carter, telephone interview, 2 September 2009.
10. Leeman Bennett, telephone interview, 26 May 2006.

11. Ray Perkins, telephone interview, 9 June 2009.
12. Phil Krueger, telephone interview, 18 May 2009.
13. Ibid.
14. Perkins, telephone interview.
15. Krueger, telephone interview.
16. David Harris, The Genius: How Bill Walsh Reinvented Football and Created an NFL Dynasty (New York: Random House, 2009), 177.
17. Brantley, telephone interview.
18. Harris, 250.
19. Brantley, telephone interview.
20. Ibid.
21. Ibid.
22. Ibid.
23. "Montana's Surgery Termed 'Successful,'" Tuscaloosa News, 16 September 1986, 14.
24. Harris, 276.
25. Bill Walsh, and Glenn Dickey, Building a Champion: On Football and the Making of the 49ers (New York: St. Martins Press, 1990), 29.
26. Harris, 277–279.
27. Krueger, telephone interview.
28. Bradley Stetz, "Culverhouse Makes Bid for Florida Commercial," St. Petersburg Times, 29 August 1987, 5B.
29. Bradley Stetz, "Culverhouse Makes Offer for Sarasota Thrift," St. Petersburg Times, 2 December 1987, 12A.
30. Zucco, "Uneven Exchange," 1C.
31. Ibid.
32. Brantley, telephone interview.
33. John Harris, "Young is Excited, But Also a Little Sad," St. Petersburg Times, 25 April 1987, 3C.
34. Ibid.
35. Ibid.
36. Walsh and Dickey, 29.
37. Paul Zimmerman, "Upset!" Sports Illustrated, 18 January 1988, 19.
38. Harris, 307.
39. Carter, telephone interview.
40. Brantley, telephone interview.

Chapter Ten

1. Scot Brantley, telephone interview, 20 September 2009.
2. Ken Herock, telephone interview, 2 June 2009.
3. Ibid.
4. Ibid.
5. Ibid.
6. Ray Perkins, telephone interview, 9 June 2009.
7. Ibid.
8. Ibid.
9. Ibid.
10. Gerald Carter, telephone interview, 2 September 2009.
11. Brantley, telephone interview.
12. John Luttermoser, "Bear Bryant Connection," St. Petersburg Times, 28 July 1987, 1C.
13. Mark Carrier, telephone interview, 10 August 2009.
14. John Luttermoser, "Bucs Escape Sting of the Road," St. Petersburg Times, 2 November 1987, 8C.
15. Brantley, telephone interview.
16. Ibid.
17. Ibid.
18. Paul Tripoli, telephone interview, 28 September 2009.
19. John Luttermoser, "Bucs Worth Only 3 Quarters," St. Petersburg Times, 9 November 1987, 8C.
20. Ibid.
21. Hubert Mizell, "Bucs' Collapse Worst Ever in NFL History," St. Petersburg Times, 9 November 1987, 8C.
22. Ibid.
23. Ibid.
24. Perkins, telephone interview.
25. Richard Williamson, telephone interview, 19 May 2009.
26. Ibid.
27. Ibid.
28. Carrier, telephone interview.
29. Ibid.
30. Rick Odioso, telephone interview, 4 May 2009.
31. Ibid.
32. Ibid.
33. Bob Chick, "Hugh Culverhouse: He Owns the Bucs," The Evening Independent (St. Petersburg, FL), 20 August 1976, 2D.

34. Paul Stewart, telephone interview, 3 August. 2010.
35. Stephen Story, telephone interview, 22 July 2009.
36. Steve Rosenbloom, telephone interview, 28 April 2009.
37. Odioso, telephone interview.
38. Ibid.
39. Perkins, telephone interview.
40. Ibid.
41. Ibid.
42. Ibid.
43. Ibid.
44. Tripoli, telephone interview.
45. Ibid.

Chapter Eleven

1. John A. Fortunato, *Commissioner: The Legacy of Pete Rozelle* (New York: Taylor Trade, 2006), 158.
2. Jack Donlan, telephone interview, 14 August 2009.
3. Ibid.
4. Ibid.
5. Ibid.
6. Ibid.
7. Ibid.
8. Ibid.
9. Hugh Jr. telephone interview, 14 May 2009.
10. Ibid.
11. Ibid.
12. Ibid.
13. Ibid.
14. Ibid.
15. Donlan, telephone interview.
16. John Luttermoser, "Fillins Are in the Money," *St. Petersburg Times*, 2 October 1987, 3C.
17. Tom Zucco, "Culverhouse Says Owners Will Not Give Up Control," *St. Petersburg Times*, 28 September 1987, 1C.
18. Ibid.
19. Ibid.
20. Ray Perkins, telephone interview, 9 June 2009.
21. Ibid.
22. Paul Tripoli, telephone interview, 26 September 2009.
23. Ibid.
24. Ibid.
25. Mike Hold, telephone interview, 5 February 2009.

26. Ibid.
27. Sankar Montoute, telephone interview, 19 September 2009.
28. Ibid.
29. Ibid.
30. Ibid.
31. Ibid.
32. Paul Zimmerman, "When Push Came to Shove," *Sports Illustrated*, 5 October 1987, 40.
33. Montoute, telephone interview.
34. Hold, telephone interview.
35. Scot Brantley, telephone interview, 20 September 2009.
36. Mark Carrier, telephone interview, 10 August 2009.
37. Perkins, telephone interview.
38. Hold, telephone interview.
39. Tripoli, telephone interview.
40. Hold, telephone interview.
41. Montoute, telephone interview.
42. Michael Janofsky, "Sparse Crowds, Heavy Picketing at NFL Games," *New York Times*, 5 October 1987, C6.
43. Hold, telephone interview.
44. Ibid.
45. David Steele, "Bucs' A Team Had Little Charity for Replacement Players Sunday," *St. Petersburg Times*, 5 October 1987, 1C.
46. Janofsky, op. cit.
47. John Luttermoser, "Culverhouse: Strike Will Last Much Longer Than Most Hope," *St. Petersburg Times*, 8 October 1987, 3C.
48. Tripoli, telephone interview.
49. Hold, telephone interview.
50. Tripoli, telephone interview.
51. Montoute, telephone interview.
52. Hold, telephone interview.
53. Ibid.
54. Ibid.
55. Ibid.
56. Montoute, telephone interview.

57. Tripoli, telephone interview.
58. Ibid.
59. Hold, telephone interview.
60. Montoute, telephone interview.
61. Hold, telephone interview.
62. Montoute, telephone interview.
63. Tripoli, telephone interview.
64. Ibid.
65. Hold, telephone interview.
66. Montoute, telephone interview.
67. Gerald Carter, telephone interview, 2 September 2009.
68. Hold, telephone interview.

Chapter Twelve

1. Pat Summerall, telephone interview, 12 June 2009.
2. Ibid.
3. Ibid.
4. Ibid.
5. Ibid.
6. Ibid.
7. John Madden, and Dave Anderson, *Hey, Wait a Minute (I Wrote a Book)* (New York: Villard Books, 1984), 25.
8. Ibid.
9. Summerall, telephone interview.
10. Ibid.
11. Ibid.
12. Madden and Anderson, 34–35.
13. Ibid.
14. Rick Odioso, telephone interview, 12 May 2009.
15. Ibid.
16. Ibid.
17. Marc Gunther, and Bill Carter, *Monday Night Mayhem: The Inside Story of ABC's Monday Night Football* (New York: Quill, 1988), 30.
18. Howard Cosell, and Peter Bonventure, *I Never Played the Game* (New York: Morrow, 1985), 131–132.
19. Gunther and Carter, 278.
20. Ibid., 279.
21. "ABC Calls 'Monkey' Remark Unfortunate," *St. Petersburg Times*, 7 September 1983, 1C.

22. Cosell and Bonventure, 131.

23. Ibid., 132.

24. Ron Martz, "Bucs Close Locker Room to Reporters," *St. Petersburg Times*, 11 August 1979, 1C.

25. Gayle Sierens, telephone interview, 7 September 2009.

26. Ibid.

27. Ibid.

28. Ibid.

29. Mike Flanagan, "Sierens May Become First Woman to do NFL Game," *St. Petersburg Times*, 27 October 1987, 1C.

30. Sierens, telephone interview.

31. Ibid.

32. Ibid.

33. Ibid.

34. Ibid.

35. Roger Fischer, "CBS' Taping of Sierens Audition Irks NBC Officials," *St. Petersburg Times*, 21 December 1987, 1C.

36. Bruce Lowitt, "I Don't Have to be Good, I Have to be Terrific," *St. Petersburg Times*, 25 December 1987, 1C.

37. Ibid.

38. Sierens, telephone interview.

39. Ibid.

40. Ibid.

41. Ibid.

42. Ibid.

43. Ibid.

44. Ibid.

45. Ibid.

46. Ibid.

47. Ibid.

Chapter Thirteen

1. Hubert Mizell, "Blame for Inept Bucs is Owner's," *St. Petersburg Times*, 4 October 1991, 1C.

2. Ibid., "Fans Bash the Bucs Brain Trust," *St. Petersburg Times*, 13 November 1991, 1C.

3. Ibid.

4. Hugh Jr. telephone interview, 14 May 2009.

5. Rick Stroud, "Walsh to Remain With NBC," *St. Petersburg Times*, 31 January 1991, 1C.

6. Ibid.

7. Culverhouse, telephone interview.

8. Phil Krueger, telephone interview, 18 May 2009.

9. Richard Williamson, telephone interview, 19 May 2009.

10. "Parcells Treated for Blocked Artery; Surgery Not Needed," *St. Petersburg Times*, 17 December 1991, 3C.

11. "Bucs on Parcells: No Talks Held," *St. Petersburg Times*, 27 November 1991, 3C.

12. Williamson, telephone interview.

13. Ibid.

14. Hubert Mizell, and Don Banks, "Bucs Likely to Hire Parcells," *St. Petersburg Times*, 28 December 1991, 1A.

15. Rick Stroud, "Krueger Leaves Bucs," *St. Petersburg Times*, 29 December 1991, 1C.

16. Mizell and Banks, op. cit., 1A.

17. Hubert Mizell, "Hugh, Bucs Left Crying at the Altar," *St. Petersburg Times*, 30 December 1991, 1C.

18. Ken Herock, telephone interview, 2 June 2009.

19. Ray Perkins, telephone interview, 9 June 2009.

20. Ibid.

21. Ibid.

22. Bill Parcells, telephone interview, 29 May 2009.

23. Herock, telephone interview.

24. Ibid.

25. Krueger, telephone interview.

26. Ibid.

27. Richard Wood, telephone interview, 20 April 2009.

28. Culverhouse, telephone interview.

29. Ibid.

30. Stephen Story, telephone interview, 22 July 2009.

31. Don Banks, "Holmgren Visits Bucs, Keeps Options Open," *St. Petersburg Times*, 8 January 1992, 1C.

32. "Report: Parcells, Bucs Talking Again," *St. Petersburg Times*, 7 January 1992, 1C.

33. Story, telephone interview.

34. Parcells, telephone interview.

35. Story, telephone interview.

36. Culverhouse, telephone interview.

37. Story, telephone interview.

38. Ibid.

39. Rich McKay, telephone interview, 10 June 2009.

40. Parcells, telephone interview.

41. Ibid.

42. Ibid.

43. Culverhouse, telephone interview.

44. Parcells, telephone interview.

45. Ibid.

46. Story, telephone interview.

47. Ibid.

48. Don Banks, and Rick Stroud, "Reports: Wyche Gets Job," *St. Petersburg Times*, 10 January 1992, 1A.

49. Culverhouse, telephone interview.

50. Ibid.

51. Parcells, telephone interview.

Epilogue

1. Hugh Jr. telephone interview, 14 May 2009.

2. Ibid.

3. Jeff Testerman, "Ex-Bucs Owner's Liaisons Detailed," *St. Petersburg Times*, 25 December 1996, 1B.

4. Doug Fernandes, "Bucs Post 'For Sale' Sign," *Sarasota Herald-Tribune*, 11 November 1994, 6C.

5. Culverhouse, telephone interview.

6. Ibid.

7. Bill Parcells, telephone interview, 29 May 2009.

8. Culverhouse, telephone interview.

9. Richard Wood, telephone interview, 20 April 2009.

10. Scot Brantley, telephone interview, 20 September 2009.

11. Tom Bass, telephone interview, 2 April 2009.

12. Rick Odioso, telephone interview, 4 May 2009.

13. Culverhouse, telephone interview.

14. Rick Stroud, "If Money Talks, Bucs Could Walk," *St. Petersburg Times*, 25 December 1996, 1B.

15. Rich McKay, telephone interview, 10 June 2009.

16. Culverhouse, telephone interview.

17. Ibid.

18. Ibid.

19. Ibid.

20. Ibid.

21. Ibid.

22. Ibid.

23. Ibid.

24. Ibid.

25. Ibid.

26. Ibid.

27. Ibid.

28. Ibid.

29. Ibid.

30. Ibid.

31. Jack Donlan, telephone interview, 14 August 2009.

32. Ibid.

33. McKay, telephone interview.

34. John Barr, "Culverhouse Has Unfinished Business," *ESPN.com*, 25 April 2010.

35. Ibid.

36. Wood, telephone interview.

37. Mark Carrier, telephone interview, 10 August 2009.

38. Ray Perkins, telephone interview, 9 June 2009.

39. Brantley, telephone interview.

40. Ibid.

Bibliography

Books

Cosell, Howard, and Peter Bonventure. *I Never Played the Game*. New York: William Morrow, 1985.

Fortunato, John A. *Commissioner: The Legacy of Pete Rozelle*. New York: Taylor Trade, 2006.

Gunther, Marc, and Bill Carter. *Monday Night Mayhem: The Inside Story of ABC's Monday Night Football*. New York: Quill, 1988.

Harris, David. *The Genius: How Bill Walsh Reinvented Football and Created an NFL Dynasty*. New York: Random House, 2009.

_____. *The League: The Rise and Decline of the NFL*. New York: Bantam Books, 1986.

Jackson, Bo, and Dick Schaap. *Bo Knows Bo*. New York: Jove Books, 1990.

Kahn, Roger. "Aboard the Lusitania in Tampa Bay." *The Fireside Book of Pro Football*. Richard Whittingham, ed. New York: Simon & Schuster, 1989.

MacCambridge, Michael. *America's Game*. New York: Anchor Books, 2004.

Madden, John, and Dave Anderson. *Hey, Wait a Minute (I Wrote a Book)*. New York: Villard Books, 1984.

McKay, John, and Jim Perry. *McKay: A Coach's Story*. New York: Atheneum, 1974.

Sports Media National. *Bucs Reflections*. Tampa: Sports Media National, 1979.

Walsh, Bill, and Glenn Dickey. *Building a Champion: On Football and the Making of the 49ers*. New York: St. Martin's Press, 1990.

Williams, Doug, and Bruce Hunter. *Quarterblack: Shattering the NFL Myth*. Chicago: Bonus Books, 1990.

Magazine Articles

Boyle, Robert H. "The 55% Solution." *Sports Illustrated*, 1 February 1982: 32–47.

"John McKay." *Pro: The Official Magazine of the National Football League (Buccaneers Edition)* 16 August 1980: 23.

King, Peter. "Young and the Restless." *Sports Illustrated*, 31 May 1993: 68–77.

Klein, Dave. "You're Wrong McKay." *Pro Football Weekly*, 24 October 1977: 6.

McDermott, Barry. "Here's Carling, Her Daddy's Darling." *Sports Illustrated*, 27 June 1983: 84–98.

Nack, William. "Give the First Round to the USFL." *Sports Illustrated*, 7 July 1986: 22–27.

Underwood, John. "A Three Hour Time Difference." *Sports Illustrated*, 23 August 1976: 16–23.

_____. "Gone With the Wins." *Sports Illustrated*, 24 October 1983: 40–49.

Zimmerman, Paul. "The Choice is Leftovers." *Sports Illustrated*, 30 April 1984: 32–37.

_____. "Pro Football '82 Scouting Reports."

Sports Illustrated, 1 September 1982: 202.
_____. "Upset!" *Sports Illustrated*, 18 January 1988: 14–19.
_____. "When Push Came to Shove." *Sports Illustrated*, 5 October 1987: 38–41.

Newspaper Articles

"ABC Calls 'Monkey' Remark Unfortunate." *St. Petersburg Times*, 7 September 1983, 1C, 9C.
"Avocations by the Millions." *Mohave Daily Miner* (Kingman, AZ) , 2 April 1985, A9.
"Baltimore's Owner Eyes Rams' Purchase." *The Free-Lance Star* (Fredericksburg, VA), 23 June 1972, 6.
"Bandits Already Ahead." *St. Petersburg Times*, 2 October 1982, 5C.
Banks, Don. "Homgren Visits Bucs, Keeps Options Open." *St. Petersburg Times*, 8 January 1992, 1C, 6C.
_____, and Rick Stroud. "Reports: Wyche Gets Job." *St. Petersburg Times*, 10 January 1992, 1A, 2A.
"Bucs on Parcells: No Talks Held." *St. Petersburg Times*, 27 November 1991, 3C.
Chick, Bob. "Hugh Culverhouse: He Owns the Bucs." *The Evening Independent* (St. Petersburg, FL), 20 August 1976, 2D.
"Colzie Joins Williams in Opposing the Strike." *The Evening Independent* (St. Petersburg, FL), 9 November 1982, 3C.
"Cosell's Testimony Entertains." *Reading Eagle*, 26 June 1986, 48.
"Culverhouse Says Wage Scale Not a Bad Idea." *Ocala Star Banner*, 6 October 1982, 3C.
"Donlan, Garvey to Resume Talks." *St. Petersburg Times*, 25 September 1982, 1C, 3C.
"Feds Say Frontiere Scalped Super Bowl Tickets." *United Press International*, 2 December 1986.
Fernandes, Doug. "Bucs Post 'For Sale' Sign." *Sarasota Herald-Tribune*, 11 November 1994, 1C, 6C.
Fischer, Roger. "CBS' Taping of Sierens Audition Irks NBC Officials." *St. Petersburg Times*, 21 December 1987, 1C, 6C.
_____. "Sierens to Audition for NFL Spot." *St. Petersburg Times*, 4 December 1987, 5C.
Flanagan, Mike. "Brrrrr!" *The Evening Independent* (St. Petersburg, FL), 2 December 1985, 1C, 4C.
_____. "It Was Different Kind of Football." *The Evening Independent* (St. Petersburg, FL), 14 February 1983, 3C.

_____. "Selling the Tampa Bay Bandits is a Job for Team Behind the Team." *The Evening Independent* (St. Petersburg, FL), 1 March 1983, 1B.
_____. "Sierens May Become First Woman to do NFL Game." *St. Petersburg Times*, 27 October 1987, 1C.
_____, and Bob Harig. "Bucs Sign ex–Bandits in Case of Strike." *St. Petersburg Times*, 21 September 1987, 9C.
Greene, Jerry. "Culverhouse Reacts to Tales of USFL-NFL Merger: 'Hogwash.'" *Orlando Sentinel*, 24 December 1985, 4C.
Gurney, Jack. "Bucs' Fame Grows With Every Defeat." *Sarasota Herald-Tribune*, 10 December 1977, 1C.
Harris, John. "Young is Excited, But Also a Little Sad." *St. Petersburg Times*, 25 April 1987, 3C.
Janofsky, Michael. "Sparse Crowds, Heavy Picketing at NFL Games." *New York Times*, 5 October 1987, A1, C6.
Johnson, Mark. "Bandit-Ball: The Thing in Spring." *St. Petersburg Times*, 14 September 1982, 6C.
_____. "Doggone, Burt, They're the Tampa Bay Bandits." *St. Petersburg Times*, 5 August 1982, 3C.
Lea, Bud. "Bucs Can't Weather Packers." *Milwaukee Sentinel*, 2 December 1985, 1, 3.
Leavy, Jane. "Special Rites: NFL Passage: A Wiser Doug Williams Will Lead the Redskins." *Washington Post*, reprinted in *Milwaukee Journal*, 14 January 1988, 1C, 8C.
Litsky, Frank. "Redskins Settle on Williams to Start." *New York Times*, 31 December 1988, B8.
Lowitt, Bruce. "Ex-Bucs Wonder What Might Have Been." *St. Petersburg Times*, 2 February 1988, 4C.
_____. "I Don't Have to be Good, I Have to be Terrific." *St. Petersburg Times*, 25 December 1987, 1C, 3C.
_____. "Is Tampa Bay Really Worst Team, or is it McKay's Incapable Coaching?" *Ocala Star Banner*, 15 November 1977, 1C.
Luttermoser, John. "Bandits Will Refuse to Play Fall Schedule." *St. Petersburg Times*, 27 March 1985, 1C, 9C.
_____. "Bear Bryant Connection." *St. Petersburg Times*, 28 July 1987, 1C, 3C.
_____. "Bucs Escape Sting of the Road." *St. Petersburg Times*, 2 November 1987, 1C, 8C.
_____. "Bucs Worth Only 3 Quarters." *St.*

Petersburg Times, 9 November 1987, 1C, 8C.

_____. "Culverhouse: Strike Will Last Much Longer Than Most Hope. *St. Petersburg Times*, 8 October 1987, 3C.

_____. "Fill-ins Are in the Money." *St. Petersburg Times*, 2 October 1987, 3C.

"Many Believe the Victory May be Fatal to USFL." *Los Angeles Times*, 30 July 1986, 1.

Martz, Ron. "Bucs Close Locker Room to Reporters." *St. Petersburg Times*, 11 August 1979, 1C.

_____. "He Didn't Pay $16 Million for a Toy." *St. Petersburg Times*, 15 August 1976, 17H.

_____. "McKay: I'm Tickled You Picked Me." *St. Petersburg Times*, 1 November 1975, 1C, 6C.

_____. "The Community Owns Nothing." *St. Petersburg Times*, 15 August 1979, 1C, 7C.

McDonald, Tim. "Culverhouse Makes Point; Where Was Counterpoint?" *The Evening Independent* (St. Petersburg, FL), 9 November 1982, 3C.

_____. "Performance Chart Says He Did it Again!" *The Evening Independent* (St. Petersburg, FL), 4 January 1983, 16C.

_____. "Potential Football Strike is on Their Minds." *The Evening Independent* (St. Petersburg, FL), 7 July 1982, 1C.

McEwen, Tom. "New Millionaire in Town." *Tampa Tribune*, 7 November 1974, 1C.

_____. "The McCloskey Progress Report." *Tampa Tribune*, 22 November 1974, 1C.

"McKay Unleashes his Wrath." *Palm Beach Post*, 10 November 1976, D2.

Mizell, Hubert. "Blame for Inept Bucs is Owner's." *St. Petersburg Times*, 4 October 1991, 1C.

_____. "Bucs' Collapse Worst Ever in NFL History." *St. Petersburg Times*, 9 November 1987, 1C, 8C.

_____. "Fans Bash the Bucs Brain Trust." *St. Petersburg Times*, 13 November 1991, 1C.

_____. "Hugh, Bucs Left Crying at the Altar." *St. Petersburg Times*, 30 December 1991, 1C, 3C.

_____. "Jacksonville Attorney Tampa NFL Owner." *St. Petersburg Times*, 6 December 1974, 1C, 7C.

_____. "McKay's Decision: Put Cards on Table." *St. Petersburg Times*, 1 November 1975, 1C, 6C.

_____. "State of Bay Bucs: Wading in Black Ink." *St. Petersburg Times*, 7 December 1978, 1C, 4C.

_____. and Don Banks. "Bucs Likely to Hire Parcells." *St. Petersburg Times*, 28 December 1991, 1A, 3A.

"Montana's Surgery Termed 'Successful.'" *Tuscaloosa News*, 16 September 1986, 14.

Murray, Jim. "McKay: Outside Looking In." *Los Angeles Times*, reprinted in *The Bulletin* (Bend Deschutes County, OR), 11 November 1977, 12.

"NFL Franchise Awarded to Tampa." *Canton Repository*, 31 October 1974, 49.

"Parcells Treated for Blocked Artery; Surgery Not Needed." *St. Petersburg Times*, 17 December 1991, 3C.

"Rams' Owner Drowns." *Ocala Star-Banner*, 3 April 1979, 3B.

"Reports: Parcells, Bucs Talking Again." *St. Petersburg Times*, 7 January 1992, 1C.

Reeves, Dave. "Bandits Finally Had to Reach for Checkbook." *Lakeland Ledger*, 11 May 1983, 1C.

_____. "Bandits Want to be Attractive." *Lakeland Ledger*, 14 January 1983, 1D, 8D.

"Robbie Calls Truce in 'Battle of Florida.'" *Ocala Star Banner*, 11 August 1979, 1C.

Scheiber, Dave. "Buc Boo-Boo Costs Bo his Baseball Eligibility." *St. Petersburg Times*, 29 March 1986, 1C, 8C.

_____. "Yes, That's Who You Think it is in a Bandits Uniform." *St. Petersburg Times*, 13 January 1983, 1C, 3C.

"Sierens to Call Chiefs Game on December 27 in Historic Debut." *St. Petersburg Times*, 17 December 1987, 1C.

Smith, John. "Bucs Owners: Million-Dollar Men With Lots of Sense." *The Evening Independent* (St. Petersburg, FL), 2 March 1976, 1C.

"Spurrier to Coach Bandits." *Ocala Star Banner*, 23 November 1982, 4C.

Steele, Dave. "Bucs' A Team Had Little Charity for Replacement Players Sunday." *St. Petersburg Times*, 5 October 1987, 1C, 7C.

_____. "Past Haunts Doug Williams." *St. Petersburg Times*, 8 January 1988, 1C, 4C.

Stetz, Bradley. "Culverhouse Makes Bid for Florida Commercial." *St. Petersburg Times*, 29 August 1987, 5B.

_____. "Culverhouse Makes Offer for Sarasota Thrift." *St. Petersburg Times*, 2 December 1987, 12A.

Stroud, Rick. "Bucs Owner Loses Fight Against Cancer." *St. Petersburg Times*, 26 August 1994, 1A, 7A.

_____. "If Money Talks, Bucs Could Walk." *St. Petersburg Times*, 1 September 1994, 1A, 4A.

_____. "Krueger Leaves Bucs." *St. Petersburg Times*, 29 December 1991, 1C, 13C.

_____. "Parcells Turns Down Bucs Job." *St. Petersburg Times*, 30 December 1991, 1A, 3A.

_____. "Walsh to Remain With NBC." *St. Petersburg Times*, 31 January 1991, 1C, 4C.

"Suit Filed by Attorney." *Spokane Daily Chronicle*, 21 December 1972, 22.

Testerman, Jeff. "Ex-Bucs Owner's Liaisons Detailed." *St. Petersburg Times*, 25 December 1996, 1B, 11B.

Tierney, Mike. "Agent Says Odds Good Williams to Join USFL." *St. Petersburg Times*, 19 July 1983, 1C.

_____. "Bucs Boss, Stalls Discuss Options." *St. Petersburg Times*, 4 October 1982, 1C, 3C.

_____. "Bucs Tabbed as a Rich, Low-Paying Club." *St. Petersburg Times*, 27 February 1982, 1C, 6C.

_____. "McKay's Preference? How About LA?" *St. Petersburg Times*, 19 December 1979, 1C, 5C.

_____. "One Owner's View: We'll Never Cancel." *St. Petersburg Times*, 30 October 1982, 4C.

_____. "Owner Urges Secret Ballot Vote." *St. Petersburg Times*, 9 November 1982, 1C, 2C.

Zier, Patrick. "Bandits on the Run as Bucs go into a Stall." *Lakeland Ledger*, 31 October 1982, 1D.

_____. "Bucs Contacting Their Players on the Sly." *Lakeland Ledger*, 10 October 1982, 7D.

_____. "Bucs Don't Care for New Kid in Town." *Lakeland Ledger*, 28 March 1983, 1D.

_____. "Bucs Select Selmon New Player Representative." *Lakeland Ledger*, 23 May 1982, 3D.

_____. "Bucs Selmon May Consider USFL Team." *Lakeland Ledger*, 28 October 1982, 1D.

_____. "Bucs Vote to Show Support." *Lakeland Ledger*, 14 August 1982, 1D, 5D.

_____. "Owners Set to Play if Players Aren't?" *Lakeland Ledger*, 26 September 1982, 1D.

Zucco, Tom. "Culverhouse Says Owners Will Not Give Up Control." *St. Petersburg Times*, 28 September 1987, 1C.

_____. "Uneven Exchange: 49ers Stole Best Bucs Had to Offer." *St. Petersburg Times*, 25 April 1987, 1C, 3C.

_____. "Super Bowl MVP? It's a Fairy Tale Come to Life." *St. Petersburg Times*, 1 February 1988, 1C, 4C.

_____. "Young, Bucs on the Brink of Finalizing Agreement." *St. Petersburg Times*, 10 September 1985, 1C, 3C.

Broadcasts, Telecasts and Websites

Barr, John. "Culverhouse Has Unfinished Business." *ESPN.com*, 25 April 2010.

Breaking the Huddle: The Integration of College Football. Dir. Mike Tollin. HBO, 2008.

Lost Treasures of NFL Films: Birth of the Bucs. Dir. Steve Sabol. NFL Films, 2001.

Minnesota Vikings vs. Tampa Bay Buccaneers. CBS. WTVT, Tampa, FL, 25 November 1979.

Small Potatoes: Who Killed the USFL? Dir. Mike Tollin. ESPN 30 for 30, 2009.

Tampa Bay Buccaneers vs. Green Bay Packers. CBS. WSAW, Wausau, WI, 1 December 1985.

Thomas, George. "20 Years Later, Williams' Super Bowl Performance Remains Fresh." *NFL.com*, 25 January 2008.

Interviews

Bass, Tom. Telephone interview. 2 April 2009.

Bennett, Leeman. Telephone interview. 26 May 2006.

Brantley, Scot. Telephone interview. 20 September 2009.

Carrier, Mark. Telephone interview. 10 August 2009.

Carter, Gerald. Telephone interview. 2 September 2009.

Culverhouse, Hugh Jr. Telephone interviews. 14, 15 May 2009.

DeForest-Stalls, Dave. Telephone interview. 5 August 2009.

Donlan, Jack. Telephone interview. 14 August 2009.

Farrell, Sean. Telephone interview. 11 January 2010.

Harris, Jack. Telephone interview. 19 January. 2006.

Herock, Ken. Telephone interview. 2 June 2009.

Hold, Mike. Telephone interview. 5 February 2009.

Krueger, Phil. Telephone interview. 18 May 2009.

McKay, Rich. Telephone interview. 10 June 2009.

McVay, Jim. Telephone interview. 11 June 2009.

Montoute, Sankar. Telephone interview. 19 September 2009.

Odioso, Rick. Telephone interviews. 7 March 2005, 4 May 2009, 12 May 2009.

Parcells, Bill. Telephone interview. 29 May 2009.

Perkins, Ray. Telephone interview. 9 June 2009.

Pupello, Frank. Telephone interview. 3 August 2009.

Rosenbloom, Steve. Telephone interview. 28 April 2009.

Selmon, Lee Roy. Personal interview. 1 November 2004.

Sierens, Gayle. Telephone interview. 7 September 2009.

Stewart, Paul. Telephone interview. 3 August 2010.

Story, Stephen. Telephone interview. 22 July 2009.

Tripoli, Paul. Telephone interview. 26 September 2009.

Williams, Doug. Telephone interview. 25 July 2005.

Williamson, Richard. Telephone interview. 19 May 2009.

Wolf, Ron. Telephone interview. 11 May 2009.

Wood, Richard. Telephone interview. 20 April 2009.

Index